Designs for Living and Learning

Other Redleaf Press Books by Deb Curtis and Margie Carter

The Art of Awareness: *How Observation Can Transform Your Teaching*,
    second edition
Learning Together with Young Children: *A Curriculum Framework for
    Reflective Teachers*
Reflecting Children's Lives: *A Handbook for Planning Your Child-Centered
    Curriculum*, second edition
Reflecting in Communities of Practice: *A Workbook for Early Childhood
    Educators*, with Debbie Lebo and Wendy C. M. Cividanes
Training Teachers: *A Harvest of Theory and Practice*
The Visionary Director: *A Handbook for Dreaming, Organizing, and
    Improvising in Your Center*, second edition

Designs for
Living and Learning

Transforming Early Childhood Environments

SECOND EDITION

Deb Curtis and Margie Carter

Redleaf Press®
www.redleafpress.org
800-423-8309

KH

Published by Redleaf Press
10 Yorkton Court
St. Paul, MN 55117
www.redleafpress.org

First edition published 2003. Second edition 2015.
Cover design by Jeanne K. Hunt
Cover photograph by Jeanne K. Hunt taken at Kids' Domain
    Early Learning Centre in Auckland, New Zealand
Interior design by Erin New
Typeset in Minion and Whitney
Interior photos/illustrations provided by the authors or programs cited
Quotation on page 263 excerpted from "A Lazy Thought" from *There Is No Rhyme For Silver*
    by Eve Merriam. Copyright © 1962 Eve Merriam. © Renewed 1990. Used by permission of
    Marian Reiner.
Appendix B, "Getting to Know the Assessment Tool" from Bloom, Paula Jorde, Ann Hentschell,
    and Jilla Bella. (2013). *Inspiring Peak Performa nce: Competence, Commitment, and
    Collaboration.* Lake Forest, IL: New Horizons. www.newhorizonsbooks.net. Reprinted with
    permission.
Appendix B, "Taking a Closer Look at an Infant or Toddler's Daily Schedule" from McCormick
    Center for Early Childhood Leadership, National Louis University (mccormickcenter
    .nl.edu). Reprinted with permission.
Printed in Canada
21   20   19   18   17   16   15   14   1   2   3   4   5   6   7   8

Library of Congress Cataloging-in-Publication Data
Curtis, Deb.
 Designs for living and learning : transforming early childhood environments /
Deb Curtis and Margie Carter. — Second Edition.
     pages cm
 Includes bibliographical references.
 ISBN 978-1-60554-372-7 (paperback : acid-free paper)
 ISBN 978-1-60554-373-4 (e-book)
1. Education, Preschool—United States—Planning. 2. Child care—United States—
Planning. 3. Classroom environment—United States.
I. Carter, Margie, 1942- II. Title.
 LB1140.23.C87 2014
 372.21—dc23
                    2014021329

8/12/15

For Anita Rui Olds
1940–1999

"Children are miracles. Believing that every child is a miracle can transform the way we design for children's care. When we invite a miracle into our lives, we prepare ourselves and the environment around us. We may set out flowers or special offerings. We may cleanse ourselves, the space, or our thoughts of everything but the love inside us. We make it our job to create, with reverence and gratitude, a space that is worthy of a miracle! Action follows thought. We can choose to change. We can choose to design spaces for miracles, not minimums."

Anita Rui Olds, 1999

For Jim Greenman
1949–2009

"Perhaps if we thought more about childhoods and less about needs, some of our programs would look less like schools and more like homes and children's museums, or like fields and parks. We might develop varied places with a genuine sense of place—of beauty, variety, and elements of surprise and mystery; places where adults and children delight at times in simply being together, messing about, and working at the tasks that daily living requires."

Jim Greenman, 1999

Kawartha Child Care Services, Peterborough, ON, Canada

Contents

Acknowledgments xi

Introduction 1

Chapter 1   Lay a Foundation for Living and Learning 17

Chapter 2   Think beyond a Traditional Classroom 35

Chapter 3   Create Connections, a Sense of Place and Belonging 59

Chapter 4   Keep Space Flexible and Materials Open-Ended 89

Chapter 5   Design Natural Environments That Engage Our Senses 127

Chapter 6   Provoke Wonder, Curiosity, and Intellectual Challenge 153

Chapter 7   Engage Children in Symbolic Representations, Literacy, and the Visual Arts 189

Chapter 8   Enhance Children's Use of the Environment 217

Chapter 9   Launch the Process of Transforming an Environment 235

Chapter 10   Face Barriers and Negotiate Quality Standards 265

Chapter 11   Seek Children's Ideas about Environments 295

Afterword 321

Notes 322

Appendix A   Tools for Assessing Your Environment 323

Appendix B   Tools to Reflect on Quality Rating Scale Components 333

Inspire New Zealand Study Tour, Auckland, New Zealand

Acknowledgments

As authors, we've been so encouraged to see the response to the first edition of this book over the last decade. Educators around the globe have sent us examples of how they have translated the principles we offered into their own early childhood environments. College instructors began to use *Designs for Living and Learning* as a textbook, and this sparked new thinking and innovation. We had the good fortune to travel across the United States, Canada, Australia, and New Zealand to visit and, in many cases, revisit a variety of programs and see firsthand how they've been diligently working to create spaces for childhood and resist standardization. We extend our heartfelt appreciation to all of you who've taken up this challenge.

As we began work on this second edition, we put out a call for contributions, particularly in the areas we wanted to offer more examples to inspire others. The response to this call was overwhelmingly generous. We heard from scores of early educators, both familiar and unfamiliar to us, and though we weren't able to use all that was sent to us, we were quite heartened by all the wonderful examples of environments that children are spending their days in. We were pleased, too, with the stories of those who are trying to insert a reflective aspect in their work with rating scales and Quality Rating and Improvement Systems (QRIS).

All of the photos in this book were gathered by us or our colleagues in the field, not by professional photographers. Each comes from everyday work of living and learning with children in an early childhood program. Our special appreciation goes out to the following people who significantly supported our efforts to create this book. The inspiring educators in Aotearoa New Zealand have significantly contributed to our thinking with their exemplary indoor/outdoor environments for their youngest citizens. Year after year they not only warmheartedly welcomed Margie to bring North American educators on study tours of their programs, but graciously allowed us to use photos and stories from their programs. We extend deep appreciation to Chris Bayes, Diocesan School for Girls, Auckland, New Zealand; Lorraine Manuela, Tots Corner, Auckland, New Zealand; Julienne Exton and Brigette Towle, Kids' Domain Early Learning Centre, Auckland, New Zealand; Therese Visser, Browns Bay Pre-School, Auckland, New Zealand; Karen Liley, Te Puna Kōhungahunga, Auckland, New Zealand; Thelma Chapman and Susan Winiata, Awhi Whanau Early Childhood Centre, Auckland, New Zealand; Jenny Jones and Adrienne

Thomson, Magic Garden Care and Education Centre, Auckland, New Zealand; Adrienne Wilkens, Sophia's Preschool, Oakura, New Zealand; Bronwyn Glass, Botany Downs Kindergarten, Auckland, New Zealand; and Heather Durham, Helensville Montessori, Helensville, New Zealand. Thanks to Andy Dean, Herb Foley, Raymond Dixon, and Barbara Ormond for allowing us to photograph the beautiful mural created by children on the University of Auckland campus. Across the "ditch" in Australia, Fran Bastion and Casula Pre-School, Liverpool City Council Early Childhood Program, Liverpool, Australia, offered us great examples for the first edition of this book and rallied contributions for this edition as well.

We are grateful to our colleagues across Canada who also provided numerous examples of wonderful environments for young children. Our Harvest Resources Associates; Lorrie Baird, Kawartha Child Care Services, Peterborough, Ontario, Canada; and Anne Marie Coughlin, London Bridge Child Care Services, London, Ontario, Canada, have worked with scores of educators in their own organizations and throughout Canada to inspire them to rethink the kind of environments young children deserve. We appreciate the contributions of Angela Woodburn, Lindsay Sparkes, and Andrea Dewhurst, London Bridge Child Care Services; Lorrie Baird and the educators of Kawartha Child Care Services; Melanie Bacon, Kerrie Isaac, Shauna Coons, and Nicole Ferguson, Saskatchewan Institute of Applied Science and Technology (SIAST) Child Development Center, Regina, Saskatchewan, Canada; Melissa Gogolinski, Isabel F. Cox School, Redcliff, Alberta, Canada; Susan Stacey, Junior Primary Programme at Halifax Grammar School, Halifax, Nova Scotia, Canada; Darlene Nantarath and Tammy Nucci, Ashton Meadows Child Care, Markham, Ontario, Canada; Tami Brandrick and Lori O'Leary, Saskatoon Early Childhood Education Demonstration Centre, Saskatoon, Saskatchewan, Canada; and Elizabeth Hicks, Halifax, Nova Scotia.

Donna King is a remarkable teacher and designer of children's environments and someday should have her own book focused on the stunning work done at Children First in Durham, North Carolina. In the meanwhile, she has significantly enriched both the first and second edition of *Designs for Living and Learning* with all her contributions. Working for many years with the centers who are part of United Way Bright Beginnings in Houston, Texas, we've seen a remarkable transformation in their environments and want to extend special recognition to Marcela Clark, Shannon McClellan, Sanjuana Frank, Kassondra Brown, Fran Brockington, and the United Way Bright Beginnings, Houston, center directors who have helped to make contributions to this book: Mitzi Bartlet, House of Tiny Treasures; Noemi Ocampo, Association for the Advancement of Mexican Americans; Leslie Jeter, Destiny Village Child Care; Francine Robinson, Waltrip High School

Child Development Center; Sharon Walker, The Bridge Over Troubled Waters; and Toni Livingston, Chinese Community Center.

In recent years Deb has appreciated the opportunity to work with administrators, teachers, and family providers associated with Preschool for All, First 5, San Francisco, California, and extends particular appreciation to the following people who made contributions to this book: Belann Giaretto, Nadia Jaboneta, and Brian Silveira, Pacific Primary Pre-School, San Francisco, California; Barbara Manzanares, Child's Play Family Childcare, San Francisco, California; Teresa Carias, Good Samaritan Family Resource Center, San Francisco, California; and Julie Fellom, Neighborhood Playgarden, San Francisco, California. We also thank other California colleagues: Kim Nave and Paula Fitch, The Learning Center, Palo Alto, California; Sue Britton and Eric Hart, Step One School, Berkeley, California; Arlae Alston, Baskin 1 Early Head Start, Santa Cruz, California; Mark Whitney, MiraCosta College, Oceanside, California; Mary Ashley, Lisa Meyers, and Lisa Curiel, Mission College Child Development Center, Santa Clara, California; Brenda Favish, Bill and Sid Rubin Preschool at Congregation Beth Israel, San Diego, California; Jo Lee, Mills College Children's School, Oakland, California; Sadie Parrinello and Robin Jurs, Ventana School, Los Altos, California; Jayanti Tambe, Pacific Oaks Children's School, Pasadena, California; Nancy Brown and Janis Keyser. For their contributions to the first edition that we carried over to this new one, we again thank Alise Shaffer at Evergreen Community School, Santa Monica, California, and Becky Candra, formerly at La Jolla United Methodist Church Nursery School, La Jolla, California.

Despite her extensive travel work, Margie has maintained a strong relationship with some centers close to home in Seattle. Hilltop Children's Center in Seattle, Washington, has made her feel like extended family; and in addition to the carryover contributions of Ann Pelo and Sarah Felstiner from the first edition, she extends appreciation to Cassie Tondreau, Joel Metschkel, Sandra Clark, and Liddy Wendell for new contributions. Special thanks to Luz Casio, Karina Rojas, and Elidia Sangerman, who always welcome Margie to engage with their work at the Southwest Early Learning Center, Sound Child Care Solutions (SCCS) Seattle, Washington, and the Refugee and Immigrant Family Center (RIF), SCCS, Seattle, Washington. Thanks go to several other Seattle SCCS center staff as well: Megan Arnim, Joyce Jackson, Jill Kennedy, Sandra Floyd, Melody Dayton, and Julie Bisson at Epiphany Early Learning Preschool, SCCS; Naomi Peterson at Pinehurst Child Care Center; Gloria Hodges at Little Eagles Child Development Center, SCCS; and Lisa Meier at Interlaken Preschool, SCCS. Hap Hanchett's design work on SCCS centers has helped us illuminate some of the principles we have included in this book.

Over the years, we have followed the transformations at the Chicago Commons Child Development Center (Head Start) in Chicago, Illinois, which has refused to let a bureaucratic mentality or an overwhelming body of regulations and requirements get in their way of creating exceptional environments that value children and families. Special thanks to Janice Woods, Kevin Durney, Jesus Oviedo, and staff at their Chicago Commons Child Development Program (Head Start) centers: Paulo Freire Family Center, Nia Family Center, Guadalupano Family Center, and Taylor Center for New Experiences. And to Karen Haigh and Peg Callaghan, who initially brought us to Chicago Commons Child Development Center (Head Start) to see their remarkable work.

While we weren't able to use all the examples they sent us, we are grateful to the following educators for showing us some lovely examples of their work: Dee Ann Perea, Children's Studio, Bellevue, Washington; Lisa Warner, Laura Edwards, Kathy Dutton, and Kelly Gant, Second Presbyterian Weekday School, Louisville, Kentucky; Laurie Cornelius and Terry Haye, Clark College Early Learning Center, Vancouver, Washington; Nancy Gerber, Little Peoples' Family Child Care, Spokane, Washington; Melanie Castillo and Sabrina Ball, Pinnacle Presbyterian Preschool, Scottsdale, Arizona; and Alison Maher and Ellen Hall, Boulder Journey School, Boulder, Colorado. Some programs featured in this book are new to us and we haven't visited, but we appreciate the examples we've seen from the following people: Vicky Flessner, Highland Plaza United Methodist Preschool, Hixson, Tennessee; Rukia Monique Rogers, The Highlander School, Atlanta, Georgia; and Shanna Kincheloe, Micky Morton, and Nikki Dolan, East Tennessee State University Little Buccaneers Laboratory Program, Johnson City, Tennessee. Thanks to Christie Colunga, Josh Trommier, and Felipe Gutierrez for their contributions from Paradise Valley Community College, Phoenix, Arizona. We extend our apologies to anyone we have unintentionally overlooked or incorrectly identified in the photo location credits. We have tried to keep good records, but it's possible we lost something in the avalanche of examples sent our way.

For helping us think through the challenging issues of working with rating scales, standards, and financing facility improvements, we extend appreciation to Lisa Lee, Kelly Mathews, Ann Hentschel, Paula Jorde Bloom, and Carol Sussman. Ann was enormously important as a critical friend helping to clarify some confusion we had with environment rating scales (ERS) and QRIS systems.

We thank Beth Wallace for the photo of Anita Rui Olds; and Carol White, Bonnie Neugebauer, Emma Greenman, and Jane Lurie for helping us track down a photo that captures the spirit of Jim Greenman. We extend appreciation to Jeanne Hunt for her wonderful photographs of centers in Aotearoa New Zealand, especially the one she captured for the cover of this second edition. We also offer deep gratitude to Sanjuana Frank and Elidia Sangerman for their ongoing translation of our work into Spanish. We enjoyed working with the team at Redleaf Press: Kyra Ostendorf, editor; Jim Handrigan, creative director; Mari Kesselring, production editor; and David Heath, director. They are always open to our design ideas, even as they continue to teach us about the world of publishing.

Lastly, for their valuable ideas and drawings about environments they especially like, we thank the children who made particular contributions to this book: Scarlet, Andrews, and Isabelle at Kids' Domain Early Learning Centre, Auckland, New Zealand; Will, Gray, Nan, Ella, Amelia, Charlie, Luke, and Charles at Second Presbyterian Weekday School, Louisville, Kentucky; Grace and Hayden at Stoneybrook Early Childhood Learning Centre, London Bridge Child Care Services, London, Ontario, Canada; Genevive at Junior Primary Programme at Halifax Grammar School, Halifax, Nova Scotia, Canada; Frankie, Ellis, Bram, Ryder, and Nora at Pacific Primary Pre-School, San Francisco, California; Eli at Clark College Early Learning Center, Vancouver, Washington; Daniel, Ella, and Yvonne at West Huron Early Childhood Learning Centre, London Bridge Child Care Services, Zurich, Ontario, Canada; Ben and Fredrick at Epiphany Early Learning Preschool, SCCS, Seattle, Washington; Everett, Justice, Lauren, Reyna, and Zella at Boulder Journey School, Boulder, Colorado; Makayla at Ashton Meadows Child Care, Markham, Ontario, Canada; and Audrey, Sela, and Lucia at Hilltop Children's Center, Seattle, Washington.

Association for Advancement of Mexican Americans, United Way Bright Beginnings, Houston, TX

Introduction

In the first edition of this book we put forward a call to early childhood care and education folks to reclaim our profession's roots, rethink what we want our programs to stand for, and transform program environments for young children. We believed then, and over a decade later continue to believe, that our profession is at a critical crossroads, with some continuing and some new challenges before us. If together we are willing to meet the challenge of taking charge of our future as a profession, we have a rich history to draw on and some new pioneers to inspire us. The alternative is for children to spend the early years of their childhoods in cookie-cutter, sterilized, commercialized settings. The choice before us is one of enriching or diminishing our human potential.

Over the past forty years, the early childhood field has formed standards to help educators and families recognize quality programs for children. For instance, mention the topic of environments and most educators have images of familiar room arrangements with the same type of learning areas and materials—easy to spot when you peek into almost any accredited child care, preschool, or Head Start classroom. Early childhood educators have established professional standards that stress the importance of an orderly, safe environment; learning areas; and materials that are culturally and developmentally appropriate. Our profession has developed rating scales and assessment tools to keep us reaching for higher quality. Most states now have implemented Quality Rating and Improvement Systems (QRIS) with Environment Rating Scales (ERS). Researchers and policy makers now recognize early childhood as a key time of life for young learners, and our government and private foundations are pronouncing early education as a priority. The tireless (or should we say tiring?) advocacy work of so many early childhood professionals is paying off, and we all have much to celebrate and be proud of.

However, inherent in most good things are the seeds of their opposites. In many cases, those who have little direct experience with teaching young children are shaping the new government emphasis on the importance of early childhood, and their emphasis is on preparing children as future citizens, rather than seeing them as today's citizens. Standards and policies are often developed with a tenor of mistrust of the actual teachers and a presumption that outside experts know what is best. This concern underlies the development of the book you are holding. With the first edition of

Designs for Living and Learning, we were seeing homogenization and institutionalization everywhere in early childhood programs with commercial, if not political, interests beginning to shape early childhood settings. The tenor of this standardization of environments has somewhat shifted over the last decade, with more attention to connecting children to nature and more use of research on the importance of lighting, air quality, and the

Children First, Durham, NC

impact of color on behavior. Though early childhood catalogs and conference exhibit hall vendors still feature an abundance of plastic, artificial, and prefabricated materials, they have started to include materials with more neutral colors and natural fibers. This doesn't diminish the danger of standardization, however, because programs typically fill their rooms with catalog furnishings. The rooms still all look the same, with no clear identity of the community the program is a part of. Busy administrators fall prey to "one-stop shopping" for their programs, eager to earn high ratings in their QRIS to secure new funding. Traveling across the United States, we've discovered that even beautiful environments with top scores on rating scales can easily lack an identity and feel soulless.

When programs rely only on commercial vendors and think only in terms of compliance with regulations, they typically forget to define the core values they need to guide their selection of materials or to help plan their environment. They fail to develop a unique identity and begin to look like an early childhood catalog, not a particular community in a particular place. Thus, though lip service is given to early childhood programs as being a home away from home and the term "developmentally appropriate" is widely used in the current climate of assessment and academic benchmarks for school readiness, too many programs continue to feel like schools or standardized institutions. True, most programs don't have children sitting at little desks, but they do regulate children's time and routines, remind children of the rules, and surround them with uniform learning materials. Early childhood programs may not implement ringing bells or have long hallways to walk down, but too many of them are organized around schedules, standards, checklists, and assessment tools.

Outside of the United States we have seen a more expansive vision for childhood represented in early education programs. But within the United States, a more enriched vision is normally only found in isolated little pockets of alternative and independent programs—programs not typically intended to remedy income and academic inequities with subsidized government funding. Of course, our field wants to close the so-called achievement gap. But with this goal, programs need to continually ask which children and families are privileged with a positive view of who they are and thus offered more expansive possibilities, and which children and families are continually viewed as deficient, "not able" and not deserving of time to play and experience the joy, rather than the stress, of learning. Addressing that inequity has great potential to erase the inequities in school achievement.

Finding Inspiration from Early Pioneers

How well do you know our field's history as a profession: the theories and philosophical and political influences that have shaped it? In studying the forebears (John Dewey, Friedrich Froebel, Maria Montessori, Caroline Pratt, Patty Smith Hill, Rudolf Steiner, and others) who laid the foundation for early care and education program environments in the United States, we find important concepts that are seldom referred to by today's practitioners outside of specialized child development circles. Perhaps this is because teacher education hasn't included this history or much about philosophy and theory. Despite any limitations in their thinking, there is much to learn from these pioneers. Postmodern thinkers and academics see the limitations and bias of the constructs that have shaped our US early childhood education practice. Overall, US constructs of "best practice" have focused more on individual developmental theories and less on sociocultural ones. Legitimate criticism has been leveled at some of these early thinkers—for instance, Jean Piaget—because each of them came out of a particular historical context and cultural setting with internal contradictions that suggest their ideas might be less relevant or unsuitable for today's world. *Designs for Living and Learning* doesn't advocate any strict philosophical stance or endorse a single theoretician; as authors, we acknowledge an eclectic set of influences.

Toward the end of the nineteenth century, several important educators began challenging the notion of sterile, passive classroom environments and launched a movement for children to have hands-on learning materials and experiences. German educator Friedrich Froebel, referred to as "the father of kindergarten," launched a far-reaching revolution in early childhood education by offering physical objects to children as the basis of their learning. He designed blocks and other playthings to be a series of "gifts and occupations" that are part of a systematic method for teaching children through manipulatives. We agree with the criticism that his approach was too structured and limited children's self-initiated engagement. However, the important idea of offering children aesthetically pleasing manipulative materials as "invitations to learning" has its roots in Froebel's idea of presenting learning materials as gifts. Maria Montessori, Patty Smith Hill, and Caroline Pratt were critics of Froebel, but they certainly built on his ideas, as today's educators have built on theirs. Our profession has Montessori to thank for the concept of child-size furnishings and materials arranged with attention to order, aesthetics, and sensory exploration. Hill's recognition of children's need for big-body activity and social experiences led to the creation of larger wooden blocks for their play, a staple of any early childhood program. Pratt further extended the idea of block play by developing sets of unit blocks with accompanying props. She suggested supplying children with an abundance of basic, open-ended materials and ample space to independently and cooperatively explore and create with them. Our profession is indebted to the early schools and practitioners who first popularized these ideas, notably Harriet Merrill Johnson and Lucy Sprague Mitchell, City and Country School and Bank Street School for Children, both in New York City. John Dewey's concept of education for democracy is one that influences our thinking as authors and, indeed, Loris Malaguzzi and the early educators of Reggio Emilia Italy studied his ideas and built on them. People familiar with the Waldorf schools founded by Rudolf Steiner may also see shades of that influence in *Designs for Living and Learning*. Steiner's general philosophical positions are open to question, but we concur with his idea that education should give children regular experiences with natural materials and the rhythms of the seasons. Waldorf schools have a strong emphasis on the arts, imagination, creativity, and moral well-being. Though Steiner lived a century ago, we concur with his critique of setting up schools to meet economic needs rather than the needs of children.

Learning from Contemporary Pioneers

As graduate students at Pacific Oaks College in Pasadena, California, in the 1980s, we were fortunate to be mentored by Elizabeth Prescott and Elizabeth Jones, who pioneered early thinking about creating homelike settings for full-time child care programs. Early on, we made use of the critical components they outlined for program settings, and we are indebted to their ideas about environments, materials, and the importance of observing children's play for our own learning. Their contributions have influenced wide sectors of the early childhood field with respect to the importance of creating environments that engage children in complex play that leads to deeper learning for both the children and teachers.

Two other significant players and organizations in the adoption of child-centered environments and materials in early childhood programs are Diane Trister Dodge and her Creative Curriculum associates at Teaching Strategies and David Weikart and his colleagues at the HighScope Foundation. In her early years of becoming a teacher educator, Margie became a HighScope trainer. In the process, she learned a great deal about active learning for adults and the potential for children and adults to reflect on their work together. Over the years, both of us as authors have appreciated the dialogue and collegial relationship we have had with Dodge. While Teaching Strategies and HighScope each have different curriculum elements and emphases, both approach children as active, hands-on learners who benefit from an attractive, orderly room arrangement with an array of materials to select from and use in open-ended ways. Because of the widespread work of Dodge, Weikart, and their associates, the early childhood field has moved away from a more scattered, informal "toy box" approach to classrooms with designated interest areas or learning centers, each stocked with well-organized materials in labeled baskets on shelves. Long before we heard the Italians of the schools of Reggio Emilia refer to "the environment as the third teacher," Dodge and Weikart had set up training programs and demonstration classrooms to show teachers how to design environments with the potential to engage children in self-initiated play. While we are not without concern about the standardization that has resulted in the rigid adoption of their curriculums, we recognize their initial work helped to make environments and routines more child-centered than adult-centered, with a strong emphasis on developmentally appropriate practices.

When we read *Alerta: A Multicultural, Bilingual Approach to Teaching Young Children* by Leslie R. Williams and Yvonne De Gaetano in 1984, we learned how to move away from a superficial multicultural approach and toward cultural relevancy in setting up environments for children. In *Alerta*, the authors emphasize the need to reflect the lives and communities of the children and families in teaching environments, which pushed us to develop concrete strategies to that end. Other pioneers who stressed the importance of cultural relevancy in the social-emotional environment include Carol Brunson Day, Louise Derman-Sparks, Janet Gonzalez-Mena, Janice Hale, Lily Wong Fillmore, and Gloria Ladson-Billings. J. Ronald Lally and his colleagues at WestEd Program for Infant/Toddler Care (PITC) have been vital champions of the important idea that working with infants and toddlers involves more than caregiving; it is a place where identities are being shaped. In our own city of Seattle, Sharon Cronin and

University of Auckland, Epsom Campus, Auckland, New Zealand

Carmen Sosa Massó have developed useful approaches to creating dual language, bicultural environments, routines, and programming. Their publication *Soy Bilingue: Language, Culture, and Young Latino Children* and ongoing teacher education work have launched an education thrust that extends beyond the Latino community, calling for cultural and linguistic democracy as a goal for education. The influence all these remarkable warriors have had on our work is deep and lasting.

Though we never met her, Anita Rui Olds is one of the strongest contemporary influences on the program environments that inspire us today. Trained as a social psychologist and self-taught in architecture and interior design, Olds taught others how to create environments for children that comfort, heal, and inspire them. For a number of years, she conducted classes and seminars that provided adults with the experiential evidence and practical guidelines to create spaces that draw the most power out of children. That has been the approach of our teacher education work from the start. Olds urged our profession to reconsider design elements often deemed luxuries and claim them as necessities. We are indebted to her fierceness in reminding us that we should be creating sacred spaces for children and planning for miracles, not minimums. Olds has laid the tracks for many future pioneers, and her *Child Care Design Guide* is an invaluable resource for architects and designers of purpose-built early childhood facilities. Carl Sussman and his associates in the Boston area have carried into practice Olds's early emphasis on child-specific environments. They have gotten significant traction advocating for investment in purpose-built early childhood facilities as a quality improvement strategy for the public and community investment agenda in the state of Massachusetts. This work is a model we should all be attentive to and learn from.

Jim Greenman was the first colleague we encountered who consistently used the term "places for childhood" as a mandate for early learning environments. His initial book, *Caring Spaces, Learning Places*, is an exemplary resource in both conceptual and practical terms. Before we wrote the first edition of *Designs for Living and Learning*, Greenman's book was the primary reference point for the college courses we taught and the consulting we did. His handbook for infant and toddler programming, *Prime Times*, now in its second edition and coauthored with Anne Stonehouse and Gigi Schweikert, will also continue to have a long-lasting impact. Greenman was involved in the design of many fine early childhood buildings and playgrounds.

The schools and educators of Reggio Emilia have had a profound influence on us as authors and across our wider profession, helping us rethink what we are doing for children. They have challenged us to reexamine every inch of our environments for the messages being conveyed. By reminding us that it is not only the needs of children we should be considering, but the rights of children, these Italian educators have helped us transform our starting place when thinking about spaces for children. Their hard, hard work of building a dream out of the ashes of a war-torn country emerging from fascism should humble professionals in this country when we are tempted to offer excuses for our lack of will in facing down budget and policy limitations or litigation-driven constraints. The pioneers of Reggio Emilia were sharp-sighted in understanding the real meaning of homeland security, and they pressed forward with a vision that has given early childhood educators around the world a living model to visit and learn from. Because of their generosity of time, spirit, and resources, many programs in North America and across the globe are redesigning their environments and programs with inspiration from Reggio Emilia. They, too, are modern-day pioneers, and visiting some of these programs has influenced our thinking and made contributions to examples offered in this book.

Over the last decade, Margie has had the good fortune to make regular visits to Aotearoa New Zealand to learn from their early and current-day pioneers and see the remarkable way their national early childhood system has embraced the idea of translating their bicultural aspirations into inspiring early childhood environments. While there is a national curriculum, Te Whāriki, in their country, this hasn't resulted in standardized programs, but rather has engaged all educators in finding a strong identity for themselves and their centers. The tradition of the indigenous Maori people introducing themselves by their lineage, including their mountain and river, has deepened our understanding of the importance of creating a sense of place for children in our early childhood programs.

Quietly, behind the scenes, in cities and conferences across the United States, Edgar Klugman, Walter F. Drew, and a cadre of "play caucus" professionals and folks from educational repurposing centers have been providing early childhood educators with firsthand experiences of the value of

playing with open-ended, repurposed materials. They have touched thousands of teachers who have, in turn, changed their thinking and practice in providing beautiful, open-ended materials to children. (Plus, their repurposing has been good for the planet.) You'll see many examples of repurposing materials throughout the pages of this book.

In the first edition of *Designs for Living and Learning*, we confessed that one of the major shortcomings in our own professional development was a lopsided focus on indoor environments. We are strong believers in the value of outdoor spaces for children and have made it a priority to learn more about creating them with as much thought as indoor spaces. We have been inspired by programs that offer a deep connection to the natural world and offer multiple opportunities for active big-body play in their designs. These programs not only include aspects of adventure playgrounds outdoors, but they bring indoor activities outside with materials that allow for ongoing investigations, building, and collaborative play to take place in fresh air and under natural lighting. We've watched with delight the free flow of children between indoor and outdoor spaces in places such as Aotearoa New Zealand and California, and indeed, when Deb returned to work with toddlers in the rainy Pacific Northwest, she designed her program in this way. We strongly subscribe to the slogan of the Scandinavians, "There's no such thing as bad weather, just bad clothing." We find the forest school movement in Europe and countries beyond to be absolutely inspiring.

While the primary emphasis in this book is on young children who are typically developing, we believe the ideas can be adapted for children with special needs, or rights, as Reggio Emilia educators remind us. Indeed, these designs bring out more competencies than we often give these children credit for.

Expanding Our Vision of What Is Possible

We have spent the last fifteen or so years traveling the United States (and a few other countries) as authors, college instructors, speakers, children's teachers, and program consultants, sharing words and images of inspiration and experiential activities. We hope to convey our respect for children and our sense of gratitude and pride in our profession—we are indeed honored to do this work. In our travels we also convey strong words of caution and concern and a reminder that we must be ever vigilant as our profession continues to grow and be regulated. The emphasis on standards, assessments, and adopted curriculums is often overshadowing the children, families, and staff because there is a tendency to apply them narrowly without careful, innovative thinking. Too many programs have been developing what author and Harvard educator Tony Wagner calls "a culture of compliance" aimed at minimums, not dreams, for children and educators.

Embracing the idea of the environment as a significant educator in early childhood programs requires expanding your thinking beyond the notion of room arrangements. You must ask yourself what values you want to communicate through learning environments and how you want children and their teachers to experience their time in your program. From the physical to the social and emotional environment, how are you demonstrating that you respect and treasure childhood and the identity of particular children and their families? Are you showing pride in your work and an ongoing commitment to developing yourself and your profession? Apart from the benchmarks of outside assessors, to what do you want to hold yourself accountable?

We have received a strong, heartwarming response to the inspiring stories and photographs of environments featured in the first edition of this book. The response we got to our call for contributions to this second edition was enormously gratifying, reassuring us that early childhood educators are on the move to create wonderful environments in their programs. We continue to encounter those who claim, "But we can't do that . . . our space isn't big enough . . . we don't have the budget . . . our licensor won't let us." We remind the naysayers that some years ago, Deb decided to leave her college teaching career to try these design ideas working directly with children. She initially worked again with preschoolers for eight years, and then for the next five years she found a new love in working with toddlers. This very personal, as well as professional, journey, along with the inspiration of countless other educators we have encountered, has taught us many lessons. We've learned that with vision and determination,

Children First, Durham, NC

you can make a way out of no way. Bigger ideas about quality are doable, and they don't require an unreasonable amount of money. Taking time, working with extraordinary diligence, and seeing yourself as creative and resourceful can help you step beyond the barriers to creating great places for childhood.

When Deb returned to redevelop herself as a practicing children's teacher, Margie continued to work as a college instructor, consultant, and coach for early childhood programs. She discovered that as inspiring as our book *Designs for Living and Learning* might be, teachers and administrators couldn't get beyond adding a bit of window dressing unless they had a process for examining why they do what they do and for exploring the values they want reflected in their work. It became clear that it wasn't just the physical environment and materials that needed reconfiguring in these programs—the daily routines, use of time, support structures, communications, and relationships all had to be rethought if the environment was to be effectively designed, cared for, and used. The social-emotional environment, what we think of as the classroom or program culture, is intricately related to what the Italian educators of Reggio Emilia call "the image" of the child, teacher, and parents together as part of the teaching and learning process. Though we don't dwell on aspects of the social-emotional environment in this book, it is an implied foundation and became a significant focus for two of our other books, *Learning Together with Young Children* and *The Visionary Director*.

Designs for Living and Learning is shaped by a particular set of values and beliefs we hold as early childhood professionals. It draws on the influences outlined above, the inventive and creative work of early childhood teachers and providers we have met and heard about, along with continual reflections on our own work over the years. Values we hold for children include the following:

Hilltop Children's Center, Seattle, WA

- Children deserve to be surrounded with beauty, softness, and comfort, as well as order and attention to health and safety.

- Childhood is a time of wonder and magic, where dreams and imagination get fueled and issues of power are explored.

- In their early years, children need multiple ways to build a solid identity and connections with those around them—their families, peers, role models, culture and community, and the natural world.

- Children bring a powerful drive to learn and understand what is around them. They learn best when offered interesting materials, ample time, and opportunity to investigate, transform, and invent—without the interruptions of a teacher's schedule.

- Children come to early childhood programs with ideas, experiences and skills that are "funds of knowledge" from their families and communities, which need to be acknowledged and drawn upon as teachers coach them into new learning. They have vivid imaginations and theories about the world, which need to be taken seriously and explored more fully.

- Children have active bodies and a desire for adventure; they have the right to show adults how powerful and competent they are.

- Children have a wide range of strong feelings; they deserve to express their feelings and be respected. Their emotional intelligence is as important to cultivate as intelligence related to academic

Tots Corner, Auckland, New Zealand

pursuits. And in fact, current interpretations of neuroscience for educational settings and the particular research we study in Alison Gopnik's book *The Philosophical Baby*, and Antonio Damasio's book *The Feeling of What Happens*, reminds us that emotional intelligence is part of a child's rapid brain development and is essential to academic learning.

When you hold these values for children, you shape their environments with a different kind of intent than just planning learning centers or striving to be compliant for high scores on ERS. Holding these values for children means you consider aesthetic components that provoke a sense of wonder and delight. You'll not only try to keep children safe, but you will put elements in the environment that encourage physical, social, and intellectual risk taking so children experience the joy and power of learning with others. Furnishings will go beyond standard early childhood tables, chairs, and shelving to include home furnishings and aspects of the children's families, culture, and the wider community and elements of nature that are around them. Your environment will reflect the unique identity of your history, who you are, and who you are striving to be.

We titled this book *Designs for Living and Learning* because we believe it is a mistake to make artificial distinctions between how young children live, play, relate, and learn. Their bodies, minds, emotions, and spirits come to your program as a package all wrapped up in an ever-accumulating set of experiences, relationships, and connections that shape learning. You must act with intention to make your beliefs about the value of children, childhood, family, community, and the learning and teaching process visible in the environments you create for children.

Navigating Your Way through This Book

In *Designs for Living and Learning*, we take early childhood educators deeper into our understandings and wider into our dreams for children's lives and communities. Our hope is to inspire an examination of the values you use to influence your work as a caregiver, educator, administrator, or teacher educator. We want to nudge you into transforming your thinking and environments with a determination to move past barriers. We encourage you to draw on your own sense of design, comfort, and aesthetics as you work with the principles and elements we offer. Take time to explore unusual materials to discover their potential and offer them with intention and curiosity to children. Turn this work into ongoing teacher research.

We suspect you will be drawn to the beautiful photographs throughout the book before reading any of the text. As you look at the photos, be aware that they can be studied further as representations of particular ideas discussed. In the first chapter, we offer an overview of the elements we feel are important to include in early care and learning environments and lay the foundation for the chapters to come. For this reason, it is worth reading first. You will find some initial snapshots to whet your appetite for discovering how these elements might look in a program. This chapter opens with an assessment tool we have created to help you look closely at how you are currently working with these elements. If you follow the guidelines of drawing a floor plan of your particular space and then coding it as directed, you will discover where you might need some fresh ideas and how you can turn to children to help you assess how your environment is experienced by them.

The remaining chapters each focus on one of the elements introduced in chapter 1. Each chapter opens with "Look Inside," a short activity for self-reflection on the topic at hand. We then offer thoughts and examples of how the larger environmental features might reflect the elements under consideration. These "macro" ideas are always under the heading "Invite

Living" and are further illustrated with photos in the "Inventors at Work" section of the chapter.

Under the heading "Invite Learning" in each chapter, we consider the "micro" environment of a program with examples of interesting materials for children and a discussion of how their presentation is designed to invite discovery and investigation. Photographs serve as examples of how children have used these materials in different settings. At the end of each chapter you are asked to consider possible environmental arrangements and inventions of your own.

If you make your way sequentially through the chapters focusing on each of the different elements, you will arrive at chapter 8, where we suggest some important ways you can enhance children's use of the

Kawartha Child Care Services, Peterborough, ON, Canada

physical environment. You will find an overview of considerations for the social-emotional environment you create to support children's ability to work collaboratively and develop a focus and intention in their use of the environment. There are ideas about organizing time and routines, helping children discover and use materials, providing meaningful jobs, and choosing different teacher roles for yourself.

In this second edition, we include a new chapter 9 with ideas on the process of transforming your environment, offering a protocol with examples of what some programs have done. Chapter 10 provides thoughts for overcoming barriers you may face, interlaced with specific stories about successful negotiations among teachers, directors, licensors, and quality rating monitors. These should refresh your determination to push for the transformations you want to make. Chapter 11 concludes the book, but it could potentially have been the starting place. It challenges us to increasingly consider children's rights, and—specific to their environments—to find ways of seeking and using their ideas for planning, assessing, and changing. This is the ultimate way we can show them respect and give them power as citizens. In the afterword, we offer a final idea about using *Designs for Living and Learning* with children themselves.

In the appendixes on the final pages, you will find assessment and reflective tools we've mentioned in the text to prompt more consideration of your environment. These are offered in Spanish and English with the hope that they will be more widely used.

As you move through *Designs for Living and Learning*, remember that it is in no way intended to be comprehensive or fully inclusive of all the considerations for creating early care and learning environments. Rather, our intent is to give you a set of values and elements to consider and a taste of how these have been translated into various settings. The examples here are from programs of many sizes and configurations, some fairly well resourced, but the majority operating with very limited budgets. Our guess is that you are looking for ideas to further your own journey of living and learning with children. Our hope is that these pages will provide you with plenty to consider and the inspiration to make your own transformations.

Kids' Domain Early Learning Centre, Auckland, New Zealand

CHAPTER 1

Lay a Foundation for Living and Learning

Assessing Your Environment

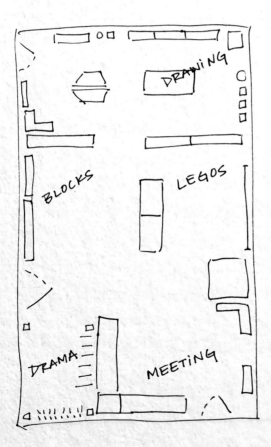

As you consider transforming your early childhood environment, start with an assessment of the way your space is designed now. First draw a simple floor plan of the room you are currently working in, one you are quite familiar with, or one you imagine using in a new job. As you sketch out the arrangements of the room, don't include a lot of detail. Provide just enough information to help you use the assessment that follows. You might want to read through the assessment first so you have a sense of the amount of detail that would be helpful.

The early childhood profession has developed many useful assessment tools and rating scales for programs to use in improving quality. However, the one you will use here is unlike the others. Instead of evaluating your space from a set of standards, regulations, or curriculum models, we will help you reconsider your environment from a child's point of view. The elements used in this assessment form the framework of a child-friendly space for living and learning; they are discussed at greater length in the rest of this book.

The components listed below are geared toward preschool or school-age children. The assessment is included in appendix A for photocopying and is available to download on the *Designs for Living and Learning* page at www.redleafpress.org. Appendix A and the Redleaf Press website also includes one assessment to evaluate your site for family-friendly environments, another for infant and toddler caregivers, and a third to assess the caregivers' and teachers' work environment. All of these resources are also available in Spanish in appendix B and on the Redleaf Press website.

Assessing From the Child's Perspective

Put yourself in the shoes of the young children who spend their days in your space. Consider the statements below from a child's perspective, and use them to assess your space. Write the number of each statement in all of the places on your floor plan where you are confident the statement is true:

1 = I can see who I am and what I like to do at school and at home.

2 = I see places that are comfortable for my tired mommy, daddy, grandma, or auntie to sit and talk with me or my teacher.

3 = The natural world can be found here (such as objects from nature, animals, or living specimens).

4 = There is something sparkly, shadowy, or wondrous and magical here.

5 = My teacher leaves a special object out here every day so I can use it many times and to try to figure out more about its properties and how it works.

6 = There are materials here that I can use to make representations of what I understand or imagine.

7 = I can feel powerful and be physically active here.

8 = I can learn to see things from different perspectives here, literally and through assuming roles in dramatic play.

9 = There is a cozy place here where I can get away from the group and be by myself.

10 = I see my name written, or I get to regularly write my name here.

11 = I get to know my teachers here—what they like, how they spend their time away from school, and which people and things are special to them.

Now examine your coded floor plan. Did you have trouble finding any of these components in your room? If so, you will probably find new ways to think about transforming your environment in this book.

Environments Reflect Values and Shape Identity

People in the United States spend most of their time in human-made environments of one kind or another. Some of these are carefully designed, while others appear to have been haphazardly put together. Spaces are typically created with some kind of purpose or intention, whether or not this is evident. Every environment implies a set of values or beliefs about the people who use a space and the activities that take place there. For example, having individual desks rather than grouping children at tables suggests that the teacher believes children learn best in isolation from one another and values individual work over group activities.

Thoughtfully planned or not, each environment also influences the people who use it in subtle or dramatic ways. People also have different preferences for the environment they feel most comfortable in at any given time. Depending on individual dispositions, experiences, cultural lenses, or needs of the moment, people may prefer to be alone or in the company of others, quiet or actively engaged, in bright or filtered light, or in an urban or wilderness setting. An environment may temporarily overstimulate or bore, calm or agitate those in it. Spending an extended period of one's life in an environment deemed unpleasant will eventually exact a toll. Because of this, a number of professional fields focus on designing spaces, from architecture to landscaping to lighting and interior design, marketing, and human psychology.

Children in the United States spend thousands of hours in early childhood programs. The early childhood profession now has assessment tools to define quality program environments. But most US programs have not drawn wisdom from those outside our profession who specialize in designing spaces. Our early childhood program spaces aren't typically put together with conscious, sustained attention to the values they communicate or the effect they have on the children and adults who spend their days in them. Perhaps this omission accounts for the awe that engulfs most visitors to the Italian schools of Reggio Emilia where the programs are housed in aesthetically gorgeous spaces that most early childhood teachers and administrators from anywhere in the world would love to live or work in. At the same time, Reggio Emilia environments deliberately reflect the community's values and beliefs about children, families, teachers, and the social construction of knowledge. Here's how Lella Gandini (2002), author and Reggio Children liaison, summarizes their intentions in designing spaces.

> The environment is the most visible aspect of the work done in the schools by all the protagonists. It conveys the message that this is a place where adults have thought about the quality and the instructive power of space. The layout of the physical space is welcoming and fosters encounters, communication, and relationships. The arrangement of structures, objects, and activities encourages choices, problem solving, and discoveries in the process of learning. There is attention to detail everywhere—in the color of the walls, the shape of the furniture, the arrangement of simple objects on shelves and tables.

While *Designs for Living and Learning* is not about the Reggio approach, Gandini's description of "attention to detail everywhere" is what we hope to provoke with this book. From our experience, when educators recognize that the spaces they design for children communicate a set of values, they begin to plan their environment differently. To do this, you won't just decorate or equip your room from a catalog, but rather, consider what equipment will communicate values such as trust and respect for children. If you believe children benefit from solving problems and negotiating conflicts, you'll provide ways for them to encounter those opportunities in the environment, perhaps by using benches at tables, rather than only chairs for individual seating. You'll recognize that learning doesn't just happen in designated areas with labels such as "Science Area" and "Writing Center," so you will offer opportunities for children to explore like scientists and find the value of reading and writing throughout your indoor and outdoor spaces. Making use of research on how color, light, and air quality impact feelings, behaviors, and well-being, you'll begin to reassign how you spend your limited budget for improving and maintaining your physical space. You'll remember that while the cultural emphasis is on getting them ready for school, the children who spend the bulk of their early years in settings away from home still deserve to have a rich and joyful childhood.

When you listen closely to the stories that adults tell of their favorite childhood memories, you get a picture of an environment in which children joyfully thrive. There are common themes in most of these memories: endless hours outdoors, fantasy play and inventions, raiding the refrigerator and cupboards when hungry, taking risks, and taking care of younger children. Sadly, too many early care and education programs don't think of themselves as responsible for creating children's favorite memories. In fact, many children today are denied some of the most pleasurable memories of childhood because of thoughtlessness or rigid interpretations of standards and regulations. Our field must go beyond the idea of equating quality to mean being compliant with regulations. We must recognize that the environments we create are shaping children's memories and their identities about who they are in the world and what they deserve.

The assessment tool at the beginning of this chapter uses common elements from countless stories of favorite childhood memories we solicited during trainings we have lead. From those stories we also identified elements that can be translated into principles to consider when planning your space:

- Think beyond a traditional classroom.
- Create connections, a sense of place and belonging.
- Keep space flexible and materials open-ended.
- Design natural environments that engage our senses.
- Provoke wonder, curiosity, and intellectual challenge.
- Engage children in symbolic representations, literacy, and the visual arts.
- Enhance children's use of the environment.
- Launch the process of transforming an environment.
- Face barriers and negotiate quality standards.
- Seek children's ideas about environments.

Each of the above considerations holds opportunities for educators to rethink the design of early childhood environments. Imagine how things might be different if you used the idea of creating a strong identity for children to design your early childhood program. When your environment engages children fully, you expand how you plan for physical, emotional, and cognitive learning. If the environment is designed to be another teacher in the program, then your work as a teacher is not only easier, but it engages more of your own creativity and learning. Embraced as a whole, this list of considerations expands understandings of how environments can be a powerful force in providing an enriched childhood that shapes children's identities as eager learners and citizens.

This book is structured around these elements, with ideas about how to use them in the larger features and arrangements of your space, and also in the specific details of the learning materials and how they are offered. The following is a brief summary of how we see the foundational elements that are required to go beyond standardized thinking about quality in designing an environment. In the coming pages, a chapter is devoted to each of these elements with further discussion and a range of specific visual examples to study. We use the word "study" here because the images go hand in hand with the text, illuminating each other with their principles and details. You can become a researcher of your own practice with these elements in mind.

Think beyond a Traditional Classroom

Early childhood programs can sometimes feel either sterile or cluttered and disorganized. Both possibilities have a negative impact on children. Using commercial catalogs to create classrooms filled with an assortment of bright primary colors and bulletin boards and walls crowded with cartoon alphabet images and look-alike art projects can easily trivialize what childhood is about and what children are capable of. For very young children our profession shouldn't even be using the language of classrooms. Jim Greenman suggests we find terms other than "classrooms"—terms such as "home bases" or "learning spaces"—to convey an image other than school for children's early learning experiences. As they learn to stand, walk, run, and jump, children need spaces for active bodies, for

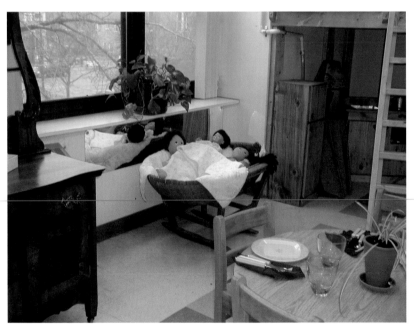

Taylor Center for New Experiences, Chicago Commons Child Development Program (Head Start), Chicago, IL

Working in the contexts of an urban center with a notable community history, along with Head Start regulations, this center meets their standards without looking at all like an institution. Here is the required housekeeping area, but it is stocked with familiar home furnishings, including china, glasses, cloth napkins, and living plants. Attention has been given to using various kinds of wood to unite the different elements of the space, making it aesthetically pleasing. All of the required materials to score well on a rating scale are part of this wider space, but none of it looks cluttered.

discovering friendships, and for exploring the wonder of the world. They need opportunities to be trusted with real tools and breakable materials. Designing environments for living and learning with children has to take into account brain research and the role of aesthetics, lighting, color, and smells in helping children focus and enjoy learning about learning. Designers have to be thoughtful in planning storage and looking at hallways, bathrooms, and outdoor places so that none of them look institutional for the one childhood our youngest citizens are allowed.

Create Connections, a Sense of Place and Belonging

Have you noticed that the strongest drive underlying children's daily experiences is the desire to have relationships with others and to be a member of a group? Because young children spend the majority of their waking hours away from their homes and families, they need us to help them maintain connections with their homes while they form new friendships and become part of a wider community. Our programs need to connect children to a sense of place in their community—the people, places, and natural world around them—and foster their growing identity.

When your environment has a cozy, homelike feel that allows for and encourages strong connections among the people there, children will experience a sense of belonging and security. Throughout your building

Association for the Advancement of Mexican Americans, United Way Bright Beginnings, Houston, TX

This early childhood classroom is designed to welcome not only the families whose children are enrolled, but those in the wider community its organization serves. Notice the objects and furniture that add beauty and softness, while plants and natural materials add interesting dimensions. The shelf and the basket filled with books invite adults to linger with their children, as do the tiered tables with things to explore. Photos of the children enrolled immediately create a sense of "who lives here," as do the smaller, framed photos of them at work and the displays of their art on the wall.

you can create a sense of softness in your selection of color, furnishings, lighting, and materials. You can add specific features that represent the interests, families, and cultures of the children and staff. Indoors and outdoors, you can create places for people to comfortably gather, get to know each other, and find avenues for further connections. Guide your selection and placement of equipment and materials to ensure opportunities for people to collaborate and demonstrate what they know.

Keep Space Flexible and Materials Open-Ended

While it's true that children need consistency and predictability, they also need program spaces designed with flexible options so that things can be moved and rearranged for specific purposes. Too often, once a room arrangement has been put into place, it rarely changes. Children are discouraged from taking things from one area to another or playing with material in unexpected ways. Being discouraged not only limits children's creativity, but it also limits the ever-deepening complexity they can benefit from in their play. Children come to early childhood programs with active bodies and imaginations. They are quick to use objects to represent things they are thinking about. Some spaces and materials will suggest dramatic themes that children are inherently eager to act out. Environments should provide opportunities for children to feel the power of their bodies and ideas.

Creating multilevel spaces inside, as well as on the playground, gives children a number of ways to explore spatial relationships with their bodies. You may envision a loft as a place for quiet reading, but when children are higher than adults, they often want to exhibit how powerful they feel. Rather than subdue their bodies, we need to find ways to help children use them as a regular part of their learning.

Here a collection of wood scraps, dowels, logs, driftwood, and old tile samples have been added to a block area with more traditional early childhood blocks. The children use these for building elaborate structures and creating games, and they take them to other parts of the room to become props for their play.

courtesy of Janis Keyser, Mountain View, CA

The guiding principle is to ensure that there are many ways for children and adults to use the space and materials. Your selections and arrangements should encourage children to pursue their interests and questions, represent what's on their minds, and build strong relationships and a love of learning. Modular furniture that can be turned and stacked in multiple ways will give you more flexibility than when everything is designed for a single use. Offering open-ended materials in a variety of areas will spark children's imaginations and speak to their desire to continually rearrange and combine materials for exploration and inventions.

Design Natural Environments That Engage Our Senses

Do you remember delighting in the smells, sounds, and textures of the world around you when you were young? It is well known that children investigate the world and learn through their senses, and things such as playdough, paint, manipulatives, sensory tables, and music devices are standard fare in most programs for young children. But many more sensory-related features can be included in program environments, ranging from engaging textures to captivating aromas. Consider herbs, flowers, leaves, naturally scented candles or soap, shells, rocks, feathers, branches, and pieces of bark and wood.

Filling your environment with aspects of the natural world can further soothe the senses and sensibilities of those present. When you contrast something as simple as a shelf of plastic baskets with a shelf containing natural fiber baskets, the different sensory experience is immediately apparent.

Children First, Durham, NC

To surround children with elements of the natural world, this program has brought the outside inside and given the children a large window with a view of an inviting outdoors where careful attention to landscaping and gardening are part of the playscapes. In the sensory table, attention is given to inviting exploration with a variety of woven and wooden materials typically found in Asian cultures. There are textures and aromas to discover as the children pursue some of their typical play themes of filling and dumping, poking, and making imprints and designs.

There are many ways to incorporate plants, water, natural light, and fresh air into your building. Outside, the landscaping on your playground should get as much attention as the equipment and toys you place there.

Provoke Wonder, Curiosity, and Intellectual Challenge

Do you recall the thrill of discovering a rainbow you created while outside playing with the garden hose? Or trying to find the source of a musical sound that caught your attention when a light wind stirred the air? Children are intensely fascinated with the physical world and how it works. You can simultaneously honor childhood and promote a love of learning by adding a wide range of engaging attractions and discoveries to your environment. This is especially effective when you include materials that provoke a sense of mystery and wonder so children become curious and intellectually engaged with objects in the world and what can be learned by manipulating them. Examples include items that play with light and its relationship to color, or pieces that reflect, sparkle, spin, make sounds, and move or are otherwise transformed by moving air. You can use natural light, air, projectors, and other simple technology to build these features into your environment. Consider various ways to discover and explore the wonder of colors. Give children opportunities to dismantle and study the parts of broken appliances and technology, help with bicycle repairs, and use real tools to build things they see in books, on the web, or have drawn themselves.

Children also love finding treasures—shells, feathers, rocks, coins, keys, flashlights, baubles, and beads. Rotate a supply of these and other intriguing objects in attractive baskets and boxes or as curiosities on a table or low shelf-top mirrors. Create nooks where you can place rocks that glitter or

Cutting off the plugs and removing any dangerous components, this center regularly offers children a variety of old technology and appliances to explore and study. The children are taught safety guidelines and invited to share their discoveries and questions.

Children's Studio, Bellevue, WA

shine, a set of costume jewelry gemstones, or holograms. Put books, cards, or photos nearby that relate to these objects to further stimulate children's inquiry. Because childhood is a time when the world seems full of magic and wonder, you can keep those brain pathways growing and expanding by placing intriguing discoveries in your environment.

Keep in mind that children need physical and intellectual engagement. Provide opportunities for them to use their bodies in safe but challenging ways.

Engage Children in Symbolic Representations, Literacy, and the Visual Arts

Early literacy has become a focus for most early care and education programs, and it is typical to see a selection of books, computers, markers, paper, signs, and labels in designated areas. But children don't just need a print-rich environment, they deserve multiple opportunities to witness and participate in the process of reading and writing, for pleasure as well

Magic Garden Care and Education Centre, Auckland, New Zealand

To expand their initial representational skills, this center has the children begin to draw their block structures, with a teacher coaching them to look closely at the details and start drawing one thing they see, then the next. Eventually the children learn to move around and draw how their structures look from different perspectives, including aerial views. The process of re-representing an idea from three-dimensional work with blocks to drawing on a flat paper not only presents children with cognitive challenges, thereby growing their brains, but also uses drawing as a pathway into the written word.

as for specific functions. Beyond the limited notions of reading and writing materials for the classroom, you can consider a wide range of other materials including magazines and newspapers, charts, diagrams, and reference and instruction books. Use technology thoughtfully as a supplement for children's research and reference work. And remember, early childhood environments should include materials that support children growing up in a multicultural, multilingual world.

Literacy involves unlocking a system of symbols and codes, and there are many ways you can expand children's experiences with this process. The wider world of symbolic representation extends into the visual arts. Adding a range of materials to explore the arts will encourage children to understand and express themselves using art materials, music, dance, and theatrical expressions. Early childhood environments should be stocked with materials and opportunities for what Howard Gardner calls "multiple intelligences," or what the educators of the Reggio approach refer to as the "hundred languages."

Enhance Children's Use of the Environment

Designing an environment with interesting materials sets the stage for investigation, complex play, and joy in learning. You also have to consider your role in the environment. If children haven't before experienced open-ended exploration of nontraditional materials or been trusted to work with adult tools or fragile objects, they will benefit from some initial encouragement, coaching, and side-by-side modeling of playing with the materials. Once the social-emotional culture of your room is established as one where children are able to engage fully with each other and the materials, your role as a teacher can shift. You begin the careful dance of allowing the children to play on their own, being present but minimizing intervention and talking only when needed. As you make this transition to a new role, find ways to meet up with the children's minds and engage them in inquiry by asking questions you are genuinely curious about. You look for when to offer additional materials and when to do behind-the-scenes cleanup so that the children can stay focused and continue to invest in their play.

Association for the Advancement of Mexican Americans, United Way Bright Beginnings, Houston, TX

The caregivers in this baby room wanted to give children opportunities to explore paint and paper in a way that would allow for it to be a sensory experience with their bodies. They believe babies deserve this kind of investigation and creatively planned for it by stretching large sheets of butcher paper from the back of a shelving unit across the floor in front of the babies. Because these babies are just learning to sit and explore their mobility, the caregiver sits close by, not only to keep the babies safe and the rug safe from paint, but also to watch closely the details of the babies' explorations and describe to them what they are doing. Do they seem to like the feel of the paint or be unsettled by it? Will they notice any change in the colors when they are combined? Will they show a preference for exploring with their hands or the brushes? Will they think the cup of paint is something to drink? These caregivers have used a number of strategies to enhance the children's use of materials, including their placement of the paper and choice of paint and using their own reassuring presence to offer a helping hand and language with rich vocabulary describing what the babies are doing.

Launch the Process of Transforming an Environment

Whether inspired by this book, a study tour, rating scale, or images you've seen online, beginning to change your environment shouldn't be about some decorating ideas or a quick fix. Be clear about the ideas, purpose, and values underpinning any changes you want to make. Significant transformation requires observing and listening, and careful thinking and rethinking, ideally through a process that gathers the perspectives and investment of others. Whether you do this work in isolation as a staff member or with the support of an outside consultant or volunteer, it is important to work with clear values and priorities. We offer in this book a protocol for launching this transformation process and a set of examples from different settings.

BEFORE

Refugee and Immigrant Family Center (RIF), Sound Child Care Solutions, Seattle, WA

AFTER

When this center came under new management, their first task was to begin to transform the classrooms. With support from a design consultation, a color pallet was chosen to soften the room and tie together different elements, such as the wall colors, bulletin boards, and rugs. Neutral wicker chairs were chosen, not only to replace the disarray of primary-colored plastic ones, but to reflect an aspect of furnishings found in many of the Asian countries their families come from. Added curtains, beads, and paper globe lights contribute to the new cozy, homelike feeling. Each of these new design elements were put into a book for the incoming teachers and families, helping them understand why these changes better serve the children. When the program's budget got replenished, their next goal was to de-clutter and replace many of the learning materials on the shelves.

Face Barriers and Negotiate Quality Standards

Some educators and administrators turn away from the ideas promoted in this book because they see more barriers than opportunities. With limited budgets, scores on assessments tied to funding, and periodic objections from regulators who think about risk as a danger rather than a benefit to children, it's tempting to forgo any attempt to be innovative and just conform to the standard way of doing things. We find that administrators and regulators alike sometimes feel disempowered. It's helpful for them to hear the voices of those who are negotiating a bigger vision and offering leadership to consider other possibilities. Seek out people who are forging ahead, find ways to reflect on the intent of regulations and assessment tools, and go beyond compliance as a definition of providing quality.

When this center initially built a loft to enhance the space in the classroom, licensors objected to the loft's height, the wide spacing of the railing dowels, and the easy access to the ceiling tiles it gave children. Through a negotiation process of augmenting the railing design; adding fabric to the ceiling; repurposing the space as a quiet, alone area; and documenting children's careful use of the loft, it has been allowed in the classroom. Each child who climbs the loft not only enjoys looking down on the room from on high, but also looking into the adjacent room through the window that was thoughtfully installed as part of the design so the children could feel connected to the classroom next door.

Southwest Early Learning Center, Sound Child Care Solutions, Seattle, WA

Seek Children's Ideas about Environments

Even when adults try to keep children's perspectives and "best interests" in mind, we often neglect to directly seek out children's ideas about the environment. Believing that children have a right to a voice and that their ideas are valuable in the planning and assessment process of an environment requires seeking out ways to understand their thinking. This is often a significant learning process for teachers who have to formulate an inquiry process to align with how children see and experience an environment. Finding good questions and inviting children to express their ideas through conversation, drawing, photographing, and building can illuminate new ideas and help teachers interpret what's on children's minds. Studying children's drawings and conversations takes practice but can be a tremendously rewarding experience for you and for the children. It is one way of committing yourself to ensuring children's rights and becoming a more significant person in children's lives.

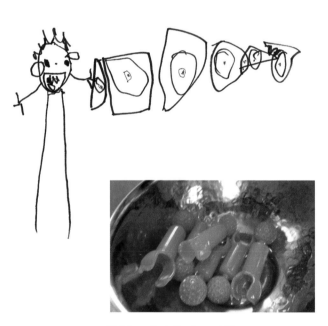

Children First, Durham, NC

Teacher Donna explored Stella's ideas about the environment in her program by asking her where she feels happy when she plays inside. Stella immediately answered, "Playing inside the loft room. Play with Zella." Donna asked Stella what she liked to use in her games with Zella, and she replied, "Build the food place." Stella went on to describe more details as Donna gently asked questions and invited her to draw her ideas. The next day Stella put together an example of where she feels happy by using blocks and creating play food; she then got a camera to photograph her work from several angles. As you look at this drawing Stella made and two of the photos she took, what stands out to you? What similar elements has she captured in both of these representations of her ideas? As Donna studied Stella's work, she recognized that she often sees Stella playing in the loft room with the wide variety of open-ended materials available there. It confirms for this teacher that things such as the red connector toys are good props because Stella sees many possibilities in them beyond what the manufacturer designed them for.

Consider Favorite Childhood Memories of Your Own

As you consider the arrangements and materials in your program, spend time with staff as a group sharing stories of the things you loved playing with over and over again when you were children—it may be a commercial toy for one person, a found object for another. What kind of play brought you joy and helped you learn about yourself and the people and places around you?

1 What were the materials like that you most enjoyed playing with? Consider the sensory aspects, the textures, the way they moved, the sounds they made, and how they connected to other aspects of your life.

2 How did you discover these materials? Where were you?

3 Who was with you? Did the materials help build your friendship with anyone?

4 How did you use the materials? Did you take them apart or combine them, build with them, or act out dramas and adventures?

5 Why do you think these materials sustained your interest over time?

As you reflect on your favorite childhood materials, you will probably discover that they relate to many of the values for children that are a focus of *Designs for Living and Learning*. As you continue reading, get ready for some wonderful ideas, both new and dusted off from an earlier time. We hope the photographs and elements they represent will inspire you. Remember to steer yourself away from the temptation to respond with "yes, but ... my space is so different ... our licensor (or director) won't let us do that ... we don't really have access to that kind of money or those resources ..." Each of the photographs in this book represents a transformation made by a teacher or administrative team, undertaken against some odds or specific barriers. When you want to design meaningful environments for living and learning with children, you can't take no for an answer. You and the children deserve no less than the biggest dream you can aim for.

Refugee and Immigrant Family Center (RIF), Sound Child Care Solutions, Seattle, WA

CHAPTER 2

Think beyond a Traditional Classroom

BEFORE

Good Samaritan Family Resource Center, San Francisco, CA   AFTER

Look Inside

What do you notice about the differences in these before and after photos of the same block area in this early childhood classroom? How would you describe your impressions and feelings about each space? What aspects of these environments help you feel welcomed, calm, and focused? What specific elements invite your curiosity and make you eager to know more? As you study these pictures, how do you imagine each area being used, and by whom?

These two environments couldn't be more different. The design of each space conveys beliefs about children and what is important for their living and learning. For the last few decades, too many young children have been spending their earliest years in institutional, commercially influenced settings similar to the photo above labeled "Before." Yet the trappings of an institution are impersonal and limited—why would anyone want to spend time in them? Institutional settings create barriers to trusting, warm relationships and are not conducive to the big ideas and actions children bring to their learning. With the technology available today, we have a wealth of knowledge at our fingertips about children and how they learn and thrive. Academics such as Alison Gopnik have contributed to the firestorm of research regarding the astonishing development of young children's brains and the immense drive and potential they have for learning. You can watch Gopnik's TED Talk on the mind of a baby at www.ted.com/speakers/alison_gopnik. From researchers such as Gopnik, we know that young children are learning machines with very flexible brains. They take in more of the world around them and can actually see, hear, feel, and experience more than adults. In fact, Gopnik and her colleagues report that children are also better learners than adults, eagerly investigating every aspect of their environment to learn about themselves and the world (Lucas et al. 2014).

By understanding this research, we can conclude that children's heightened sensory awareness and talent for learning allows them to see more details in the world around them, which means they can also become easily overstimulated in environments that are harsh, loud, and cluttered. Because they bring movement and big-body energy to most all their experiences, it's no wonder that cooped-up children in cramped spaces with little attention to their physical needs can surely experience anxiety and become aggressive.

Other research that has been available for decades suggests that children's social and emotional experiences play an enormous role in their learning and development. Dr. Stanley Greenspan's work on children's social and emotional development reminds us that when children feel irritated, stressed, and emotionally overwhelmed, they literally can't pay attention to anything else (1999).

All of this research on children's enhanced learning abilities, active bodies, and social-emotional sensitivity should be influencing how we design environments. Yet most early childhood programs are still stuck in a confining, regimented school-like model, creating classrooms with hard surfaces and furnishings, primary-colored bulletin boards, and walls crowded with cartoons that diminish an image of who children are and either bore or overstimulate them. In our consumer society, teachers often feel compelled to bring more and more "stuff" into their classrooms despite limited storage space or the lack of skills to organize it all. With the ever-growing attention to assessment tool ratings to enhance quality, teachers focus on the checklists rather than the actual experiences children are having in their environment. As the influence of commercial and political interests expands and the pressure for academic performance increases, the result is a focus on surrounding children with materials and displays they don't benefit from or need. This creates cluttered spaces and contributes to a sense of disorder, making it hard for children to focus. Children come to feel more and more agitated in these environments and not welcomed for who they really are.

Most adults have the ability to block out the activity going on around them. Think about how often you can ignore background noise and distractions or an uncomfortable seat you are sitting on and still stay with a task. Because of our adult accommodation to sensory input, we may not even realize the impact busy walls, cluttered shelves and countertops, bright colors, harsh lights, hard furnishings, crowded spaces, and irritating sounds have on children's learning and well-being.

The Power of Sensory and Aesthetic Elements in an Environment

Color, lighting, and other classroom design choices have a huge impact on children's experiences. According to Peter Barrett, professor in the School of the Built Environment at the University of Salford in the United Kingdom, six design parameters—color, choice, complexity, flexibility, connection, and light—have a significant effect on learning (et al. 2013). To enhance children's intellectual, physical, and emotional experiences, we must turn our attention to learning more about elements of aesthetics and design from other professions. Architects, interior designers, gardeners, artists, and even chefs use aesthetic elements to create inviting, positive experiences for people. There's no reason for us educators not to, and so many reasons why we should embrace the power of aesthetics.

Teachers who take on the task of redesigning their environments with attention to the sensory and aesthetic elements, as well as the organization and relationship between spaces and materials, will immediately notice the changes in children's responses to the environment, as well as their own.

Color, Texture, and Living Things

Warm colors, carefully chosen textured fabric, artwork, baskets and wooden bowls, plants, water, fish, and gardens create an atmosphere where people feel emotionally and physically at ease. Other professions and businesses, in places such as shopping malls, grocery stores, hotels, and office parks have taken great advantage of the research on environmental and interior design. They use color, texture, and nature to enhance employee comfort and productivity and customer satisfaction. When neutral, warm colors are used on walls, floors, and furnishings in children's environments, they become a clear backdrop for careful placement of interesting materials, documentation of the children, art, and other beautiful objects. These colors enhance the children's ability to relax and be present, rather than bombarding and distracting them. When carefully chosen and applied, repeated colors and patterns can work to unify and highlight aspects of a space. Textures from plants, fabric, and natural materials offer many ways to engage children. Children can immerse themselves in the soft translucence of a sheer cloth to feel the silkiness or peek through for a different view of the world. A wall or floor covered with a smooth, shiny surface of rocks and tiles beckons children to engage with their eyes, hands, and feet. Animals and plants in an environment evoke the vibrancy of being alive. Children are naturally drawn to living things, eager to have relationships with them. Plants and animals need to be cared for, which gives children

Association for the Advancement of Mexican Americans, United Way Bright Beginnings, Houston, TX

the opportunity to feel useful and find the joy in sharing the world with other living beings.

Lighting

Many early childhood programs are relegated to church basements or school districts' portable buildings with few windows or natural lighting options. The overhead fluorescent lights in these spaces usually hum and glare. A more calming feeling can be created even in these less than ideal settings by using a variety of direct and in-direct lighting sources to help soften and define spaces and create a focus for children. Clamp-on lights, track light-ing, or a floor or table lamp can be placed near a couch, chair, or table to highlight an area and add coziness to a dark corner. A large, well-lit aquarium can have the same effect. Mirrors hung on walls and placed on countertops can enhance the existing natural light and make spaces feel larger. Many kinds of string lights can add beauty and whimsy to a room, as well as more light. Whatever lighting options you are considering, take care with cords, sock-ets, and secure placement. Industrial Velcro can be used effectively under many lamps and mirrors. Having an electrician install additional outlets, particularly along the floor in central areas of the room, opens up many new options for using lighting effectively and safely. Try to have separate light switches for each part of the room, and make use of dimmer switches to provide even more lighting options as the natural light and the level of activity in your program changes throughout the day.

Tots Corner, Auckland, New Zealand

Sound and Noise

Classrooms with groups of children and adults have the tendency to be noisy places. Children surrounded by loud sounds all day become fatigued and irritated (and often damage their hearing). Loud noises interrupt concentration when children are working alone and make communication with others difficult. Sometimes children have to yell to hear each other, and this, in turn, causes more yelling, and the noise grows out of control. Many of the aesthetic elements, such as a sense of order, warm colors, texture, and items from nature, can help children feel more relaxed and engaged and less likely to use loud voices. Add softness to the environment with quilts on the walls and rugs on the floors, which will absorb sound and help to quiet the room. If the space has tall ceilings, lowering them with hanging fabric or trellises with plants can also absorb the sound and add beauty and coziness to the room. If the sound still feels overwhelm-ing and out of control, consider contacting an expert who could help you

Magic Garden Care and Education Centre, Auckland, New Zealand

learn about sound baffles and other strategies to control the noise in the environment.

The ideal way to address noisy environments is to open the door to the outdoor space so children can move in and out throughout the day. If you have this possibility, consider arranging your schedule and supervision plan to allow an indoor/outdoor flow during busy—and noisy—times of the day. That way children with active bodies and exuberant voices always have access to an outdoor space to express these vital aspects of themselves.

Sound can also bring lovely aesthetic experiences to the environment. Trickling waterfalls, soft chimes tinkling in the breeze, and calming music playing softly in the background can all offer intrigue, as well as soothe the ears and the mind.

Smells and Aromas

Our olfactory sense has a big impact on how we experience the aesthetics of an environment. Nothing is more off-putting than walking into an early childhood program to encounter a whiff of disinfectant, urine, or dirty diapers. The power of these odors can last a lifetime, as our sense of smell is stored in the long-term memory of our brains. You may have had the experience of walking down the street and suddenly smelling something that takes you back to an experience from long ago. It's not enough to cover up offensive odors; you need to diligently attend to them. Adequate ventilation and storage that keeps out odors are important considerations. Taking dirty diapers out of the room immediately is another strategy.

Providing wonderful aromas for children is part of building their memories. Consider children's experience if you take time to offer them the smell of bread and cookies baking or the comforting aroma of soup cooking. Steeping teas, such as mint or orange spice, or a naturally scented candle burning are surprise encounters and aesthetic delights for the children and others in your building. Be careful with artificial fragrances that may be overpowering and irritate the eyes and throat of sensitive people.

Hilltop Children's Center, Seattle, WA

Order and Organization

Corners crowded with stuff and cluttered walls, shelves, and countertops create a chaotic feeling. Since children have a heightened ability to take in more information, jumbled, messy spaces are distracting and make it difficult for them to pay attention to the value and purpose of what's available. Disorganized places communicate to children that the environment and materials are not respected.

Children First, Durham, NC

Sterile environments with limited aesthetic qualities may feel orderly, but they don't offer children multiple ways to invest in the space. Children in these environments might climb the furniture, fight, or break the limited toys that are available because the environment doesn't attract more interesting possibilities.

Young children are often characterized as having no attention span or ability to regulate their own behavior. But when children are viewed as easily attracted and eager to engage with an interesting environment, environments are carefully designed to communicate to them that there is order and purpose in the space. Creating an organized, orderly environment can go a long way in positively impacting how children feel and engage in a place. Offering materials with multiple possibilities in an organized fashion will entice children's flexible brains and their quest to investigate.

Storage

To create order and keep things organized, early childhood programs must tackle the hordes of stuff that seem to accumulate. Our profession has been underfunded for so long that many of us live with a scarcity mentality and we can't bear to get rid of anything. Many creative teachers can always see another possible use for every paper towel roll or dried-up, old paint jar. Others don't have the disposition or skills to sort and organize materials in useful ways. Even as we repurpose materials for children's use, all of us have the ongoing work of keeping the environment clean, rotating materials, and creating a place for everything so we can find it again.

One of the primary reasons early childhood programs look cluttered, chaotic, and uninviting is because there is too much stuff and inadequate storage space—in and out of doors. With limited square footage for living and playing together, it is often tempting to shortchange storage. The results can have the opposite effect of what is intended, with usable space taken up by supplies, broken equipment, or miscellaneous items with no designated home. In her seminal work the *Child Care Design Guide*, Anita Rui Olds developed an extensive chart of all the storage needs of a typical early care and education program. This is well worth studying when doing any redesign work. Storage options can be creative and attractive. Both indoors and outdoors, storage space can be developed that doubles as some other architectural feature or furniture element.

Destiny Village Child Care, United Way Bright Beginnings, Houston, TX

If our programs are to be attractive and comfortable places where children can concentrate and engage, then we need to have out-of-sight places for extra equipment, supplies, appliances, tools, and things that need repair. These areas need to be well organized and accessible to the busy staff. Devoting staff time to learning skills for purging, sorting, and organizing could prove a useful professional development focus.

Green and Healthy Environments

Taking care of the environment and working toward green early childhood programs are important features for the health and well-being of the children and adults, as well as the planet. Fresh circulating air, natural light, and living things are all part of a healthy environment—and are easy for nearly all programs to accomplish. Another aspect of being green is the absence of toxic chemicals and odors. Focusing on green practices helps children learn the value of taking care of themselves and the larger world around them. We recommend Phil Boise's books, *Go Green Rating Scale for Early Childhood Settings* and the companion handbook, as valuable resources on this topic.

Kawartha Child Care Services, Peterborough, ON, Canada

Outdoor Spaces

Many of the ideas discussed for indoor spaces can be applied to outdoor play areas as well. Study your outdoor space, whatever the size, and consider how to add multilevel areas or create cozy enclosures and interesting textures, smells, sounds, and colors. Use landscaping catalogs to find ideas. Consider allocating more of your budget for trees, berms, sand, water, and durable, scented (and of course nontoxic) plants. Spend less on bright-colored plastic toys and equipment. Make sure that there are comfortable places for children and adults to sit and converse together, as well as places for large-body challenges and sensory exploration. This applies to spaces for babies through school-age children. Approach the outdoor play space as an extension of your classroom—it is a place for children to investigate, feel powerful, and build relationships. For shade, consider plants, a trellis, or an arbor. For inclement weather, consider some of the interesting tent or canopy designs used by commercial vendors or outdoor event planners. Art, made by children or professional artists, can add interest and beauty to your outdoor space. Include interesting tiles, cement creations, sculptures, or fountains for children's open-ended investigations.

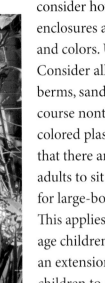

Pacific Primary Pre-School, San Francisco, CA

Sensory Elements Provoke Aesthetic Responses

Sensory elements in an environment include the things we can see, hear, touch, taste, and smell. Beyond the five senses, humans also experience *equilibrioception*: the sensing of movement and balance and finding our bodies in space. Our senses can entice and soothe us as well as bombard and swamp us. Broadly defined, the concept of *aesthetics* comes from a branch of philosophy dealing with the nature, creation, and appreciation of beauty. Beyond pleasant sensory experiences, aesthetic environments, situations, and materials have the power to engage children's minds and hearts.

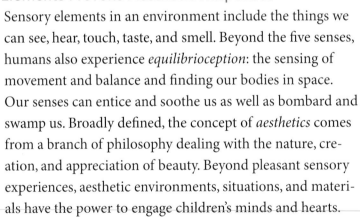

Magic Garden Care and Education Centre, Auckland, New Zealand

Think about the last time you were out in nature. Perhaps you were at the beach as the sun was setting. You looked out at the brilliant, changing colors emanating from the sun through blue skies and white clouds. You felt the soft sand under your feet as you breathed in the crisp ocean air. You noticed the breeze on your face as the wind gently moved your hair. As a part of this moment, you became filled with joy and your thoughts turned to questions about the larger meaning of life. Rather than solely a pleasant sensory experience, this reflects the fullness of an aesthetic experience. Consider how such an experience affects your mood, your attention to what's around you, and your relationships and actions in such a setting. Being in an aesthetically pleasing environment reduces stress and promotes a sense of well-being.

Relationships and Responses as a Part of Aesthetic Experiences

Those of us who have been inspired by the stunning environments in the schools of Reggio Emilia, and perhaps by some of the programs featured in the first edition of *Designs for Living and Learning*, have been working to add more beauty and wonder to our early childhood programs. As authors we have worried that people would just look at the beautiful photos in the first *Designs* book and try to recreate them without reading and thinking more carefully about the values underneath the designs. Our continued study of aesthetics has helped us to understand more fully the importance and impact of offering children beautiful spaces and materials. Continued study is the key to creating environments that are more meaningful for you and your group of children. Rather than just trying to copy someone else, be inspired by new ideas and images then adapt them to reflect your values and vision for your program.

Sometimes seeing lovely early childhood environments provokes people to say or think, "This isn't a place for children." This response could be a result of not seeing children as competent enough to benefit from, appreciate, or care for a beautifully organized environment. Other times people have the mistaken notion that child-centered environments should be messy, bright colored, and noisy because children like it that way. There are also beautiful program environments that are not truly suitable for children because they are filled with decorations and lack the elements that invite children to personally explore and engage.

An aesthetically pleasing environment for children draws them to have a relationship with the space, and the people and objects in it. It speaks to children's innate drive to connect to people and the world around them. It appeals to children's alert, flexible minds, and their desire to move. An aesthetically pleasing environment also calls on children to investigate the possibilities for how they can fully participate in the experience by immersing themselves in the environment and making contributions by adding to or changing it in some way.

Examine the photos here again and consider these questions about the elements of aesthetics as you compare the two environments:

BEFORE

Good Samaritan Family Resource Center, San Francisco, CA　　　AFTER

1　Does the choice of colors work to unify and highlight aspects of each space, or does the space have a disjointed, distracting quality?

2　How does the quality of light and color in relationship to the equipment and materials make you feel? How does each space invite your curiosity and attention?

3　Describe the variety of textures and materials you see in each space. What impact might these aspects—or lack of them—have on engaging with the space?

4　What aspects of these spaces feel institutional and commercial? What impact does this have on your response to the space?

5　What do you notice about the size and organization of the space, equipment, and materials? How might these elements in each space impact how it is used?

6　What in each of these environments might you immerse yourself with, change, or add to in order to enhance the feeling that this is a space for you?

The insights you gain from carefully examining these photos can help you begin to see the elements of aesthetics that you will use to assess and change your own classroom environment. What elements of aesthetics are you particularly drawn to: color, lighting, texture, or order? Deepen your understanding by noticing and responding to what you see and respond to in the environments where you spend time.

Invite Living and Learning with Elements of Aesthetics and Design in Places for Children

Children are remarkable beings, filled with curiosity and wonder, always ready to use their heightened senses, and eager to dive in and learn. We have found that when teachers come to deeply understand and appreciate the profound nature of childhood, they make a commitment to create environments worthy of children's immense capacities. Our hope is that this book will help you reach this level of commitment too. This requires a bigger and different vision for what is possible and a willingness to dive in and make changes. It is big work, yet it can be accomplished through simple acts and attention to details.

Programs that understand the remarkable minds and hearts that young children bring to their living and learning are inspired to create spaces worthy of this profound time of life. Study the following examples to inspire changes in your program.

Aesthetics All Around

As you study the series of photos that follow, notice how each of these teachers—no matter what the age of the children they work with—have paid close attention to order, organization, beauty, magic, and wonder in the arrangement of the space, as well as in the materials they have provided. The children have calm places to relax, interesting materials to engage with, plenty of space to move around, and invitations to engage with others.

The teachers in this toddler room have thought through the elements of an aesthetically engaging place for toddlers' lively minds and bodies. Notice the way the space is organized for openness, yet areas are defined with a few shelves, tables and chairs, and carpets, which helps the children see how to move in the space. The repeated patterns and colors of the carpets are inviting and give the room a feeling of connectedness without being overstimulating. The neutral wall and furniture colors create a calm feeling in the room. Cozy corners offer the children places to be comfortable and work alone or in small groups. There are open-ended materials on the shelves and walls, such as nature items and other interesting things that invite children's investigation of textures, lights, shadows, and sparkles.

Destiny Village Child Care Center, United Way Bright Beginnings, Houston, TX

Destiny Village Child Care, United Way
Bright Beginnings, Houston, TX

The infant educators in this room know the importance of a soft, inviting environment for their babies along with elements that will enhance the babies' growing attention. Study the ingenious ways the teachers have hung fabric to create cozy yet dramatic spaces in the room. The sheer cloth over the climber is hung with the bars of a crib they no longer use. There are interesting textures, shapes, and sizes of materials for the children to investigate on the floor, walls, and ceiling. The climbing loft offers a place for children to challenge their bodies as well as their minds while they notice the sparkly lights, prisms, and mirror hanging in the area.

This preschool classroom is designed for focus and relaxation. The soft chairs and lamp communicate that this is a place to curl up with a book. The table and orderly shelves help the children focus on writing, drawing, and dramatic play. The blue painted stripe around the room, along with the repetition of blue carpets on the floor, helps define the space and create connectedness among the different areas of the room.

Second Presbyterian Weekday School, Louisville, KY

Indoor Storage

Organized, orderly, attractive storage is critical for both children's and teacher's focus and well-being. Objects can be stored in an appealing manner by using baskets and other pleasing containers. Study the following examples of carefully stored materials to design your own orderly presentations.

courtesy of Deb Curtis, Seattle, WA

The Learning Center, Palo Alto, CA

Tots Corner, Auckland, New Zealand

Flat, open baskets and containers help children see what is inside so they know what is available and possible for their play. Storing materials in similar containers, such as baskets or like-colored tubs, creates a feeling of order and calm and helps people see what is available.

Outdoor Storage

Just like indoor storage, outdoor storage needs to keep materials organized and accessible; plus it needs to cover and protect them. The photos here offer a variety of examples of how two programs accomplished this.

These programs store a wide variety of materials in outdoor storage that is attractive and accessible to the children.

courtesy of Deb Curtis, Seattle, WA

Children First, Durham, NC

Aesthetics Outdoors

Attention to order, beauty, and engaging materials is just as important outdoors as it is indoors. Study the following examples to inspire your own work.

The Learning Center, Palo Alto, CA

The teacher in this infant program has created an aesthetically interesting place in the small yard adjacent to her classroom. The fabric, pillows, and outdoor carpet she used create an intellectually inviting and emotionally soothing space. Plants, shells, drums, and colorful water bottles invite investigation of texture, sound, movement, and light.

Located in downtown San Francisco, this program worked thoughtfully to create an aesthetically pleasing outdoor environment in their small narrow yard that is surrounded by apartment houses and other buildings. Notice how they have created different levels to expand the space, including a hillside garden and sand area, an area for playing under the deck, and a garden that begins on the ground floor of the yard and moves up the small hill. Imagine the calming and intellectually stimulating experiences that this environment offers children living in a busy, urban area.

Pacific Primary Pre-School, San Francisco, CA

The Use of Light

Lighting is a significant factor in how children experience an environment. When light is used thoughtfully, it can invite a calm feeling, highlight and define a space or materials, and be used to create a magical ambiance. In the following photos, notice the many kinds of light and how the programs have purposefully used it.

Magic Garden Care and Education Centre, Auckland, New Zealand

*Hilltop Children's Center,
Seattle, WA*

Notice the various ways these programs use light in their environments to create a focus, calmness, and invitations to magic and wonder.

This dramatic four-poster bed is covered with flowing fabric and twinkling lights. Imagine the feelings of wonder children experience as they look up into the canopy.

Pacific Primary Pre-School, San Francisco, CA

This large mirror above the inviting collection of natural materials reflects the natural light, making the space feel larger. It also invites the toddlers in the room to see multiple perspectives as they explore the texture, shapes, and colors both through their senses and in the mirrored reflection.

Maitland Early Childhood Learning Centre, London Bridge Child Children's Services, London, ON, Canada

Chicago Commons Child Development Center (Head Start), Chicago, IL

Maitland Early Childhood Learning Centre, London Bridge Child Children's Services, London, ON, Canada

The teachers in these classrooms take advantage of the natural light streaming into their environments by offering materials that are enhanced through their interaction with the light.

Inventions for Your Program

Walk through your own environment to assess it for aesthetic qualities.

1. Does the choice of colors work to unify and highlight aspects of the total space, or is there a disjointed, distracting quality?

2. How does the quality of the light in the environment make you feel? How does the light invite curiosity and attention?

3. Describe the variety of textures and materials you see in each space. Where do you see nature, magic, and wonder? What impact might these aspects—or lack of them—have on how you and the children feel in the space?

4. What aspects of your space feel institutional and commercial? What impact does this have on your and the children's response to the space?

5. What do you notice about the size and organization of the space, equipment, and materials? Where do you see order and organization, and where is there clutter? How might these elements in each space impact how it is used?

6. What in your environment might children immerse themselves with, change, or add to that enhances the feeling that this is a space for them?

Use the information you discover from assessing your own environment to spark your creativity and take action. Clear out the clutter and organize closets, shelves, and materials. Use color, nature, light, and the other aesthetic elements to create a peaceful and engaging environment. The children and you deserve to spend your days together in a beautiful, nourishing space.

Guadalupano Family Center, Chicago Commons Child Development Program
(Head Start), Chicago, IL

CHAPTER 3

Create Connections,
a Sense of Place and Belonging

Look Inside

Imagine this is the first space you encounter as you enter an early childhood program. How would you describe your impressions? What specific elements make you feel welcome and eager to know more? What elements of this environment convey a sense of belonging for children and families? As you study this photograph, how do you imagine this area being used, and by whom?

courtesy of Deb Curtis, Seattle, WA

Although the Look Inside photograph comes from a full-day child care program, this is not a typical scene of an early childhood program entryway. Sadly, the majority of children today are not spending their days in homelike environments with vibrant neighborhoods, grassy backyards, or nearby parks or woods to explore. Instead, children are growing up in harsher, less-inviting settings, away from fresh air, the natural world, and in many cases, their neighborhoods and homes. The lives of today's children are filled with plastic, concrete, metal, electronic media, and other materials controlled by commercial interests. Most adults sigh and accept this as a given. But does it have to be? Aren't we who set up early care and learning programs in a position to invent something different?

In the early 1970s, when the expansion of early childhood education was in full swing, training programs for caregivers emphasized creating a home away from home. In fact, many centers actually searched for homes and neighborhoods in which to establish their centers. In their landmark book *Planning Environments for Young Children: Physical Space*, Sybil Kritchevsky and Elizabeth Prescott (1977) urge educators to provide furniture, equipment, and materials to create an environment that is responsive to the child. Their suggestion is that hard, institutional, school-like surroundings give children the message "you better shape up and do what this environment requires." They warned nearly forty years ago that, especially in full-day programs, children would suffer, experiencing fatigue and tension in such an atmosphere. When we fast-forward to the twenty-first century, we clearly see what Kritchevsky and Prescott predicted. Early childhood programs have drifted away from these early guidelines, with commercial interests and political agendas rushing in to steer us away from responding to the children. Children are frequently tense, stressed, or emotionally strained in group environments.

Early Childhood Environments Today

For families using early care and education programs, each day begins with a significant transition from home to another setting. If the program is a family child care home, the transition has the potential to be a bit less dramatic in its contrast—although many family child care providers are now pressured to create programs to be more like school than home. If it is a center-based program, the transition is likely to feel more like stepping into an institution, a far cry from home. Whatever the setting, children who are on a tight schedule to leave their families and homes each morning experience a major shift from one world to another. Eventually this daily transition process becomes a familiar routine that everyone accepts or becomes resigned to. If the transition is a bumpy or less than desirable experience, children and adult family members typically find a way to tune it out and get on with their day.

The predominant stance of early childhood professionals in response to this strained transition has been to regard it as a developmental stage. Literature and staff training on "separation anxiety" has proliferated, offering strategies to help children adjust to "our" programs. Seldom is there a discussion of the importance of helping children remain connected to their families while they are in early childhood programs. We believe this needs to change. A central focus of our profession's thinking should be on strengthening the connection between children, their families, and community settings, rather than emphasizing separation from them during the long days children spend with us.

Young children come into the world seeking relationships for their comfort, identity development, and learning process. From their youngest years, they find great interest in other people and animals. Very young babies are attracted to other babies, their own images in a mirror, and large photographs of human faces. By the time they are preschoolers, watching older children and teenagers fascinates them. It's not surprising that recent research on young children's development shows that children grow and learn best in the context of relationships with the people and places that reflect their families, cultures, and communities. Research on brain development and emotional intelligence also suggests that children must feel comfortable and secure for healthy development and learning to occur (Shonkoff and Phillips 2000).

Despite all this, center-based early childhood programs typically isolate children based on their ages. The babies, waddlers, and toddlers are in separate rooms, and the two- through five-year-olds and school-age children occupy different spaces with self-contained activities. In the typical early care and learning program, siblings of different ages spend most of the day apart. With each new birthday or school year, children often must leave a familiar space and move to a new room and caregiver or teacher. This practice of shifting children is often explained by children's growing physical needs and the program's economic issues. However, this approach to grouping and moving children creates separations and disruptions that aren't conducive to the relationships so central to building trust and to the learning process.

Adults as well as children deserve to feel comfortable in early childhood environments. Parents often view classrooms as the domain of children and teachers, and they typically drop their children at the door. Many programs even discourage parents from lingering in the classroom, citing separation anxiety or an undesired distraction from the routines or curriculum under way. Staff members only have opportunities for conversation with each other during brief exchanges on the playground or during their short breaks from the children. Teachers and caregivers often spend more time in these environments than in their own homes. Working with groups of children is demanding and stressful, and should be mediated with opportunities for collaborative dialogue and genuine social interactions with other adults, as well as with individual children.

In addition, we would do well to reconsider the professional notion that employees should leave their own lives at the door when they report to work. Saying that professionals shouldn't share any personal aspects of themselves counters the important goal of building strong relationships in early childhood programs—with the children, with their families, and with coworkers. Relationships go two ways. To build trust and meaningful connections, providers and teachers must be able to share appropriate aspects of their lives and have something of themselves reflected in the environment. Most administrators want more than lip service given to family involvement and staff retention. To achieve this, they must create environments that say to the adults, "This a place for you too."

How different most early childhood programs are from the home or neighborhood settings early childhood educators first envisioned years ago! Yet many teachers and directors and even family child care providers accommodate the current conditions as "the way it is." They dare not allow themselves to dream of any other options, wanting to protect themselves from feeling dissatisfied, disgruntled, or powerless to change the way things are. But stop and reconsider this: Is this really how you want to be living your life? If there were a different physical and social-emotional environment in your program, would you experience your work differently? Would you garner more meaningful relationships, involvement, and support for your program? Could early childhood programs reduce staff turnover, build stronger partnerships with families, and give children the experiences of childhood they so deserve?

In the early childhood community's effort to be professional and keep children safe, healthy, and learning, we have used public health standards, fears about litigation, and public school thinking to design group environments for young children. Ironically, this approach deprives children of a key element for safety and security (and for optimal learning) in their early years—a cozy, homelike environment.

Young children not only benefit from but deserve to be surrounded by softness, comfort, and meaningful relationships in their childhoods. Filling a program with commercial equipment and materials designed only for the size, safety, and sanitation of young children also hurts adult relationships, because it creates an environment that is hostile or neutral to families and staff. In light of what we know about learning and development, and in our desire to show respect for children, families, and our work as caregivers and educators, it is imperative that we shape a different vision for designing early childhood environments.

Over the last decade since the first edition of this book was published, hundreds upon hundreds of early childhood educators have been inspired to make their environments more beautiful and inviting. Many have gone on study tours to Reggio Emilia or Aotearoa New Zealand, and returned with inspiration to replicate what they've seen. But trying to replicate how someone else has designed an environment is going down the wrong path, just as replacing early childhood catalogs with those home décor ones doesn't necessarily result in a better place for children. Being homelike is much more than the furnishings. In the best sense of the word, *home* means a place of familiar comforts and traditions where memories and identity are formed.

Reggio Emilia educators remind us that their schools reflect not just any place, but a particular place. Likewise, in the United States, David Sobel, Ann Pelo, and other advocates of place-based education persuade us that meaningful learning best happens when schools are actively connected to the communities and natural elements of the environment in which they are situated. This approach creates roots, meaningful relationships, and a focus on learning who we are and what we can do together. If your goal is to replicate, you might just end up with a beautifully furnished place that still feels lacking because it has no soul or clear identity of who spends time there. We have found that when educators grasp the deeper meaning of a Reggio Emilia-inspired approach or the ideas offered in this book, they take time to explore who and where they are, and how their environments can reflect their core values and connections with their community. Our hope is that this happens for you!

Kawartha Child Care Services, Peterborough, ON, Canada

Invite Living with Elements for Belonging and Connections

Programs need to make conscious efforts to help the children and adults who come together in their sites to develop relationships of trust and confidence with one another. We suggest that you reconsider both the inside and outside of your building with the goal of creating a welcoming first impression and an ongoing invitation to deeper relationships. The arrangements and provisions in the physical environment create the context for the social-emotional climate and the quality of interactions among the people there. What follows are many ways to intentionally design environments to encourage connections, collaboration, and an experience of community.

As the Look Inside photo opening this chapter suggests, the first impression one gets in a building helps set the stage for a sense of comfort and belonging—or not, depending on the environment. The welcome feeling that a comfortable entry-way provides should be continued with other physical elements threaded throughout the halls and individual rooms. That way, as people move through the space or settle in, they will experience a climate of comfort and belonging. To evaluate your own welcoming environment where people can create identity and experience comfort, belonging, and connections, walk through your program with your colleagues and ask yourselves these questions:

1   Who are we? Where do we come from? Where do we see ourselves reflected or represented?

2   Where in this space do we learn more about each other and create more connections?

3   How can children and families regularly contribute to the environment so that it reflects their values, interests, and lives?

4   What elements might encourage family members to linger before leaving each day?

5   In what ways can the environment convey the history of our program and wider community, reflecting a sense of what we value in it?

Discussing questions such as these with colleagues and parents can lead to new ideas for creating a sense of belonging, connections, and identity in your environment. The vision underlying these questions creates an inviting, inclusive community rather than an institutional setting that belongs to sanitation workers, prosecuting attorneys, or commercial interests. Creating this atmosphere generates its own energy and involvement. It doesn't require a huge budget and can be accomplished through simple acts and attention to details.

Drawing inspiration from a variety of places, including close observation of children's play endeavors, early years educators are reinventing environments to have a unique identity, be aesthetically pleasing, and enhance connections with and a sense of belonging within the community. Study the following examples and consider how you could build some of the elements into your program.

Connect Home with the Program

Imagine yourself as a young child making that daily transition between home and an early childhood program. With this in mind, consider including homelike elements in your environment to help make this transition go smoothly. This should include comfortable places for family members to linger briefly with their children to begin the separation process and to reunite at the end of the day. Find objects to include that will keep children connected to their families while they are apart during the day.

Stepping Stones Children's Center, Burlington, VT

As you enter this center, you discover you are in a small kitchen with a welcoming adult-sized table where you're invited to ease your way into the program. The program invented the role of the "transition teacher" (whom the children renamed "the kitchen teacher"), who uses this space to greet families as they arrive and keep track of special circumstances and medications, as well as organize snacks and lunch and assist the children with self-care activities. Throughout the day, you may find a small group of children gathered around the kitchen table engaged in an activity, or perhaps a parent and teacher conversing over a cup of coffee.

Hilltop Children's Center, Seattle, WA

Remodeling the first level of an office building with cement floors, this program used several approaches to make the environment more cozy and homelike. They added couches, rugs, fabric, soft lights, and home furniture.

Entries and Hallways

Too often the entry and hallways are thought of as places leading to the program, not actually part of it. Thus, they can easily become cluttered with things that aren't wanted in the classrooms, such as strollers, car seats, broken toys, and discarded items that no one takes responsibility for. Instead, you should consider these as a first encounter that communicates what you care about. In very large programs, a number of these welcoming spaces can be scattered throughout the building, creating "pods" or "neighborhood hubs." Creating architectural connections between rooms is also possible with features such as sliding doors or windows that look into other rooms or into shared hall spaces.

These programs use their entries and hallways as community gathering places—they have the feel of a living room, community center, or neighborhood park.

Refugee and Immigrant Family Center (RIF), Sound Child Care Solutions, Seattle, WA

Hilltop Children's Center, Seattle, WA

Communication Stations

In places where people are continually coming and going, take care to create communication stations for required postings and logs, as well as information and announcements about current happenings in the program and wider community. These can easily look institutional or cluttered, so designing them to be inviting and user friendly is key. In hallways, classrooms, and staff rooms, be sure to use images and text that highlight what you are learning together in your program. Just as you would do at home, consider carefully how you want to balance the use of technology, print, and images to communicate news and information in your environment.

The communication stations in these programs are thoughtfully planned to be attractive and useful for families.

Magic Garden Care and Education Centre, Auckland, New Zealand

University of Auckland Early Childhood Centre, Auckland, New Zealand

Hilltop Childen's Center, Seattle, WA

Design the Outdoor Areas

The feeling of home should be extended outdoors, too. In Aotearoa New Zealand, educators give special attention to both the outdoor and indoor environments for children. They create a sense of belonging for all children and families and create a sense of place with their natural elements and cultural heritage. These examples of outdoor spaces offer familiar elements to what the children might experience at home.

A large outdoor shed has been filled with softness by draping flowing fabric that matches twin couches; a perfect place for children to develop dramatic stories within an enchanting setup.

Botany Downs Kindergarten, Auckland, New Zealand

Here a large gazebo tent provides the dual purpose of adding shade protection while creating a defined space in the yard for more focused play, even as larger big-body activities take place around it.

Magic Garden Care and Education Centre, Auckland, New Zealand

Create Retreats in the City

Early childhood educators in urban settings need to be mindful of creating quiet spaces where children and adults can retreat from the hustle and bustle of the city. With centers throughout low-income neighborhoods in Chicago, Chicago Commons Child Development Center (Head Start) operates child development and Head Start programs in a variety of buildings, some purpose-built and others older, renovated buildings. Each one has managed to create a unique, welcoming identity with its design and use of documentation, art, and natural materials in the hallways and classrooms.

Guadalupano Family Center, Chicago Commons Child Development Program (Head Start), Chicago, IL

Rather than viewing hallways as separate from the classroom community, this center uses their hallways as a way to collectively gather teacher bio-boards and attractively display them. A nearby water feature, plant, and baskets of treasures invite families to slow down and engage with their children.

Taylor Center for New Experiences, Chicago Commons Child Development Program (Head Start), Chicago, IL

Paulo Freire Family Center, Chicago Commons Child Development Program (Head Start), Chicago, IL

Tucked at the end of a hallway is a seating arrangement that encourages children and families, and even staff, to pause for a while and have a few moments of rest or quiet conversation with one another. A basket of books encourages family members to read with their child.

As you enter this center, you are encouraged to stop and take a load off your feet with an inviting lounge chair, rug, table lamp, and wicker stools. This aesthetic sets the stage for access to a bulletin board full of required postings, each carefully arranged for easy reading. Notice the bottom half of the board allows for documents to be removed and read while comfortably seated.

Store Belongings

Creating a sense of belonging involves children having a place to store their belongings. You can move away from an institutional feel of school that traditional coat cubbies create by using other kinds of furnishings that serve the same purpose.

Magic Garden Care and Education Centre, Auckland, New Zealand

Photos of children placed in the areas where they store their belongings send a message that those areas are a place for them. Putting up family photos in the same areas expands the welcome message. If you are open to having children go barefoot during the day, it helps to have an organized place to store shoes, as might be done at home. Placing comfortable seating nearby provides an easier transition for families as they keep track of belongings when they bring and pick up their children.

Southwest Early Learning Center, Sound Child Care Solutions, Seattle, WA

A Sense of Place

As early educators learn more about the importance of giving children a sense of place, particularly in relationship to their natural surroundings, they employ different strategies for infusing this into their environments. Some name and furnish their programs, classrooms, and outside areas to reflect the local surroundings.

The Highlander School, Atlanta, GA

In her play yard, this director designed a stream of water to reflect the Chattahoochee River that flows in the area. Children have learned that it flows all the way down to the coast.

Awhi Whanau Early Childhood Centre, Auckland, New Zealand

Honoring the importance for the Maori people to identify with a mountain and river, this center features a mural in their play yard.

Highland Plaza United Methodist Preschool, Hixson, TN

Various areas of this center's play yard are designed to represent specific features of the surrounding area, such as the area's nature center, the Riverbend Amphitheater, and the Bear Trail that winds upward through the Great Smoky Mountains. The children can easily hike up through the woods by pulling themselves along a knotted rope. The director says, "That rope was the best $15 I ever spent! They love it."

Te Puna Kōhungahunga, Auckland, New Zealand

Throughout their center, this program features representations associated with their surroundings, such as the silver leaf fern and Maori symbols.

Spaces for Eating, Sleeping, and Caregiving

Providing child care means caring for children's bodily needs as well as their emotional well-being and curious minds. Places for eating, sleeping, toileting, and diaper changing can be viewed as pit stops or sanitation stations, or they can be designed with beauty, taking care of our bodies and relationships. Examine these photographs and consider the care that went into making these routine places beautiful and comfortable for children as they transition into these activities.

courtesy of Deb Curtis, Seattle, WA

courtesy of Deb Curtis, Seattle, WA

Diapering becomes an inviting experience for mobile babies and toddlers when they get to navigate the pull-out stairs up to the changing table and watch butterflies flap their wings above them. Along with some special moments with the caregiver, the child sees photos of his or her friends and the activities of the program. At the foot of the table, a bench with more photo documentation encourages other children to hang out nearby.

This area is available for dress up most of the day, but to ease toddlers into a group naptime, a soothing nest has been created with hanging fabric, a rug that can accommodate nap mats, and lovely photos for each child to see him or herself sleeping as they are settling down for their nap.

Sophia's Preschool, Oakura, New Zealand

People in warmer climates often share memories of having a sleeping porch when they were children. This Aotearoa New Zealand multiuse outdoor building reflects the Polynesian culture and architecture of a *fale*. Built in collaboration with a parent and from wood that was reclaimed and restored from one of the parents' worksites, this center uses the Maori term *Te Whare Rakau* to describe the house of wood. Open windows are covered with transparent covering to add protection during the windy season while still allowing the children to sleep with fresh air. The director says, "There's nothing like the sense of cosiness when you shelter from the winter elements in the *whare* with the children whilst still being part of the whole naturescape surrounding us."

Sophia's Preschool, Oakura, New Zealand

Tables on the porch of this center are set for eating when mealtime arrives. The center takes care to include the children in creating beautiful place settings. A bird's-eye view of the table on a typical day reveals the place mats that the children make when they start attending the center, along with healthy food, much of which comes from the center or parents' gardens, including lemon balm tea, green beans, broccoli, and waffles made with corn and zucchini.

Create Connections, a Sense of Place and Belonging ❧ 75

Toileting is major learning for young children, and while there may be differences between bathrooms in children's homes and in an early childhood center, the design of a bathroom can still create a homelike feeling and sense of comfort. Each of these educators has made some aspect of their bathroom aesthetically pleasing as well as functional for the children's use.

Kids' Domain Early Learning Centre, Auckland, New Zealand

Evergreen Community School, Santa Monica, CA

Children First, Durham, NC

Furnishings

Specific places where relationships are fostered should be part of your early childhood environment. Include adult-sized furniture to offer comfort to the staff and parents and provide spaces for laps for children to sit on. Comfortable furniture does not need to be expensive—you can find suitable items at thrift stores, in classified ads, and at garage sales. Sanitation concerns can be addressed by using slipcovers that can be easily removed and washed. Seek out couches, love seats, overstuffed chairs, gliders, rockers, large floor pillows, and hammocks. Create a unifying, comforting effect by coordinating the colors of the pieces you choose. Be selective about high-quality child-sized furniture from early childhood vendors. Whenever possible choose neutral colors and wood over plastic. Remember, a room furnished entirely from one of these vendors will look institutional and convey the identity of a catalog, not your specific place.

The Learning Center, Palo Alto, CA

The cushions are beautiful and inviting—and they provide a comfortable place for children and adults to sit together.

Magic Garden Care and Education Centre, Auckland, New Zealand

The furniture in this dramatic play area is unique and practical. The children can access and return materials easily.

Studio Spaces

Many educators exposed to the schools of Reggio Emilia are astounded by the artwork the children create and thus lobby for including studio spaces in their own programs. Without a deeper understanding of the intent of these studio spaces, however, they can easily become misused, neglected, or a wasted space. Beyond "doing art," studios should provide a protected space for a small group of children, their educators, and sometimes family or community members to focus on a particular investigation over an extended period of time. This may involve such things as scientific experiments, representational art, music, dance, or theater work. During such times, children engage in relationships that serve as apprenticeships, learning to use adult tools under the guidance of someone with mastery. When used with intention, studio spaces can foster powerful connections between children with different abilities, as well as between children and adults. Out of these encounters a strong sense of identity can develop from the skills and relationships developed, as well as in the discoveries and creative output.

Nia Family Center, Chicago Commons Child Development Program (Head Start), Chicago, IL

The children who use this studio instinctively understand that it is a special place for them. Notice the softly filtered natural lighting and the adult-sized, beautiful table and chairs. All the children's supplies are accessible on the shelves, and the sink is at just the right height to wash messy hands.

Children First, Durham, NC

This studio looks out on the play yard, providing an inspiring view for the children while they work in the studio.

Adult Work Spaces

In an effort to be child- and family-centered, programs shouldn't neglect the spaces that administrators and educators need for their work apart from the children. Similar to children, staff need space for lively collaborative work as well as a quiet place to think, plan, and regroup. A sense of belonging and connection with each other and to a profession can contribute to sustainability and retention for educators and administrators.

Association for the Advancement of Mexican Americans, United Way Bright Beginnings, Houston, TX

Isabel F. Cox School, Redcliff, AB, Canada

Hilltop Children's Center, Seattle, WA

These programs have created spaces with great attention to order and organization, comfort and aesthetics, and furnishings and technology so that staff feel they belong as professionals and community members.

Invite Learning with Materials and Activities for Belonging and Connections

The materials and activities educators provide, and how we provide them, can help children make connections with their homes, other people, and ideas they want to explore. Our profession has long been promoting social-emotional learning, attachment and bonding, identity development, problem solving, and conflict resolution as central to academic learning. We know the importance of providing children with housekeeping areas with multicultural dress-up and food props, block props, puzzles, books, and songs to help them play out and extend their understandings of their world.

With families from a multitude of cultures and individual circumstances and who speak many languages entering our programs, we must become increasingly intentional about the materials we put in the environment. The materials need to invite children to have further connections with their families, develop friendships across differences, and see themselves as part of a wider community.

Children's identity development begins at home, with their families. As they begin to spend time away from their families, their sense of self and their family connections are tested. To support children through these tests, programs need to remind them of the strengths of their families and heritage. Children whose lives at home are stable, secure, and predictable generally have a better time of building new relationships than those whose families face poverty, continual upheaval, and traumas, such as divorce, refugee experiences, violence, expressions of racial hatred, or unfair treatment due to skin color, religion, or family circumstances. Early childhood programs should be places where all children—regardless of family circumstances—can be themselves, with all their feelings, interests, knowledge, and desires. At the same time, programs can invite children into new relationships and understandings through interactions with their peers, adults, and engaging materials. Programs can make sure children find familiar things in the environment and also pique their curiosity with new things. As children learn the language and culture of schools and other institutions of power, early childhood programs should help them develop strong individual, family, and cultural identities. Teachers should also plan materials and activities with the goal of helping children expand their empathy, emotional intelligence, and desire to learn from different perspectives.

Children are very concrete thinkers, but they also have fantastic imaginations and the ability to understand things that seem removed from their lives. This especially happens through children's books when adult guidance is provided to connect the stories to the children's own experiences. Materials and activities that help children make these connections include visual images and physical objects. With regular opportunities to see, touch, and investigate, children acquire experiences with people, places, and things that are both familiar and unknown. They become less hesitant or fearful and more at ease when encountering something or someone new.

Photos and Stories

Displaying images from children's home and family life in the early childhood environment creates a continuous reminder of the home-to-program connection. These photos can be displayed in a variety of ways, such as plastic sleeves secured on the outside of cribs, photo stands and frames, notebook binders, bulletin boards, or handmade books. Some of these images should be portable so that children are free to move them around and incorporate them into their play or turn to them when they need comfort or reassurance. If the photos are accompanied by short written stories, they invite children into literacy experiences as well. Including photos and stories of the caregivers and teachers reminds children that these adults are important members of their own families as well.

Hilltop Children's Center, Seattle, WA

Children First, Durham, NC

Magic Garden Care and Education Centre, Auckland, New Zealand

The examples here are some of the ways programs use photos to create a sense of belonging and to build connections between home and the child care program.

Documentation

Posting curriculum plans has been a long-standing requirement in early care and education centers, with the intention of demonstrating that teachers are thinking carefully about children's learning each day. Programs working with an expanded notion of what constitutes learning and using a more emergent approach to curriculum can regularly post documentation of what has been unfolding in the learning process.

*Epiphany Early Learning Preschool,
Sound Child Care Solutions, Seattle, WA*

This documentation display is placed to be accessible for the children to view, which helps them not only revisit what they have been doing, but also remember stories to share with their families.

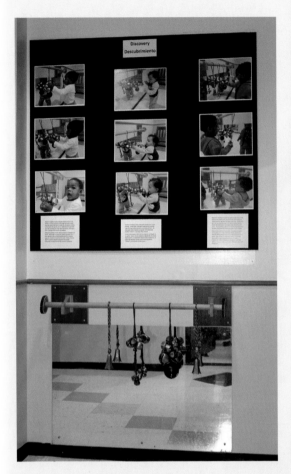

Nia Family Center, Chicago Commons Child Development Program (Head Start), Chicago, IL

Posting documentation right next to the materials featured in the display board promotes an understanding of what goes on in this area. Family members and center visitors can see the competencies of the children as well as the value of the materials.

Tots Corner, Auckland, New Zealand

This program, similar to many others, is integrating new technology into their documentation displays of children's work. This can be accessible to the children as well as adults.

Family Objects and Cultural Artifacts

Along with your own selections of objects for your program, you can invite families to contribute things that will keep children connected to their homes and help build connections across families. Thought should be given to whether these are intended for display only, or if they are suitable for incorporation into the active life of the classroom. Posters and art, textiles, and woven objects or baskets reflecting the families' cultures add beauty and also provide a way to share lives.

With a culturally and linguistically diverse population, this center places reflections of the children's culture throughout their rooms. Their selection of books represents a variety of cultures, and the music and art activities they do with the children try to build on the children's cultural heritages.

Southwest Early Learning Center, Sound Child Care Solutions, Seattle, WA

Tots Corner, Auckland, New Zealand

When teachers share artifacts from their lives, they have the opportunity to deepen relationships with the children and their families. Here a teacher shares her love of horses, which the children immediately connect with and explore for an extended period of time.

Te Puna Kōhungahunga, Auckland, New Zealand

Children's cultures can be represented both indoors and outdoors. Here an outdoor water fountain has been designed with a Maori statue as its motif.

Guadalupano Family Center, Chicago Commons Child Development Program (Head Start), Chicago, IL

This program places the mask as a cultural artifact alongside the children's self-portraits to connect them to their lineage and their community's expression of culture.

Family Contributions

Beyond asking for objects and artifacts from families, consider using some of your family meetings to generate collaborative contributions to your environment. When families work together to make a contribution, their relationships with each other and with the program grow stronger.

Second Presbyterian Weekday School, Louisville, KY

As a way to honor the death of Charles, a child in their program, this center worked with his family to keep his memory alive with a gift related to two things he loved: frogs and boots. Lining the hallway are green frog boots children can wear when going outside in wet weather. Adding flowers to a boot continues to remind Charles's family that they still belong in the center.

Epiphany Early Learning Preschool, Sound Child Care Solutions, Seattle, WA

After an extended exploration of yarn with her group, this teacher invited the parents of the toddlers in her class to study the documentation of their work and then create a gift of yarn for the program. Tremendous excitement mounted as the families did a "yarn bombing" on the play yard.

Inventions for Your Program

As you consider your own environment and your goals for creating a cozy, homelike space where everyone has a sense of belonging and feels a sense of place, what are some of the easiest changes you can make? How could you better create a connection between children's homes and the program? What long-term goals might you have? Consider these elements to decide where you might start making some improvements:

- entries and hallways
- communication stations
- furnishings
- a sense of place with the natural world
- spaces for eating, sleeping, and caregiving
- work places for adults
- photos and documentation stories
- objects from home and cultural artifacts
- collaborative contributions from families

Once you have defined a starting place, revisit the pages of this chapter related to that element and make some notes. Find a colleague or families in your program to help you brainstorm ideas. Search unconventional stores, catalogs, and secondhand shops for ideas. Move slowly. Each change will suggest others, and it's useful to keep the big picture in mind as you begin to tackle the details.

Hilltop Children's Center, Seattle, WA

CHAPTER 4

Keep Space Flexible and Materials Open-Ended

Look Inside

In what areas of this preschool classroom do you think these photos were taken? Are the children in the block area, the drama area, or the large-motor area? How have their teachers offered possibilities for each of these kinds of play and let the play expand by being flexible with how space is used?

Stoneybrook Early Childhood Learning Centre, London Bridge Child Care Services, London, ON, Canada

In designing early childhood classrooms, it's useful to start by identifying learning areas for specific activities. This sets the stage for the organization of the room and materials and assists with group management as children learn what is available and where things are stored for easy access and cleanup. Children and adults benefit from having a visual logic to a room. However, far too often teachers stop there and become rigid in the way they think about and control the use of space in a classroom. Environment rating scales, standardization, and rules begin to take over as teachers remind children, "Remember those dishes belong in the dress-up area," "Climbing is for outdoors," "Don't build those blocks higher than your shoulders," or "Let's keep our books in the book area."

While we want our spaces to be safe, clean, and organized for children, we should also be eager to design an environment that meets up with children's flexible minds and energetic bodies. Children repeatedly have ideas about how they want to use materials or spaces that are different than what teachers could ever imagine. We need to encourage and support children's ideas by being careful observers. When we watch and listen closely to children, we see that they are fluid, creative thinkers who engage in dramatic and active play, construction, and design with many kinds of materials and in many areas of a room.

Young children bring their active bodies with them wherever they go, and their physical development is a critical aspect of their cognitive, social, and emotional development. Children deserve to be allowed to use their bodies to explore space and their own competency—climbing to a high loft, jumping off logs, going up and down steps and ladders, running or riding fast on a pathway, squeezing into a small box, or hiding under a blanket or behind a bush. These are favorite and vital activities for children.

In programs increasingly focused on providing an "educational" environment, the natural physical desires of young children are often ignored. For the sake of safety and noise control, too many programs limit children's indoor large-motor activity, and on behalf of more "learning" time, they further limit the time children have for outdoor activity. Indoor environments are typically designed with areas for small-group play, and "use your walking feet" is a constant refrain. However, for young children learning is a physical activity. They use their whole bodies—in motion— to learn. If we limit their activity, we limit their learning, as well as their joy and well-being. As children spend most of their early years in our programs, we have to continually raise these questions: Are we providing enough places for their active bodies? How can we negotiate our concerns about learning and safety with children's innate desire to challenge their brains and bodies?

Of equal significance, when young children are spending most of their days in a group situation, it is essential that we provide them time to be alone or with a small group of friends. Being in loud, large group environments can add to a child's stress, sense of invisibility, and difficulty concentrating. Our environments must provide quiet, restful places to gather emotional as well as physical replenishment. Children flourish in places where they can get away and work with small groups to explore their relationships and ideas without interruption.

If we initially design our spaces with more flexibility in mind, we will be better able to accommodate a range of varied activities and we wouldn't feel so obliged to keep children from rearranging things to suit their interests.

Flexibility and accommodation are what the teachers had in mind in the photos in this chapter's opening. Rather than using standard materials in completely separate areas for block play, dramatic play, and large-motor activity, they intentionally provided space, shelving, and open-ended materials for children to use in a multitude of ways. This freedom to move to different spaces using materials in open-ended ways is a prerequisite for children to be able to engage in complex problem solving and collaboration. Inspired by a read-aloud chapter book and conversations with their teachers, the children came up with a desire to help some animals get across a river. They had many conversations to discuss their different ideas, and their determination to find a possibility was fueled.

One group had the theory that the animals needed steps and worked with teachers to move furniture to try this out. The children ultimately created a structure that crossed over the river, with one set of steps to go up and another set of steps to go down, and a platform that linked them to span the water. The other group worked on a theory to create logs to step on across the water. They ultimately placed tall posts that could be walked on to cross the water. The flexibility built into the design and use of the space and materials helped the children invent strategies and try out their brilliant ideas. The teachers supported the children's risk taking in pursuit of these intellectually and physically challenging ideas. Interestingly, the children came up with two ways in which bridges are actually constructed: a beam across the water or supported by pillars that are anchored in the water.

Invite Living with Elements for Keeping Space Flexible and Materials Open-Ended

When children are offered flexible furnishings and open-ended materials, they engage in the range of activities that best foster their development and learning: moving, manipulating, investigating, building, representing, creating, communicating, and problem solving. With these kinds of activities, children become more competent in their physical abilities and develop self-confidence and independence. Meanwhile, their self-awareness increases and they become more alert and gain respect for others around them. Open-ended materials encourage children to use their flexible brains and become responsive playmates. As you consider how your environment lends itself to these important areas for growth and learning, ask yourself these questions:

1   What message does your environment give children about how they should use their bodies?

2   Are the indoor and outdoor areas flexible enough to be transformed for a variety of uses?

3   Can children expand their play and move materials into other areas of the room?

4   Where are the opportunities for individual children to get away from it all and relax?

5   Is there a space where a small group of children can work without interruption?

6   Are you satisfied with the balance of open-ended materials and single-purpose ones?

7   Where can you add unusual loose parts for children to use, both indoors and outdoors?

8   What is your disposition toward children's eagerness for challenge and risk?

Working with these questions will help you think differently about your environment and lead you to plan spaces geared toward the wide range of children's desires and abilities. Keep in mind that you are creating an environment for the remarkable children you work with to inspire a rich and active childhood for them.

As you design your room into learning centers, make sure some of the areas can be expanded when the need for bigger groups or building projects arises. With portable screens or dividers, you can also instantly create smaller spaces within larger ones for cozy gatherings or individual work. Two-tiered steps or risers against walls and movable platforms or risers allow children to create various arrangements and scenes. Provide large, hollow blocks of different shapes and sizes, heavy cardboard tubes and boxes in assorted sizes, card tables or other lightweight tables, pillows, and covered foam furniture for children to easily move around to suit their play ideas. Large pieces of fabric can be attached to structures with rods, clothespins, or curtain rings, enabling children to design hideaways and habitats.

Most early childhood programs have less than desirable spaces to begin with, but creative thinking will allow you to invent some new possibilities. To start, take a visual survey of the room from various angles: stand at your door, stand on a table against a wall, and lie down in the middle of the room. In each perspective, imagine you are a timid child, an uncoordinated one, and a group of physically active young friends. How would each space work for you? Study the examples that follow to see how some providers and teachers have invented fun and engaging ways to offer flexible spaces and open-ended materials.

Dedicate Indoor Space and Equipment for Active Play

Children ought to have indoor as well as outdoor places for their active bodies. Consider lofts and ladders for climbing high, logs and blocks for jumping, beams for balancing, and perhaps a rope or trapeze for climbing and swinging. This large-motor equipment isn't just for children to blow off steam, but rather to develop strength, sensory integration, and a sense of themselves as competent and powerful. Their ability to learn is enhanced when they use their bodies.

What better or more thrilling way to explore strength, motion, speed, gravity, and balance than with your own body? This teacher of two-year-olds has created an exceptional opportunity for sensory integration activities. He so values the excitement, joy, and learning to be found in jumping, swinging, and flying that he has hung rings from the ceiling. In another area, he has created a giant space for jumping. A large mattress, pillows, and floor mats, as well as conversations with the children, keep this a safe and exhilarating place to move!

Step One School, Berkeley, CA

Create Play Places at Various Levels, Heights, Perspectives, and Angles

When you vary the space in your program, you create out-of-the-box experiences for children. As you arrange furniture, try to create interesting angles and entry points into different areas of the room. An extended platform area in one part of the room, reached by one or two small steps, will expand the sense of space available. Likewise, a loft or two in a room multiplies the possibilities for how children can be alone or together. Window seats, the area under countertops, and empty open closets provide some other ways to create spaces at different levels with varied perspectives.

courtesy of Deb Curtis, Seattle, WA

When this program decided to add a toddler class to the school, the teacher in this room lowered a loft that had been built for preschoolers and repurposed a bed frame with railings to make a ramp. The children use the comfortable spot at the top to rest and read books. The ramp is used for sliding, climbing, and exploring gravity by rolling balls and cars down the slide.

courtesy of Deb Curtis, Seattle, WA

This platform offers the children a different height and focus for building with blocks. The children and teachers also gather around the platform for group times where their meetings have the feel of a family sitting around a dining-room table.

To allow for the flexible minds and bodies of toddlers, this room has been organized into zones rather than specific learning centers. There is a place for relaxing with a teacher and a book and a low table for exploring building toys and puzzles. Nearby there is space and equipment for active play, and behind the couch is a small dramatic play area. The other half of the room has linoleum and tables for messy sensory play and eating.

The Learning Center, Palo Alto, CA

Include Flexible, Varied Experiences Outdoors

Many programs confine outdoor play to typical playground equipment with an emphasis on safety and controlled activities for large-motor skills. Often teachers see the outdoors as just a place for children to let off steam. Rarely is there attention to interesting loose parts beyond sandbox toys, nor are there places to get away to a quiet place or for a big adventure. The following programs aren't settling for this limited view of outside play. Study how they have expanded the possibilities for deep engagement with the sensory and natural world, exciting dramas, and exhilarating challenges.

The Learning Center, Palo Alto, CA

The Learning Center, Palo Alto, CA

Rather than offering traditional playground equipment to their group of toddlers, this program has created places for the children to climb, jump, ride, run, focus, and rest. Notice the large ramp, boulders, and tree stumps. Do you see places where children can hide but still be supervised? Surrounded by nature and offered open-ended materials, this is just the place for toddlers to be busy or quiet and to use their energetic bodies and curious minds.

Tots Corner, Auckland, New Zealand

It doesn't take expensive commercial equipment to engage children in learning. Can you envision the ways children might invent dramas and adventures, build and construct, and strengthen their bodies as well as their spirits in this simple yet multifaceted outdoor space?

Step One School, Berkeley, CA

On the hillside in their play yard, this program has built an amazing, circulating creek where water runs down through the rocks. The children spend hours using the long gutters to capture the water and direct it to the sandpit.

Neighborhood Playgarden, San Francisco, CA

This family child care provider has created a parklike setting in her backyard for the children. Accordingly, she named her program Neighborhood Playgarden. Lush plants and flowers surround the children. The enchanting tree fort has an astonishing view of San Francisco and a bird nest inside that the children helped create by collecting twigs and branches from trees while on neighborhood walks. And a special treat is being able to use the slide to exit the house.

Arrange Quiet Spaces for Children

Protected areas away from the larger classroom allow children opportunities to have focused discussions and work cooperatively. Studio spaces, quiet coves, and corners work well for this. These can be created with hanging fabric or canopies, the arrangement of shelving units, or transparent room dividers made of Plexiglas or garden lattices. Some nooks, crannies, crawl spaces, and seating areas should be available for individual children to get away from the fray of the large group, indoors and outside. You can arrange these with transparent fabric or plant arrangements, which will still allow for supervision. A private place to get away is especially important for children in full-day programs.

Taylor Center for New Experiences, Chicago Commons Child Development Program (Head Start), Chicago, IL

This enchanting corner of a Head Start classroom invites one or two children to get away from the hustle and bustle to focus, think, and relax.

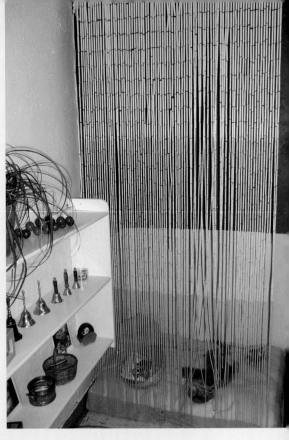

Pacific Primary Pre-School, San Francisco, CA

A sheer canopy gives the children in this room the feeling of hiding away in a magical space. Notice the use of sheer curtains to cozy up the space and keep the area visible for adults to supervise the children.

courtesy of Deb Curtis, Seattle, WA

The teacher took the door off of his closet to create a place for the children to be alone or with a friend. The beads offer the children the feeling of being away from the group while still allowing the teachers and children to see in and out. The beads also make a delightful tinkling sound when they move.

Children's Studio, Bellevue, WA

Creating cozy places outside is another way to help children get some time alone or special time with a friend. Here some old tights have been repurposed and hung from an outdoor climbing structure to create a secret place to hide.

Pacific Primary Pre-School, San Francisco, CA

Children who spend their days "in public" need a place to retreat and regroup. These places on two playgrounds provide children with spaces to get away, whether you are a crawling baby or active preschooler.

Browns Bay Pre-School, Auckland, New Zealand

Invite Learning with Flexible Activities and Open-Ended Materials

As you develop your space and design activities with flexibility in mind, you also need to think about providing a balanced selection of typical and nontraditional materials. In addition to keeping children safe, you want to challenge their minds, bodies, and social skills with materials that invite more complex play, collaboration, problem solving, and creativity. Children are capable of building elaborate structures with intricate landscaping and interior designs. With open-ended materials, they can design intricate patterns and detailed settings for their dramatic play. They can work with more than one type of building material and combine a standard set of unit blocks with Lego blocks and toy people and animal props. The skills and knowledge children possess and are eager to acquire usually surpass the limited learning opportunities of most early childhood materials designed for specific uses.

You can gather open-ended materials, items from nature, and other loose parts from the cardboard recycle bin, junk shop, garage sales, thrift stores, kitchen cupboards, beaches, woods, or parks. These undefined materials invite children to engage their imaginations, see themselves as inventors, and move toward more complex and challenging endeavors. Loose parts call out to children, saying, "Use me to show your ideas and creations." An ongoing supply of carefully selected open-ended materials, some common and some unusual, should be organized and displayed in various parts of your room and outdoor area.

As we look at what will be necessary for living in the twenty-first century, shouldn't our learning outcomes be focused on the ability to think flexibly, invent, collaborate, and problem solve? Don't we want to nurture people who will value conserving, preserving, and repurposing? The following are examples of thoughtful, open-ended materials teachers have offered and the kinds of activities they provoked in children.

Open-Ended Materials in the Block Area

Using traditional unit and large, hollow blocks along with well-chosen animal and people props, you can enrich the block area with open-ended materials that extend children's involvement and learning. Finding interesting materials to add to the block area is not difficult. Wander through garden, hardware, and craft stores; frequent garage sales; visit thrift, surplus, and repurposing stores for treasures that children can use in their construction and design work. Look for materials that offer interesting shapes and textures. Find things that can be used for extending the length, width, and height of a structure and items that can be used to enclose or cover it.

Offer children props they recognize from the adult world around them. These can spark the creation of constructions or additions to a structure, or inspire new ideas for dramatic play. Objects such as street signs, license plates, and exit signs enhance a building project as well as literacy skills. Hoses, tubes, and plumbing pipes all suggest a multitude of uses. You can get various lengths and widths of pipes and tubing at a hardware store or find old vacuum cleaner hoses at a thrift store. Steering wheels, small tires from wheelbarrows or bicycles, flashing lights, and traffic cones encourage inventions of vehicles and transportation structures. Repurposed computer keyboards, remote controls, calculators, and small air pumps can become controls, dials, or tools for buildings and vehicles.

When you add interesting design props to traditional blocks, girls are typically more eager to get involved. Natural materials and things that are colorful, sparkly, and attractive to children can be added as design elements and decorations for constructions. Be on the lookout for interesting materials such as tiles, marble pieces, carpet squares, cardboard tubes, industrial spools, sheer and opaque fabric, fur pieces, scarves, rope, elastic, pieces of Plexiglas, and artificial flowers and leaves. Many of these are available free as samples from creative surplus or home supply stores. When you provide materials from nature, such as rocks, twigs, driftwood, pieces of tree branches, and small tree stumps, they will find their way into children's constructions, designs, and unfolding dramas.

Tots Corner, Auckland, New Zealand

These programs have inviting block areas, using familiar and new materials to engage the children in thoughtful play.

Maitland Early Learning Centre, London Bridge Child Care Services, London, ON, Canada

After observing the girls in her group use the artificial flowers, fabric, and colorful tiles in their block buildings, this teacher created an inviting setup in the block area that will encourage these items' continued use. The girls use the materials to create amazing structures with beautiful elements of design, enhancing their dramatic play.

courtesy of Deb Curtis, Seattle, WA

Finding stones, fabric, carpet, and toy animals in the block center, this boy and his classmates create beautiful designs and habitats for the dinosaur babies and their mama and a bridge for the goat to cross the water. Their work is layered with complexity as they use the materials to explore math skills such as enclosure and one-to-one correspondence, in addition to inventing dramas.

Magic Garden Care and Education Centre, Auckland, New Zealand

Notice how this preschool boy uses the sheer fabric, stones, and tiles to create an elegant design on top of the Plexiglas mirror. It's obvious he has reverence for these materials, as he is working with them so purposefully.

Child's Play Family Childcare, San Francisco, CA

Repurposed Materials

An "invention center" or "creation station" is an area of the room supplied with loose parts and repurposed materials for children to use in building and creating representations of their choice. Unlike the loose parts in the block or drama areas, invention center or creation station materials are primarily consumables—the children make creations for a onetime use or as an ongoing prop in dramatic play or an in-depth study project.

You can find an array of repurposed materials once you begin scouting for them. At home, collect things such as paper tubes, small boxes, food packaging, and corks. Most communities have creative surplus and recyclable stores; scout out one in your area. The wonderful book *Beautiful Stuff! Learning with Found Materials* describes how one program had families collect loose parts for a studio space they set up. This process began an extended project of organizing and displaying the materials, learning about their properties, and then using them for a variety of representations, storytelling, and projects.

Recognizable objects such as bottle tops, corks, straws, craft sticks, buttons, wood scraps, and fabric pieces all lend themselves to creative use. Plastic and metal odds and ends spark children's thinking, and the way they use these items often surprises adults. The children use these smaller items to attach things together or create details in their representations. Look for a variety of materials that can be used to connect things—all kinds of tape (including masking tape, clear tape, and colored masking tape), twist ties, wire of all kinds, pipe cleaners, string, paper clips, ribbon, yarn, and pieces of modeling clay. The variety encourages different approaches to construction, invention, and problem solving. Provide tools such as scissors, hole punches, wire cutters, tape dispensers, and staplers to use with consumable loose parts.

For children's representations to be stable and potentially more permanent, offer larger items for bases or foundations. Keep a supply of clean egg cartons, boxes of all shapes and sizes, pieces of cardboard, foam core or poster board, plastic tubs and lids, paper plates, old computer disks, and CDs. Natural materials such as shells, twigs, pebbles, and leaves add a different kind of texture, color, and form than manufactured materials.

courtesy of Deb Curtis, Seattle, WA

To avoid a cluttered look while inviting exploration of loose parts, the teacher at this school stores them in flat baskets that are similar in construction and color. Objects of similar colors or shapes are sorted into the baskets and containers. This display reminds both children and adults that what appears to be throwaway, useless objects can be transformed into remarkable creations.

courtesy of Deb Curtis, Seattle, WA

When this program ordered new blocks, they also received packing material and cardboard tubes. The children eagerly began using these materials with as much concentration as they did the expensive new block set, so the teachers decided to permanently keep these materials in the building area along with the blocks.

Loose Parts with Infants and Toddlers

Study the following photos closely and you will see natural materials, shiny tubes that came from the middle of sports trophies, gorgeous sparkly ribbon, boxes wrapped with aluminum foil, decorating samples from the hardware store, and tree pieces with holes drilled in them for lacing games.

Certainly you will need to supervise when you offer small parts to infants and toddlers and you also want to avoid any materials that may be toxic. Your search and attention will be well worth it when you see the enthusiasm and apt focus these items cause young children to bring to their explorations.

Destiny Village Child Care, United Way Bright Beginnings, Houston, TX

courtesy of United Way Bright Beginnings, Houston, TX

Loose parts and repurposed materials are just as valuable for infants and toddlers. Notice in these photos the variety of possibilities for offering even the youngest children intriguing materials for their investigation.

Child's Play Family Childcare, San Francisco, CA

The young toddlers in this family child care home were just as engaged in playing with this offering of loose parts and repurposed materials as the older children. The children showed great skill and persistence playing with these items. The little boy in the red shirt was able to get the napkin and curtain rings to spin around and around on the stick. And the girl in the purple shirt stuck the tips of the spiral shells in the bamboo cylinders, filling every tiny hole she discovered.

Materials for Design

Young children are continually classifying, sorting, matching, and transforming the objects and materials around them. Because children have a natural eye for design, they can make good use of attractively displayed, diverse open-ended materials. As they explore the textures, shapes, colors, and sizes, they notice how things are alike and how they are different. They pay close attention to filling spaces and sometimes will create recognizable representations if an object reminds them of something they know. Open-ended materials also lend themselves to sorting, counting, one-to-one correspondence, seriation, and other mathematical concepts.

You can intentionally locate and offer materials that inspire children to investigate, design, and learn. Objects from nature provide an array of texture, color, and shapes that can be used in children's designs and constructions. Collections of almost any kind of natural material, presented to children in inviting ways on trays, in baskets, or on neutral fabric, can lead to many wonderful creations. Here are some suggestions that can be offered both indoors and outdoors:

- rocks, stones, and pebbles (natural and polished)
- shells of all sizes and shapes
- leaves of all sizes, shapes, and colors
- twigs, branches, driftwood, and rounds and lengths of tree trunks
- flowers, petals, and herb sprigs
- feathers of all shapes, natural colors, and sizes (find these at craft stores rather than using real bird feathers, as they may be unsanitary)
- pinecones, pods, and nuts and seeds in their shells

Scout out interesting treasures that children can use in design work at creative surplus, repurposing, thrift, or craft stores. Look for items that have beautiful colors and interesting shapes and textures that, either alone or in combination, suggest possibilities for classification and order. These kinds of items engage children hour upon hour:

- beads, buttons, beach glass, plastic and glass gems
- tiles, marble pieces, linoleum samples
- ribbon, fabric samples, spools of thread
- napkin rings, candleholders, votive candles
- marbles

Pacific Primary Pre-School, San Francisco, CA

When teachers in this program offer playdough and a variety of loose parts and natural materials, the children enthusiastically work to spread the dough over their trays and then use the materials to make intricate designs. As they work they describe dramas that are taking place in the awesome habitats they made.

Buttons are a source of endless hours of sorting, categorizing, and designing for preschoolers. These children are offered an exciting array of buttons and small cups, which they use to create many intricate configurations with attention to size, shape, color, texture, and stability.

courtesy of Deb Curtis, Seattle, WA

Open-Ended Materials and Props for Dramatic Play

Children find it natural to use open-ended materials as invented props for their dramatic play. Pinecones quickly become food to feed the family. A house is built from scarves and chairs, carefully secured to protect the family from the "bad guys." Through dramatic play, children represent what they see and construct their own understandings. They recreate familiar scripts to work out issues of security and fear. As children act out their ideas with their bodies and props, they acquire the ability to think symbolically, a prerequisite for literacy and math concepts. They also learn co-operative skills as they negotiate complex play scripts and try out roles and differing points of view. Materials that get incorporated into rollicking adventures help them face fears and feel powerful and competent.

Teachers of young children can enhance this natural flair for drama by providing thoughtful collections of props and materials. Younger children and children less able to use symbolic representation in their dramas benefit from props that look similar to the real thing. When they use props they recognize from their daily lives, children have a shared experience to play out. But as they become experienced play negotia-tors and more able to use symbolic representation in their play, it is important to expand props beyond the traditional—and recognizable—housekeeping items found in most early childhood programs. Open-ended, less-prescriptive materials suggest different kinds of drama and offer children opportunities for divergent thinking.

To become a good provisioner of props for dramatic play, it is important to learn about the children's family life and to listen and observe them closely to uncover the issues and concepts they are pursuing. Understanding the developmental themes that drive children's energy and eagerness for high adventure, noise, and bravado can help teachers expand children's minds, as well as the space and materials for this type of dramatic and often big-body play.

When collecting props for dramatic play, look for a combination of items: objects that come from the children's daily lives, new items to expand their experiences, and open-ended materials that encourage divergent thinking. Examples of these types of materials include:

- hats, shoes, boots, and a few items of clothing that reflect the people and places in the children's daily lives
- a variety of fabric lengths, including fake animal fur and prints, sheer fabric, shiny fabric, ethnic prints, and sequined fabric
- a variety of colors and lengths of scarves
- capes in a variety of colors and lengths
- a sampling of simple masks
- ribbon, sashes, elastic rounds, Velcro, clips, and other kinds of ties children can use to attach fabric to costumes, habitats, and buildings

- interesting loose parts that can become part of a drama, including telephones, binoculars, cameras, magnifying glasses, sunglasses, combination locks, keyboards, and flashlights

- large pieces of cardboard, wooden boards and ramps, tubes, vinyl gutters, and hollow blocks that can be moved and used for dramas.

- boxes, bags, purses, and luggage that can be used in a variety of ways, including storing and transporting things

- a tool kit and a medical kit with as many safe, real objects as possible

- open-ended materials from the inventors' repurposing bin and other found, natural materials such as twigs, shells, and rocks

Tots Corner, Auckland, New Zealand

Props for drama should be neatly and logically organized so children can see what is available and how things might be combined and used together. Flat baskets or containers can be used to display materials in an attractive, orderly way to help children approach their play more intentionally. Locating mirrors near the dress-up props gives the children immediate visual feedback.

Children First, Durham, NC

courtesy of Deb Curtis, Seattle, WA

Hilltop Children's Center, Seattle, WA

Each of these programs—two center-based and the other a family home—challenges children to invent and imagine their own costumes and dramas by displaying capes, masks, and a selection of fabric pieces rather than predetermined clothing or costumes.

Guadalupano Family Center, Chicago Commons Child Development Program (Head Start), Chicago, IL

As the toddlers in this program use these recognizable but open-ended areas for pretend play, their caregivers discover what the children already know and get ideas for other things to offer.

Kawartha Child Care Services, Peterborough, ON, Canada

Child's Play Family Childcare, San Francisco, CA

Expand dramatic play opportunities by offering miniature drama-scapes. You can design inviting backdrops to enhance pretend play by offering collections of materials focusing on children's play themes and unfolding interests. In these photos are examples of a bird and nest drama-scape, butterfly drama-scape, and a farm drama-scape.

Keep Space Flexible and Materials Open-Ended 𝓰 117

Open-Ended Materials Outdoors

Watching children play outside is a testimony to their curiosity and inventiveness. Even on an asphalt surface, children will search for a hole to poke and prod until they get to the loose dirt underneath. Whether we grew up in cities, small towns, suburbs, or rural areas, most of us can remember what it's like to be a child out of doors.

But children's curiosity is no excuse for outdoor play areas in early childhood programs to consist of nothing more than flat surfaces, a climber, sandbox, some plastic toys, and trikes. It's our responsibility to ensure that the children experience a more dynamic playscape. Children need materials for invention, discoveries, and experiments. It isn't difficult to gather a collection of loose parts for your playground. The following are some props that you can make available, paying attention to modifications that need to be made and maintained for safety (sharp edges that need to be removed or covered and so on):

- large and small pieces of driftwood
- tree rounds, stumps, and branches—both large enough to climb on and small enough to carry and build with
- smooth rocks and boulders for climbing on and carrying
- pieces of marble and stepping-stones that can be moved by the children for constructions
- wooden pallets
- bales of hay
- large wood scraps and planks
- different lengths of portable vinyl gutters
- portable ladders and step stools
- large milk crates or other plastic bins
- barrels, buckets, and wheelbarrows
- sawhorses and planks
- poles with pulleys, clotheslines, and buckets
- shovels, rakes, boots, brushes, brooms, sifters, and trowels of various sizes
- spray bottles, hoses, sprinklers, and spigots with water fountains and dog licks
- pinecones, needles, and pods of all sizes
- measuring tapes, rain gauges, thermometers, and air pressure gauges
- wheels, tires, and spools

Loose parts on the playground can become a pile of broken junk without a watchful eye, thoughtful planning, and an adequate, well-organized storage system and maintenance plan. As with indoor materials and curriculum planning, setting up and maintaining outdoor materials should be part of a teacher's paid planning time. Programs can dedicate a portion of their play area to storage of large items and another area to shelves and boxes or bins for smaller items. Store similar items together for easy location and regularly discard broken items and clean heavily used ones. Have maintenance tools handy, along with outdoor cleanup supplies.

Children can create "dinoramas" using traditional materials, such as toy dinosaurs, combined with a variety of loose parts on the playground, like pipes, ramps, and tree branches.

La Jolla United Methodist Church Nursery School, La Jolla, CA

Everyone remembers building forts with wood, tree branches, and other found objects as a child, which is exactly how this group of children use the loose parts available to them in their play yard.

courtesy of Deb Curtis, Seattle, WA

Mills College Children's School, Oakland, CA

These flexible planks and sawhorses can be arranged in a variety of ways to challenge the children's physical skills. The teachers help ensure safety by closely observing the children's competence and confidence while staying near to help when needed. The jumping area is in a sandpit, and the mattress and pillow provide extra cushioning for landing. If you study this photo closely, you'll see children who are capable of engaging in play in a big way. Imagine the powerful, exhilarating feelings they have as they take the leap.

This inviting outdoor building platform has a variety of sizes and shapes of driftwood and boulders. The children gain confidence as they construct, invent dramas, and lift and carry the heavy objects.

Browns Bay Pre-School, Auckland, New Zealand

Study the variety of loose parts that these programs make available to children. How are the children using them, or what do you think the children might do with them? What benefits do you think the children gain from engaging with materials and equipment like these? What role could a teacher play to support the children's work?

The Child Development Center at Mira Costa, Oceanside, CA

Botany Downs Kindergarten, Auckland, New Zealand

Saskatoon Early Childhood Education Demonstration Centre, Saskatoon, Saskatchewan, Canada

Children First, Durham, NC

This family child care provider highly values children spending time outdoors with open-ended materials to use their minds and their bodies fully. She has several options for children to use loose parts for building complex structures, creating elaborate dramas, and pursuing intellectual and physical challenges and risks. Imagine being a child in this "place for childhood."

Repurposed Materials

The amount of stuff that we accumulate and throw away in our society is shameful. Scouting thrift stores and garage sales for interesting, usable items can be an enjoyable treasure hunt. You can also use your arts and crafts skills to provision for children and invite them into the fun. Repurposing materials to be used in creative ways not only helps the environment, but it also grows flexible thinking skills. There are many resources these days for using everyday objects in new ways. Pinterest and other websites offer suggestions and directions for using things such as discarded wood pallets, furniture, dishes, and water bottles, just to name a few. The following are examples of inventions from several child care programs.

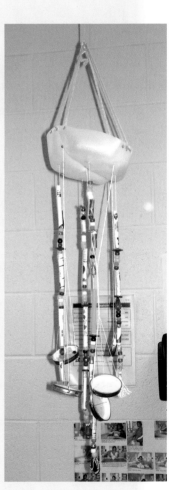

The Bridge Over Troubled Waters, Inc., Pasadena, TX

This child care program for children living in a homeless shelter offers many opportunities for staff and children and their families to work together using repurposed materials to create beautiful things. Here you see three examples of stunning hanging curtains that they have made from water bottles, milk jugs, rolled-up magazines, and metal and plastic lids. The curtains move, sparkle, and make lovely sounds, creating magical surroundings for the children, as well as a sense of pride in their contribution to the projects.

Rather than the standard early childhood catalog sensory table, this teacher has adapted a coffee table for sensory exploration. It is often filled with beautiful white sand and different rotating collections of materials for the children's sensory exploration.

Children's Studio, Bellevue, WA

Second Presbyterian Weekday School, Louisville, KY

After studying the work of glass artist Dale Chihuly, the school-age children in this class created their own version of one of his stunning glass installations. Theirs isn't made of glass, but is just as impressive made from plastic water bottles.

Inventions for Your Program

If you think your environment needs an infusion of open-ended materials, consider where you might find a selection. Carefully study early childhood catalogs or visit discount and museum stores, garage sales, and thrift shops. Request help from your friends and the children's families in locating creative repurposing materials. Reading the book *Beautiful Stuff!* will give you some ideas about how you might turn this gathering process into a long-term project. As you consider adding loose parts to various areas of your room and play yard, keep these ideas in mind:

- Keep furnishings and arrangements flexible.
- Add different levels, heights, and angles to your space.
- Provide open-ended equipment that can be transformed by the children's interests.
- Create places for individual children and small and large groups of children.
- Provide spaces for both quiet and active pursuits.
- Establish an invention or creation station with recycled, repurposed, or "one-time use" materials.
- Create invitations for building and construction, dramatic play, and creative design work by providing natural, loose parts.
- Supply your outdoor area with a selection of attractive and well-maintained loose parts.

With this list of possibilities, commit to a starting place for you and your coworkers. Remember, not only will you be providing children with the tools and materials they deserve for an unforgettable childhood, but you will also be encouraging stewardship of the planet and equipping future inventors with the skills and dispositions to solve the ever-increasing problems of the world.

Nia Family Center, Chicago Commons Child Development Program (Head Start) Chicago, IL

CHAPTER 5

Design Natural Environments That Engage Our Senses

*Baskin 1
Early Head Start,
Santa Cruz, CA*

Look Inside

In this toddler program, the teachers created an invitation of natural materials in their room. If you were these teachers, what might be on your mind as you selected materials and planned this environment for the toddlers? As you reflect on the photo, to what do you think the children might be drawn? How would you describe the colors and textures available here? What role might the hanging photos have in how the children use the materials?

If you think back to your own childhood, depending on your age and location, you probably spent the majority of your time outdoors. Your fondest memories may be of the times you spent in the natural world, scurrying after bugs and frogs, romping with your dog, or building a fort with rocks, twigs, leaves, dirt, and pods. Perhaps your family had a vegetable garden. Maybe you dared to stomp in the mud left behind after a big downpour. If you grew up in an urban setting, perhaps you scouted for sources of water to play in, gathered sticks and rocks, or watched the clouds roll in or the silhouette of trees or buildings change against the sky with the seasons. Parks were no doubt a favorite destination.

The natural world provides an abundance of opportunities to engage the senses. Outdoors, you can usually find a hint of an interesting aroma coming from something in bloom; experience the pleasure of touching plants, shells, feathers, dirt, and sand; and hear the sounds of birds, running water, wind, and rustling leaves. With the changing seasons and angle of the sun, you can discover an ever-changing array of shadows. A fresh falling of snow or icicles dangling from the edges of roofs or tree branches can conjure up the feeling of a fairyland.

Watching children at any park, woods, or beach, we can see that they are especially drawn to the opportunities the natural world provides to use all of their senses: they stomp in puddles, dig in sand, climb trees, build snow forts or bridges across gullies, create adventures, explore, transform, and invent. And yet beyond some brief outdoor play period, a classroom aquarium, gerbils, or a water table, few early childhood programs offer children extended opportunities to experience the natural world. With adult concerns about unfavorable weather and health and safety issues, children spend less and less time outdoors and have little sense of the natural world around them. They not only don't know the names of birds, bugs, and animals in their community's natural habitat, but they are afraid of them.

With the publishing of *Last Child in the Woods*, Richard Louv (2008) warned of the growing dangers of what he calls "nature-deficit disorder." He helped launch the Children and Nature Movement, through which a host of individuals and organizations around the world have been working to reverse this trend. You can do an online search and find a way to get involved with organizations such as World Forum Foundation's Nature Action Collaborative for Children and the Children and Nature Network, cofounded by Louv. Wherever you are located, early childhood programs can join this movement and play a daily role in getting children reconnected to the natural world. You can bring children out into nature but also bring nature inside the doors of your center.

Invite Living with Elements for Creating Natural Environments

Whatever your program setting—urban, suburban, small town, or rural; church, school, or portable building; grass or wood chip, blacktop, or concrete playgrounds—you can still surround children with Mother Nature and natural objects that engage their senses. As you consider including the natural world in your environment, use these questions to guide your thinking and discussion with coworkers:

courtesy of Ann Pelo, Montesano, WA

1. How can we learn more about the natural elements in our environment, begin to learn their names, and become more connected to them?

2. What natural materials in our community can be brought into our program?

3. Who in our community can assist us with food resources and botanical, landscaping, and animal knowledge?

4. How could we gather natural loose parts for our play yard and indoor environment?

5. What sources of water do we have available, and how can we make them accessible and safe for the children's use?

6. What seasonal traditions or rituals could help children become more closely connected to Mother Nature and the life cycle?

We suggest you revisit these questions each year to set new goals for your program to continue to find new ways to connect children to the natural world around them.

Saskatoon Early Childhood Education Demonstration Centre, Saskatoon, SK, Canada

The United States is geographically diverse; every region's weather is different, and plants and animals vary from one location to the next. For this reason, the work of connecting children to the natural world will change from one program to another. Still, there are some basic elements that most programs can consider, as demonstrated in the following examples.

Furnish Your Building with Natural and Sensory-Rich Objects

It is simple and inexpensive to collect things from nature to enhance and beautify your environment. For starters, try using natural fiber baskets and bushel bins for storage rather than plastic ones. These can be continually replaced at a nominal cost from thrift stores. Well-placed shells, rocks, and interesting pieces of driftwood or marble can be made available to look at and touch. Tree branches can be hung and large bark pieces mounted as natural sculptures. Put smaller collections of rocks, feathers, leaves, pinecones, bird nests, and dried herbs in baskets around the building; use good judgment with safety concerns in mind. Young children also love coffee-table books and calendars with photos of the natural world and landscape designs. These can provoke further investigation when accompanied by a basket of natural materials featured in the picture. And of course, all kinds of nontoxic plants in hanging baskets or on windowsills and countertops will add beauty, texture, and calmness to a room, as will open windows and fresh air!

Baskin 1 Early Head Start, Santa Cruz, CA

courtesy of Deb Curtis, Seattle, WA

Toddlers love to fill baskets and carry things around in them. This toddler room offers beautiful African woven baskets for this purpose and includes natural materials of different textures and weights to be included. By including a related book as part of the invitation, children become exposed to the idea that books are a source of information as well as a source of visual interest.

When a storm blew down a big tree in their play yard, parents, children, and teachers worked to claim pieces of it that could be brought inside. The result was a beautiful loft reminiscent of outdoor tree houses. The children not only have a fun place to perch and see the room from a different perspective, but the opportunity to stay connected to the play yard tree they had loved.

Offer Natural Materials Indoors for Study, Design, and Play

Try adding large and small driftwood logs to your block area. You can include small branch pieces, rocks, shells, leaves, pods, marble, and tree bark contained in baskets in your block area or on the manipulative toy shelves, or for use in playdough and the art area. Children love to study these objects' textures, sizes, and shapes. They also focus on sorting, classifying, designing, and constructing with natural materials. Rotate natural things such as these in the sensory table: fall leaves, gourds, pine needles, cones, nuts, seeds, grass clippings, straw, and rose petals. Be sure to obtain a listing of poisonous plants and any allergies children and staff in your program have.

Mission College Child Development Center, Santa Clara, CA

A collection of natural materials are always offered on an inside table in this toddler room so the children can explore and compare the various textures, colors, smells, and weight of each object.

When your program is in the middle of an urban setting, it is especially important to bring elements of the natural world inside for children to experience. Here a program uses large plants in the room, along with a shelf of collected materials from trees that includes branches, bark, and driftwood.

Paulo Freire Family Center, Chicago Commons Child Development Program (Head Start), Chicago, IL

*Paulo Freire Family Center, Chicago Commons
Child Development Program (Head Start), Chicago, IL*

*Casula Pre-School, Liverpool City Council Early
Childhood Program, Liverpool, Australia*

Tree stumps indoors can serve as stools for sitting and surfaces for using materials.

Botany Downs Kindergarten, Auckland, New Zealand

Believing that learning to humanely care for animals leads people to treat each other well, this program incorporates a number of animals into their program. They currently have a turtle, fish, canaries, quail, monarch caterpillars, guinea pigs, and a worm farm. Not all children have pets at home; this program offers an opportunity to care for animals in life and in death. The children do most of the pet care, and they keep the housing well above standard. The guinea pigs live in a "grotto" that has seats for children to sit in when they are petting them. Usually the animals are in their "snuggle bag" so that they feel secure and the children can manage them easily. The teachers find that the children with special needs are especially drawn to the animals. Just as the children do, all the animals have portfolios, and the children frequently write learning stories about them.

Landscape with Textures, Colors, and Scents

Before you spend your budget on playground equipment, invest in landscaping features: create hills and plant trees, edible plants, and shrubs. While children can benefit from encountering and learning to identify and take care of plants with thorns or prickly leaves, do take care to avoid landscaping with any poisonous plants or those known to cause skin irritations. Plant fragrant herbs that spread quickly and can handle heavy traffic, such as mint, lavender, rosemary, and creeping thyme. (A simple web search can help you find what grows in your region.) These herbs can be planted around the grounds, and periodically bouquets can be brought inside for sensory investigation and to set on meal tables or in bathrooms. Berry bushes or a garden, fruit tree, or grape arbor offer children a chance to see and pick their own produce instead of buying it at the grocery store. Even temporary landscaping is something to consider. For example, each January Bev Bos has families bring their used Christmas trees in buckets of sand to create a temporary forest in her California yard.

Sophia's Preschool, Oakura, New Zealand

Thoughtful attention was given to landscaping the fence area around this preschool using natural plants, bushes, and wood to create a sense of mystery and a space for adventures. As the children venture behind the plantings, they discover a mirror in a mosaic frame, giving further depth and perspective to the play yard.

Children First, Durham, NC

The garden in the play yard of this family child care home provides multiple opportunities for children to watch the growing process and discover the scents of different herbs, which they often cut to bring inside.

Design Outdoor Playscapes

Consider using wood in its rough or natural form when constructing such things as fences, platforms, and benches in your play yard. While it may not seem as durable as plastic, the texture of natural wood is valuable for children to experience. They also benefit from seeing how wood weathers and changes over time. Research the toxicity of any wood preservative you consider using.

Here a platform for a slide was created out of tree branches that were cut in a way to make them safe around children. The use of indigenous large plants adds to the natural feel of this play equipment. Flax plants in particular have been used for centuries by indigenous peoples of the Pacific Islands and have symbolic as well as functional purposes for the Maori families and educators at this center.

Awhi Whanau Early Education Centre, Auckland, New Zealand

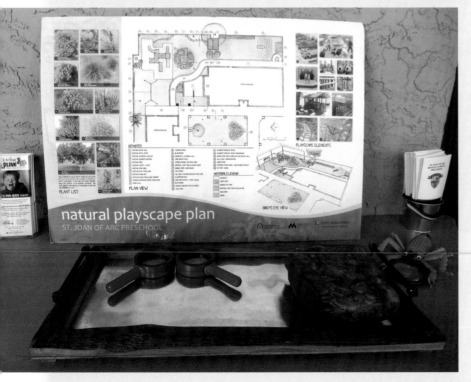

Designing outdoor playscapes for the extreme heat of the Southwest requires identifying native or desert-adapted plants that are safe and appropriate for children. It also requires a shift in thinking so that there is a desire to go outside. To build enthusiasm for an upcoming landscaping project, this preschool began engaging the children and families with the landscape design and some of the materials they will be able to explore.

courtesy of Josh Trommler, Phoenix, AZ

Tots Corner, Auckland, New Zealand

Here a program has used gathered driftwood as a railing for a little bridge and landscaped with beach grasses, both natural elements the children commonly see in their community.

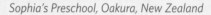

Sophia's Preschool, Oakura, New Zealand

Using gathered vines, branches, twigs, fronds, and branches from the surrounding area, this program created a nest in their play yard, adding some shiny balls to entice the children to check the nest and see what might have hatched.

East Tennessee State University Little Buccaneers Laboratory Program, Johnson City, TN

A permanent feature inside the fence of this child development center is a rack for books and charts about things found in the natural world. The children use these as field guides when they want to learn more about things in nature they are discovering.

Places for Sand Play

Outdoor sandboxes are disappearing in early childhood programs due to concerns about health and animal feces. But would you—or could you—keep children away from a sandy beach even though they might encounter bird poop, feathers, or dead fish? Children can be taught to join adults in watching out for and removing unsanitatry elements. Sand can also be brought inside and its sensory properties used for smaller-scale work.

Children First, Durham, NC

Part of what makes this sand play so inviting is the interesting shape of the sand bed and the availability of water and sturdy shovels. The children spend endless hours discovering different ways the sand can be moved, shaped, and transformed.

Helensville Montessori, Helensville, New Zealand

Sand play in this center is expanded by a two-level box with a connecting ladder and plank. Notice the rain barrel, shovels, gutters, and platforms that invite the children to expand their sensory exploration to the fullest.

*East Tennessee State University
Little Buccaneers Laboratory Program,
Johnson City, TN*

This program has chosen to mound sand into a hill and add gutters and buckets the children can use to add water and discover more about how both the sand and the water change when they interact with each other and gravity.

Highland Plaza United Methodist Preschool, Hixson, TN

This preschool's sandpit is adjacent to a cement area supplied with water and a variety of natural loose parts. Children can experiment with ways to combine and transport the materials. These materials offer the children many textures to explore.

Provide Sources of Water

Water in early childhood programs should not only be for drinking, washing up, or occasional play in the sensory table. Water should be made available for looking at, listening to, and touching, as well as for playing in and with. It is one of the most soothing and engaging substances that we can offer ourselves and children. Provide water by including hoses, pumps, faucets, sinks, and even showers in your play yard. A river rock creek bed with a source of water will provide hours of exploratory and dramatic play outdoors. Remember that with climate change, water is a precious commodity in many communities, so offer water in an environmentally conscious way, such as using rain barrels and pumps that recycle water.

The Highlander School, Atlanta, GA

Large stones create a streambed across this program's play yard, and the teachers provide a hose for the children to feel the cool sensations of the water and listen to its sound as it splashes down.

Children First, Durham, NC

A simple circle of stones around a patch of dirt becomes a mud kitchen with endless possibilities when water and cooking utensils are made available.

Highland Plaza United Methodist Preschool, Hixson, TN

With watering cans placed next to an outdoor rain barrel, children at this center learn to care for the plants in their play yard. They also learn the importance of gathering rainwater in this way.

Children First, Durham, NC

Children at this family child care home program have a number of ways they can use and explore water. Over time, they learn to move the hose around to discover how water interacts with different materials, sometimes causing the materials to move or creating a spray.

Awhi Whanau Early Childhood Centre, Auckland, New Zealand

Because the children here are free to explore the natural elements (sand, mud, water, plants) of their play yard, the designer of the yard included an outdoor shower so the children and teachers can wash off any residue from their play they don't want to track inside.

Provide Natural Loose Parts in Outdoor Spaces

If your playground is mostly concrete and has stationary climbing structures, try adding natural items such as driftwood logs, large rocks, shells, pinecones, hay bales, and tree stumps and branches for the children to explore, move, and use to create constructions. Monitor these items for safety to make sure there aren't such things as sharp edges that could cause any serious injury, but let the children use them freely in their play. Look for new natural elements to introduce in the play yard. For instance, vines that grow to create tunnels with scented flowers or hanging fruit, potted or hanging baskets of tomato plants and herbs, a collection of large tree branches, or bamboo sticks vertically secured in the sandpit or buckets.

East Tennessee State University Little Buccaneers Laboratory Program, Johnson City, TN

Tree trunks provide a number of valuable experiences for children. Children can climb and balance on them, jump from them, and negotiate space and safety with peers. Adding additional props such as ladders expands these opportunities. The ecosystem of the bark invites discoveries and possibilities for research.

A row of tree stumps in a play yard encourages climbing, jumping, and balancing, but they can also serve as a platform for investigating materials brought from other places around the yard. Rocks, sticks, leaves, and hay all add possibilities to explore weight, texture, sound, and smells.

courtesy of Janis Keyser, Mountain View, CA

Children First, Durham, NC

This program periodically has campfire days with the children. They learn to build the fire by first placing a layer of newspaper balls, adding some smaller sticks, and then topping with broken-up branches. One time, while they were creating the fire pyramid shape, the children discovered a stick in the shape of the letter "y." Once the fire is lit, the children get to experience smoke and see the sticks gradually turn from brown to black to gray. With lots of practice being safe with fire, they become savvy fire keepers.

Paulo Freire Family Center, Chicago Commons Child Development Program (Head Start), Chicago, IL

Baskin 1 Early Head Start, Santa Cruz, CA

Tree stumps can be used as loose parts to be moved around or fastened in the ground to provide outdoor climbing and leaping adventures.

Invite Learning with Natural Materials and Sensory Activities

Along with sensory-rich natural features in the overall environment, teachers can continually invite children to connect to the natural world with specific materials and activities. Sensory materials can often change in shape and form. Water changes as it freezes, food as it cooks, wood as it burns, and sand and clay as it is molded. As children work with these materials, they are learning about themselves and their role in using the physical properties of their world. Children are transfixed by looking at, smelling, touching, tasting, and moving and rearranging things. These experiences are as vital to young children as eating and breathing. As they absorb the rich sensory information around them, children's brain pathways are making connections that will be the foundation for a lifetime of experience and learning.

Sensory experiences are a traditional part of most early childhood programs. Teachers offer children water tables, fingerpaint, and playdough. Sand tables, if not outdoor sandboxes, can be found in some early childhood program environments, and natural materials are typically offered on a science table. The possibilities of materials and the ways to explore and transform them are unlimited if we open our eyes and our mind to the joy and importance of the natural world and sensory activities. Yet many adults limit these activities because of the mess, noise, and spread of germs associated with them.

Are you enhancing or limiting the learning possibilities for children's involvement with natural and sensory materials? For instance, is the same substance left in the sensory tub or tray for weeks at a time with little thought given to the tools offered for exploring and designing? Do you provide materials that are already made and mixed rather than allowing children to combine and transform them, such as involving the children in making playdough? Do the tools for playdough go beyond rolling pins and cookie cutters? Have you ever offered natural materials for use in construction, design, and art projects? Do you have beautiful displays in your room featuring natural materials with a variety of textures, colors, shapes, and sizes that children can study, manipulate, arrange, and rearrange?

Turn to your observations of children for ideas and you will see the many ways they study, design, or transform the materials they use. As children work with these materials, they are discovering the materials' properties and how they can change them. To enhance this investigation, you can look for materials, as well as tools and utensils, with interesting textures and features.

When you include natural materials in early childhood environments, the possibilities are endless. Some of them can be offered just for children to explore and appreciate their sensory properties, while others can be offered in combinations that provide learning opportunities similar to those created commercially as early childhood materials. Rocks, shells, pinecones, and gourds can be used for classifying and sorting, seriating, designing, and transforming. Nearly all of early childhood "schema theory" can be explored with thoughtfully combined natural materials.

Develop Wonder and Scientific Thinking

Rather than limiting your science curriculum to a table focused on a science concept, offer opportunities to develop scientific thinking and behaviors throughout your environment. A scientist is a person who wonders, asks questions, and tries out different ways to answer them. When you offer natural materials in ways that provoke wonder and curiosity, you start the process of scientific investigation. Children begin to practice scientific thinking and behaviors when they do the following (Lehn 1999):

- wonder and ask questions

- learn from their senses

- observe closely and notice details

- compare and sort by looking carefully

- experiment by trial and error and test predictions

- keep trying over and over

- count and measure to make comparisons

- describe, draw, and write what they see and think

- collaborate with others to build on each others' ideas

Nia Family Center, Chicago Commons Child Development Program (Head Start), Chicago, IL

Shadows naturally occur as the angle of the sun dances with different objects in its path. This urban program decided to bring shadows into their toddler room by placing a detailed leaf on a projector. It's larger-than-life silhouette creates a sense of awe in the room, and the children continually study and try to reach for it. They ask questions with their eyes and hands. They notice details and begin to test things out. Children use their finger to trace the outline edges and try to slip their fingers under the shadow to see if they can pick up the leaf. They cast their eyes around the room as if looking for the tree and source of the big leaf.

An Early Head Start program takes advantage of the toddlers continual desire to stack things by replacing plastic stacking toys with these smooth, heavy rocks, each of which has a hole drilled in it for fitting onto a metal rod. These materials engage children as scientists as they explore properties, cause and effect, and experiment over and over again. In addition, the children might learn some geology or anthropology while playing with the rocks. These lessons can be further provoked by photos of stacked rocks reminiscent of those found across the Canadian Arctic, called *inukshuk* and created by the Inuit people to mark their paths. Closer to this program's location, in the Southwest United States, similar stacks of red rocks called *cairn* mark paths across the desert canyons.

Baskin 1 Early Head Start, Santa Cruz, CA

Nia Family Center, Chicago Commons Child Development Program (Head Start) Chicago, IL

Early childhood programs are reminded to give babies some supervised "tummy time," so why not make that an experience with nature? Here an inner-city program has landscaped the outside play area so that children have safe opportunities to engage with dirt, bugs, and plants.

courtesy of Felipe Gutierrez, Phoenix, AZ

Along with playdough, children benefit from exploring natural clay taken from the earth. Very young babies delight in the way their little fingers can pinch off pieces and poke holes in the clay. Many find joy in the cool feel of the clay on their bodies. As they gain more fine-motor skills, older children can experiment with using pencils as tools for making holes and work on skills with other clay tools. Peeking through the holes he made was a serendipitous discovery of delight for this child!

Hilltop Children's Center, Seattle, WA

Food Items as Learning Material

Playing with food has long been a controversial idea among early childhood educators. Children explore food first with their senses to discover its texture, temperature, and taste. Cooking with children is a wonderful learning experience as food items are transformed: flour is turned into cookie dough and then baked to make cookies, or cream is churned to make butter or ice cream. But food is a scarce commodity for many families, and some educators feel it is disrespectful to use it as a play object. Each early educator needs to explore these issues carefully and make thoughtful decisions about incorporating food into their explorations for children. The following are a couple of ways programs have incorporated their values into providing sensory experiences for children.

Baskin 1 Early Head Start, Santa Cruz, CA

A large bag of birdseed provides a plentiful backdrop for different kinds of freshly picked squash to be explored in this toddler sensory table. After the children enjoy a time of swishing the birdseed around with their hands, filling little clay pots with it, dumping it out, and hearing the sound it makes, they transfer the squash to a table and an adult cuts the squash open so the children can see the moist seeds tucked inside the flesh. Then the children help roast the seeds and bake the squash for a tasting party.

The Highlander School, Atlanta, GA

To support local farmers and help the children understand where food comes from, this program has contracted with a small farm "food to table" group to receive a weekly delivery of fresh food. Before it is made into meals for the children, they have a chance to closely examine it. They learn the names, textures, and smells of various local fruits, vegetables, and herbs.

courtesy of Janis Keyser, Mountain View, CA

Wanting children to recognize food in its natural state before it is transformed through peeling, cutting, seeding, and cooking, this program regularly engages children in the preparation and serving of food they will eat.

Kids' Domain Early Learning Centre, Auckland, New Zealand

This program's intention is to introduce sustainable living practices into the center by developing a "food forest," a garden where the children grow food by nurturing it from seed to harvest. This photo captures the early stages of introducing children to what will be planted and harvested in their food forest. As the children explore, their descriptions and observations are documented and pointed out to their peers. The teachers challenge the children to look closer and offer additional ideas. Along the windowsill are the children's broad bean seedlings that they water and monitor for daily changes before they are put into the ground.

Invite Children's Explorations

The presentation of materials makes a difference in how children respond to them. Make sure the arrangement is orderly and attractive. Baskets, trays, tubs, mirrors, or other surfaces define the area and help children focus their attention on what is available. Avoid the cluttering effect of combining different-looking implements and utensils together in one arrangement. Offer sets of things that match and complement each other so the children have a clearer view of what is there and how the items may be used. Try offering things at various levels by propping trays and platforms for the children to work on. The following are examples of invitations with sensory rich and natural materials.

Children First, Durham, NC

Here the less commonly seen shimmery red sand has been put in a sensory table surrounded by baskets of natural materials to use with it—rocks, feathers, wood pieces, twigs, and lavender stalks. Notice the careful way this child is choosing and arranging these materials, spending long stretches of time in focused work.

Create Art with Natural Materials

Combining opportunities to design, draw, and paint with nature as the focus helps children look more closely, notice details, and have a sensory experience with yet another media. Following are examples of programs that have invited children into that experience.

Children First, Durham, NC

As spring arrives and buds form on the trees, small branches are brought inside for the children to smell and draw.

Clark College Early Learning Center, Vancouver, WA

After their play yard was redesigned to better replicate aspects of the special Pacific Northwest experience of climbing on rocks and experiencing the flow of water down a creek bed, the teachers found this child drawing the details of what he noticed. As you study his drawing, you will see the hand pump he knows is located at the top for the children to pump the water and watch it run down the creek bed into a drain at the bottom.

Inventions for Your Program

Look around your environment both indoors and outdoors for possible places to include the natural world, sensory elements, and living things. Discuss options for care and maintenance with your colleagues. Visit a garden or landscaping store with them, or sift through magazines and take field trips to woods, fields, and bodies of water to locate more natural materials for your program. Consider the following possibilities:

- natural materials, objects, and visual elements
- pleasant aromas
- sources of water
- landscaping, edible plants, and gardens
- loose parts from Mother Nature (indoors and outdoors)
- animals

As with any change, be sure to think through all the issues related to the values and improvements you want to make. Remember to stay attuned to allergies and health and safety issues as you introduce new elements of nature. Also, there is a delicate balance between exposing children to Mother Nature and avoiding dislocating things that should remain in their natural habitat. We want to help children become environmentally conscious and respectful, and sometimes this involves conflicting choices. Ongoing dialogue, clarifying values, and research will help you make thoughtful choices.

House of Tiny Treasures, United Way Bright Beginnings, Houston, TX

CHAPTER 6

Provoke Wonder, Curiosity, and Intellectual Challenge

Look Inside

Imagine walking into this preschool room. What feelings would doing so invoke in you? Do you notice the light, reflections, and colors? Do particular elements or treasures capture your attention and imagination? Is a sense of wonder and curiosity evoked by what is here? If so, how?

courtesy of Deb Curtis, Seattle, WA

Children are intrigued with natural phenomena and the world of physics and chemistry—things such as light, color, reflection, sound, and motion. On the one hand, these things are mysterious and magical to them. But children are also eager natural scientists, full of wonder. They observe closely and take action to try out their theories about how the world works. They are drawn to sparkles and shadows. They are attuned to the sounds around them—they stop to look up and listen when a bird or an airplane flies overhead.

Have you noticed how children seem to do the same actions over and over again with a variety of materials? You have probably discovered that toddlers are avid about dumping and filling and putting things inside other things, and preschool children continually sort, classify, and connect things. Child psychologist Jean Piaget identified these actions as schemas. A *schema* is a line of thought that is demonstrated by repeated actions and patterns in children's play. These repeated actions suggest that the play is a reflection of inner and specifically directed thoughts. Schemas build cognitive structures. When children explore schemas, they are building on their understanding of abstract ideas, patterns, and concepts (van Wijk 2008). Nikolien van Wijk reminds us, "The idea of schemas helps us to see the intellectual continuity in children's play that we might otherwise think is random or mercurial, and therefore, overlook" (2008, 104). When you provide children with materials that invite them to explore schemas, they are intellectually challenged and fully engaged, and you are able to see their emerging cognitive structures. Here are some of the schemas van Wijk, Piaget, and other researchers have identified:

- transporting: picks things up, moves things, puts down, or dumps

- transforming: uses materials to explore changes in shape, color, consistency, etc.

- trajectory: explores the horizontal, vertical, and diagonal movement of things and oneself; makes things fly through the air, moves own body in these ways

- rotation and circulation: experiments with things that turn, such as wheels and balls; explores curved lines and circles

- enclosing and enveloping: surrounds objects with other things; uses self to get inside a defined area such as blocks, boxes, etc.; hides, covers, or wraps self and other things

- connecting: joins things together and ties things up

- disconnecting: takes things apart, and scatters pieces and parts (van Wijk 2008)

Provisioning your environment with experiences for children to explore schemas is an interesting way to think about materials. Educators find their own intellectual stimulation as they learn more about different schemas or patterns of thought and action that children pursue. Understanding schemas shifts your focus from "behavior issues" to cognitive endeavors. Many of the ideas described in this chapter related to motion involve the schemas of trajectory and transporting. Here are some other materials that absorb children in exploring schemas:

- Coaster sets, napkin rings, hair curlers, paper towel tubes, and candleholders can be used for enclosing and connecting.

- Textured tiles and shiny wooden wedges encourage children to connect and disconnect the items in rows and lines, possibly using shape, color, and size as a reference.

- Bamboo cove molding, plastic or wooden troughs, balls, spools, and other objects that roll invite children to explore trajectory in a focused way.

- Colorful bracelets, round containers with lids, and paper towel holders offer children the opportunity to explore rotation and circularity.

- Colored water in small containers, pipettes, and ice cube trays invite children to explore transformation and transporting as they change the color of and move the water from the bowls to the pipettes and then into the ice cube tray.

- Gak or flubber (homemade) and a wire rack intrigue children with their ability to transform the magical substance.

- Wheeled toys, baskets, and buckets with handles invite children to transport items around a space.

When teachers fill classroom environments with standard materials aimed at teaching with achievement-oriented outcomes, the message conveyed to children is that learning is dry and boring. It also suggests that you have a narrow understanding of what is valuable to learn and provide for. The use of cartoon images and commercial figures in classrooms suggests that learning should always be entertaining. These kinds of things disregard and disrespect children's innate eagerness to explore, inquire, and make meaning of what is around them. Instead, set up environments to take advantage of children's passionate quest to investigate and theorize about things that provoke a sense of magic and wonder and intellectual challenges.

Invite Living with Elements of Magic, Wonder, and Intellectual Challenge

Embedded in the seemingly magical phenomena of rainbows, shadows, gems, and the rustling of trees in the wind are important concepts related to physics, science, and math. Being surrounded by these elements can spark children's imagination, focus their attention and inquiry, and calm their spirits. With these ideas in mind, consider the following questions to help you integrate a sense of wonder and curiosity into your program:

1   What natural sources of light do we have, and how could we make better use of these sources to explore shadows, reflections, and color refractions?

2   Where does air naturally move in our room, and what could we place nearby to make magical moments of sound and motion for children?

3   What more useful ways can artificial light and sounds be used to provoke children's curiosity?

4   How can we use nooks and crannies, windowsills, or countertops to display natural or scientific phenomena or treasures that might capture children's attention and imagination?

Planning for children with these questions in mind will ensure that you are thinking outside the typical early childhood box—your environment can become a place that speaks to the magical world of childhood as well as applying valuable research on brain development.

In a variety of settings, some more encouraging than others, providers and teachers are inventing ways to inspire children's natural drive to investigate the marvels of the world. As they provide these opportunities for children, their own adult lives have become more enriched by and they have become more alert to the small wonders that are part of everyday life.

Use Light and Color

Consider how natural light moves across your room and interacts with the materials that are there. It can change the apparent color of the paint on the wall during the day and over the seasons. Think carefully about this as you choose paint colors for your walls and for anything else you might be tempted to add to them. Many paint stores or websites will help you explore color possibilities, and some cities have lighting labs that help architects and interior designers explore how to best use light in their building. In addition to natural light, consider adding well-placed track lighting to help define the space, create interesting shadows, and highlight certain features of the space or materials placed in the room for children to discover.

Watching light as it moves, sparkles, refracts, and creates illusive colors and whimsical shadows will usually capture children's interest and provoke a joy in learning. The use of different kinds of mirrors for light and reflection adds so much to the intriguing feel of a classroom. Putting mirrors not only on walls, but also on and under tables and counters, inside shelving units, and on block building platforms creates opportunities to see things from multiple perspectives. Consider mirrors of all shapes and sizes, including those that change the reflection with curves and magnifiers. Be thoughtful about your use of glass and Plexiglas mirrors. Each is suitable for

The Learning Center, Palo Alto, CA

These dramatic, shiny beads entice the babies in this room to observe them closely and reach for them to make them move, which in the process, causes the beads to make a delightful tinkling sound.

different purposes and age groups. Plexiglas is very expensive, scratches easily, and provides a hazier reflection than glass. To eliminate safety hazards with glass mirrors, you can attach them to surfaces with industrial-strength Velcro or mirror hardware. Most people find that children learn to work respectfully with fragile items and there is very little breakage.

Prisms, holograms, and transparent color paddles present endless opportunities for exploring light and color. The educators of Reggio Emilia have shown us the wonder of placing strings of glass beads or bottles of colored water in a window or in front of a mirror. The programs featured in this section have given thoughtful consideration to the use of light.

Tots Corner, Auckland, New Zealand

Mosaic mirrors light up a space with color and sparkle. This mirror is hung in the bathroom, inviting a moment of magic amid the daily routines.

courtesy of Deb Curtis, Seattle, WA

The colorful milk jug lids and sheer fabric strung across this area create a festive feeling on the playground as they sway in the breeze or respond to the children's interactions with them.

Provide Treasures

Placing special objects in unexpected spaces draws children's attention and focus. Children's eyes and hands are always scanning the environment for something interesting to encounter and investigate. Most of the time when children discover these "treasures," they are told, "Don't touch," "Be careful," and "Don't break that." Yet, when children come upon something magical, beautiful, fragile, or complicated that has been carefully collected and arranged for them, they know that they themselves are respected and treasured. With this understanding, they are more likely to treat the objects with care. Special treasures can be selectively hung from the ceiling, light fixture, or door frame. They can be accessible to children in niches, boxes, and baskets or on mirrors placed on tabletops and counters. Treasures can also be discovered in the sandbox or water table. They are a wonderful addition to bathrooms and hallways. Special caution: remember to be alert to choking safety standards when providing small treasures for infants and toddlers.

Awhi Whanau Early Childhood Centre, Auckland, New Zealand

This alluring collection of bright green leaves and sparkling stones in the entryway of this program welcomes children with a clear message: "This is a place of wonder."

Tots Corner, Auckland, New Zealand

The teachers in this program want to make sure their outside area is as rich with possibilities for wondering and curiosity as their indoors, so they created this lovely display of plants and a large mirror on the fence.

Include Motion

Children love to watch things in motion and make things move, including their own bodies. They are fascinated by gravity, speed, and any phenomenon that stimulates motion. From the time they are babies, children find a million ways to use their bodies and objects around them to zoom, whirl, race, spin, roll, float, bang, pound, swing, hop, leap, and crash. It often seems that children can defy gravity—or at least are on a quest to challenge it as much as possible. As they pursue their exuberance, children are involved in important brain development and learning, including the relationship between cause and effect; predicting and hypothesizing; problem solving; and exploring spatial relations, physics, and other mathematical concepts. Make use of ceiling fans and air vents, and rotate interesting installations that offer opportunities for children to observe and participate in the physics of movement.

Tots Corner, Auckland, New Zealand

courtesy of Deb Curtis, Seattle, WA

Imagine a child coming upon either of these wall mountings, one simple and one complex. However, each wall mounting offers opportunities to explore gravity and sound: dropped balls race at different speeds, and racing water flows and splashes back and forth.

Plan for Sound

Most children stop to notice the sounds around them and investigate how they can make sounds with just about any object. While some are very sensitive to noise and cover their ears during joyful banging and pounding, other children robustly create noise whenever possible. Making loud sounds is a powerful experience, helping children feel big in their small bodies. Children make sounds in their play more often than they use words. They eagerly imitate the roar of an engine or the sweet meow of a kitten. Observing how they use sounds can teach adults so much about what children understand and feel. We can take advantage of their interest and alert sense of hearing by intentionally providing installations that create interesting sounds. A trickling fountain or delicate wind chimes can add whimsy and wonder to any room or outdoor environment.

This program mounted a permanent installation of objects that the children can interact with to create sounds and music. There are hooks on the wooden frame so the objects can be regularly changed for different explorations.

Association for the Advancement of Mexican Americans, United Way Bright Beginnings, Houston, TX

Offer Real Tools

When children have the opportunity to use real tools and materials of high quality, they feel respected and taken seriously. When they are trusted and shown how to use and care for these tools and materials, children live up to the responsibility of using them and as a result bring more focus and intention to their work. Consider the daily tasks that need doing and offer children the real tools and time to do them. Help children learn to use tools to accomplish big work and creative projects. Provision your classroom with items that will help the children feel like important, contributing members of the group, drawing on the following list:

- adult-sized brooms and dustpans
- spray bottles, buckets, and sponges
- feather dusters, cloth, and nontoxic furniture oil
- tool set: hammer, clamp, saw, nails, screwdriver, electric drill, and glue gun
- sewing kit: sewing machine, scissors, needle, thread, and pin cushions
- cooking tools: toaster oven, hot plate, electric fry pan, electric blender, oven mitt, bowls, and measuring cups and spoons
- garden tools: shovels, racks, and watering cans
- documentation tools: clipboards, pens, and cameras

Do children in your program have access to these tools? If not, what would it take for you to offer these things to your group?

Built into the outdoor environment is a real woodworking shop. Children show reverence and care when using real building tools such as hammers and saws.

Neighborhood Playgarden, San Francisco, CA

Invite Learning with Intriguing Materials and Intellectually Challenging Activities

Along with ongoing installations and nooks and crannies around the room filled with elements of magic and wonder, teachers can arrange materials and plan specific activities for children to engage with these phenomena more actively. For instance, you can purchase or build materials to explore light, shadows, transparency, and color. Light tables or boxes can be found in photography or art stores or in early childhood catalogs. You can also build them for very little expense by studying the designs in the catalogs or by going to the archives of the Reggio Emilia Listserv for designs.

Collecting materials that speak to children's natural intrigue for a world of wonders can enhance the joy teachers find in planning experiences for children. You can't help but heighten your own attention to our awesome world when you strive to help children discover it. See how the following teachers have found simple and creative ways to provide enchanting experiences of light, color, sound, and motion for children and themselves. Use their ideas as inspiration for your own treasure hunts.

Engage with Light and Color

Overhead projectors and shadow screens are also useful tools for exploration of light and shadows. Prisms, magnifying glasses, jeweler's loupes, holograms of all shapes and sizes, mirrored disco balls (large and small), garden reflection balls, color paddles, color cubes, jars and bottles filled with colored water, plastic and glass beads, and stones and jewels can all be collected from a variety of sources, including discount and museum stores, garage sales, and thrift shops. Following are some examples from a variety of programs.

courtesy of Deb Curtis, Seattle, WA

Teachers in this preschool classroom have created a dazzling collection of mirrors and colored objects for the children to use for exploration, design, and construction. The variety of mirrored and reflective surfaces enhances the reflections of light and the colorful objects and designs.

courtesy of Deb Curtis, Seattle, WA

Here is an example of teachers arranging an invitation for children to mix and explore colors. Notice how the possibilities are clearly communicated with a different watercolor in each container and with eyedroppers for mixing. Clear ice cube trays offer a way for children to explore the transformation of colors.

courtesy of Deb Curtis, Seattle, WA

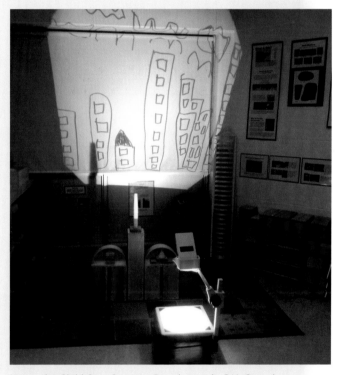

Kawartha Child Care Services, Peterborough, ON, Canada

Teachers can rotate a supply of purchased or collected materials that are well suited to a light table or an overhead projector. Painting, designing, drawing, and constructing are enhanced when light shines from beneath or projects shadows of the work above. Transparent and translucent objects and paper with color and embedded designs work well for exploring on the lighted surfaces. Slides from photos or transparent copies are also engaging.

Create Sounds

Offering interesting opportunities for children to experiment with sound keeps their investigative skills alive. It also leads to an intuitive understanding of rhythm and melody that can enhance an interest in learning music. Teachers can provide materials that make softer, melodic sounds indoors. Outdoors they can create opportunities for loud banging and drumming. Look for sound-making materials that can be explored alone and in relationship to each other.

Homemade and commercial bells, chimes, and gongs of all sizes and varieties are intriguing and, in many cases, inexpensive. Shakers and drumming instruments of all kinds, including rain sticks and maracas made with a variety of materials, offer different sounds. Metal garbage can lids and cans of all sizes make a variety of sounds. Consider using pieces of tubing, hose, and pipes, as well as conventional musical instruments.

courtesy of Deb Curtis, Seattle, WA

House of Tiny Treasures, United Way Bright Beginnings, Houston, TX

The toddlers in this classroom are enchanted with this collection of bells, homemade rattles, and music boxes provided on a shelf for them to investigate a variety of loud, soft, and melodic sounds.

This program offers musical structures in its outdoor play area. The children make music for dancing and marching, sing, and integrate music into their active pretend play.

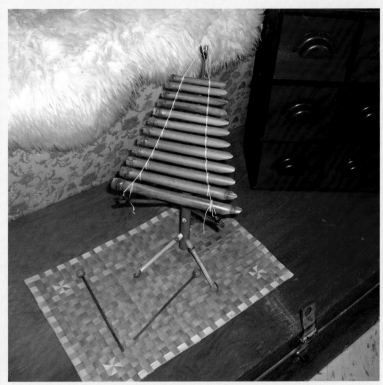

Bamboo and metal instruments, whether homemade or commercial, small or large, make a beautiful sound when hit with a stick. You can get these materials in a variety of sizes, widths, and lengths. They are inexpensive and easy to find in most hardware and garden stores.

courtesy of Deb Curtis, Seattle, WA

Kawartha Child Care Services, Peterborough, ON, Canada

Provoke Wonder, Curiosity, and Intellectual Challenge ♪ 167

The teachers in this infant classroom make sure the babies are able to access and manipulate these interesting objects to make many different sounds. Notice how the teachers have created a focused corner for the instruments and further capture the babies' curiosity with mirrors.

Destiny Village Child Care, United Way Bright Beginnings, Houston, TX

This teacher knows that in addition to invented musical instruments for exploring sound, classic adult-sized instruments, such as this violin, particularly captivate children. In addition to listening and singing along, children love to try their hand at plucking sounds from the strings.

Hilltop Children's Center, Seattle, WA

Make Things Move

With simple props and materials, you can invent elaborate ways for children to explore motion and gravity. Balls of various sizes and materials such as Ping-Pong balls, yarn balls, marbles, golf balls, rubber balls, cotton balls, bouncy balls, and whiffle balls are easy to collect and can be used along with ramps, racetracks, planks, slides, gutters, pipes, and tubes of various lengths, widths, and circumferences.

Cars and other toy vehicles with wheels of various sizes, wheelbarrows, wagons, scooters, tires, and hoops can move and be moved in many ways. Things that spin, including tops, rotating trays (lazy Susans), yo-yos, salad spinners, eggbeaters, turntables, gyroscopes; pulleys; pendulums; and metronomes all have interesting motions to explore. Objects that can move using air from fans, straws, balloons, balloon racers and flyers, tire pumps, and air mattresses provide yet another form of energy for motion and sound exploration. Windsocks, windmills, and kites are always captivating for young children. Study the following interesting examples of collections of materials designed to capture children's attention for making things move.

courtesy of Deb Curtis, Seattle, WA

Taking cues from the children's ongoing fascination with marbles, the teachers at this program went to their local dollar store and bought twenty-five bags of marbles for a dollar a bag. They filled their sensory table with nearly two thousand marbles and added various props for the children to use with them. The tubes and ramps enhance the children's investigation of moving the marbles. They roll as many marbles as they can as fast as they can down the ramps and through the tubes, onto the floor, and occasionally into the basket.

The object in the middle of the sensory table is an adaptation of a design from a toy company. It has a series of Plexiglas petals of various sizes attached along the length of a piece of wood. The children release marbles onto the top petal, and as the marbles move down the other petals, they make a musical sound that changes as each marble strikes a larger petal. The marbles magically reflect light and color off the Plexiglas as they fall and make a melody of raindrops.

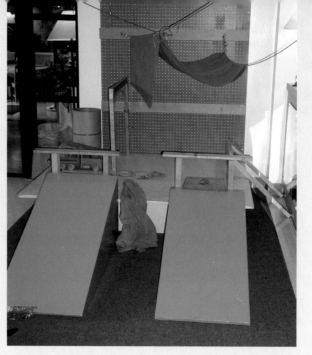

courtesy of Deb Curtis, Seattle, WA

Evergreen Community School, Santa Monica, CA

Here are examples of ramps with collections of simple props that invite children to investigate the differences in speed and motion.

Child's Play Family Childcare, San Francisco, CA

Tots Corner, Auckland, New Zealand

Saskatchewan Institute of Applied Science and Technology (SIAST) Child Development Centre, Regina, Saskatchewan, Canada

Study the variety of "water works" invitations that these programs have invented. They are places to play with the physical science of moving water. Children spend hours experimenting with funnels, ramps, and tubes, as well as cups and containers for pouring and catching the water. They use problem-solving skills to get the water to go where they direct it. They have fun while learning physics concepts such as gravity, volume, and displacement.

Step One School, Berkeley, CA

Children First, Durham, NC

These two programs have provided fascinating installations of hanging baskets with flubber inside. The slow movement of the flubber as it drips out of the baskets is another way for children to learn about movement and gravity, this time at a slow speed.

Association for the Advancement of Mexican Americans, United Way Bright Beginnings, Houston, TX

Children First, Durham, NC

Magic Garden Care and Education Centre, Auckland, New Zealand

Using pulleys and ropes, this teacher has invented contraptions where children can take action and make something interesting happen. The pulley system invites the children to explore how objects move in space and how one action causes another action. As they pull on the ropes, different things happen. It's a tricky and engaging task, and with practice children construct the understandings they need to be successful.

courtesy of Deb Curtis, Seattle, WA

Shaking simple, colorful feather dusters provides a captivating study of the movement of the feathers. The feathers feel soft and tickly on children's skin and create a tiny, quiet breeze when shook. The children enjoy using them while dancing to music. These feather dusters are interesting to babies, toddlers, and preschool-age children.

Provoke Wonder, Curiosity, and Intellectual Challenge 173

The teacher in this toddler classroom is engrossed with the knowledge that the very young children she spends her days with actually hear, see, and experience more than adults. Through observation she saw how keenly the children notice the smallest details in the world around them, and she decided to create an environment that captivates the children's innate sense of wonder. She hangs a variety of appealing mobiles from the ceiling so the children can reach them to explore how they feel, move, and sound. She places surprises in the corners, such as a mirror, a tinkling wind chime, or a mobile they can spin, stretch, and change. Sheer fabric hangs above the heater vents so the children can dance with the fabric as it moves with the warm air. The children excitedly investigate the teacher's provocations and return again and again to the fascinating objects planned just for them.

courtesy of Deb Curtis, Seattle, WA

Provoke Wonder, Curiosity, and Intellectual Challenge ℘ 175

Explore Schemas

When you observe children closely, you will see them engage in the same explorations over and over again. In fact, if you study many of the examples shared in this book by our inventors, you will see schema theory at work in most of them. Children love to carry things from one place to another, fill up containers and dump them out again, transform substances, connect and disconnect objects, line things up, and stack things tall. They love to throw things and find many ways to create action and movement. Often these behaviors seem inconsequential to adults and sometimes even annoying. Piaget's schema theory helps us to see the significance in these ordinary actions. If we plan for these actions, we are meeting up with children's minds in a way that will help them focus for hours (see earlier in the chapter for a fuller discussion and sample list of schemas). The following collections of materials were gathered and offered with schema theory in mind. Each example is followed by its correlating schema in parentheses.

courtesy of Deb Curtis, Seattle, WA

This sensory table filled with craft balls and containers is the perfect combination of materials to explore several schemas. Children can scoop the balls and transport them to the various-sized clear containers. They can fill the different heights and widths of containers all the way to the top and then work to dump them out. They can enclose the balls inside the long tubes and watch them move down and back out. The balls themselves are also wonderful for throwing in the air and watching as they bounce. (transporting, enclosing, and trajectory schemas)

Magic Garden Care and Education Centre, Auckland, New Zealand

This large, divided tray calls out to children to fill it up with the gorgeous rocks and stones sitting near by. The children can also use the materials to create a line of stones and jewels across the floor. (enclosing, lining up, and connecting schemas)

Playful Possibilities, Seattle, WA

This collection of industrial-looking loose parts suggests many possibilities for filling the different sized containers with different sized objects. Children can also stack, roll, and line up the materials. (enclosing, connecting trajectory, and lining up schemas)

House of Tiny Treasures, United Way Bright Beginnings, Houston, TX

Colorful boxes with lids provide serious work for toddlers as they spend long periods of time taking the lids off and putting them on again. (enclosure) They also find treasures to put inside. (enclosing schema)

This invitation of hair curlers, industrial sewing machine spools, wooden board, and sticks captures children's attention. They cover the sticks and put the curlers and spools inside each other (enclosure). The cylinder shape of the curlers and spools allows children to spin and roll them. (enclosing, rotation and circularity, and trajectory schemas)

Playful Possibilities, Seattle, WA

Homemade flubber or gak are great substances for children to explore the transforming schema. They can fill cups with flubber and watch it hold the shape of the container and then change back when removed (enclosure, transforming). Offering a way for the flubber to flow and drip from the raised shelf is also a fascinating study of transforming for the children. (transforming and enclosing schemas)

Use Real Tools

Even the youngest children approach the work involved with using real tools seriously because using tools requires skill and knowledge to get them to work successfully. Children return to this work again and again because they understand that adults use these tools and they strive to be competent members of the adult world. Inviting children to make contributions such as this when they are young and eager will likely build their disposition to be responsible, contributing members of a group into the future. Following are some possibilities for offering this important work.

Children First, Durham, NC
The motivation for this corkboard activity is what the children love about it: they are offered thumbtacks and pushpins, things usually "forbidden" to them. The teachers trust the children to figure out how to use the tacks and pins safely on their own. The children love using these things and seem to interpret this offering as a gesture of respect.

These smaller shovels are easy for children to handle and are sturdy enough to dig deep holes. Having real tools and materials available all the time spurs children on to accomplish big tasks with collaboration and persistence.

Neighborhood Playgarden, San Francisco, CA

courtesy of Deb Curtis, Seattle, WA

Children have apt attention for adults who want to coach them to use these tools properly and safely. The programs shown here see the children's competence to learn, so the teachers take the time to create a careful learning environment; they supervise, coach, and support the children's serious and satisfying efforts.

Children First, Durham, NC

Magic Garden Care and Education Centre, Auckland, New Zealand

These centers have real sewing machines and supplies in their dress-up areas.

Botany Downs Kindergarten, Auckland, New Zealand

courtesy of Janis Keyser, Mountain View, CA

The studio space in this center is primarily stocked with fashion and sewing books, along with sewing machines, scissors, measuring tapes, and a wide range of fabric, needles, and thread. The children draw out costume ideas for different characters and then are coached to measure, pin, cut, and sew their designs. The process of envisioning the idea and going through the steps of representing it in fabric is a challenge the children are eager to take up. As with learning to write, draw, or create a sculpture, using real tools for this representational work builds children's confidence and flexible brains.

Epiphany Early Learning Preschool, Sound Child Care Solutions, Seattle, WA

After trying to get her group to investigate simple machines by drawing their understandings, preschool teacher Megan recognizes their drawings usually feature pirates and treasures. She decides to offer something in the environment that uses those interests to further children's investigations of simple machines. When the children arrive one day, they find a treasure map Megan has drawn. They are immediately motivated to learn to read this map to search the playground. Once they find the treasure box buried in the sandbox, they discover it is too heavy to lift without the aid of simple machines. Megan offers photos of their previous investigations and drawings of simple machines, and they begin to apply this knowledge by gathering the tools and machines they need to raise the treasure box and get it back to their classroom. The children regularly use the shovels and ropes on the playground, so it is a logical decision to use them for this task. They work hard using the tools and are successful in the end.

Children First, Durham, NC

In this program, children use cameras every day for various purposes. Each child also takes a series of photographs for the welcome books showing what they think a new child coming into the school should know. They take photographs of their families early in the morning or at the good-bye window, which create very dear and empowering images. The children also take photographs of each other, of the play they see unfolding, and of their completed work. Taking photos gives them the experience of stepping back and looking again at their work and allows them to "save" their work for later viewing. Revisiting each other and their work through photography grows a classroom culture of reflection and learning about learning.

*Pacific Primary Pre-School,
San Francisco, CA*

This program frequently invites children to cook. Often they use the food they grow in the planter boxes on their urban playground. Study the photos to see the children earnestly at work with real tools. The teachers believe the children are competent enough to learn the important life skill of cooking with real tools. And the children step right up to the responsibility.

Uncover Treasures

Materials that are offered as treasures can include things with interesting textures, smells, colors, sparkles, or patterns. Combining particular materials invites children to explore and interact with them, perhaps touching, designing, building, or learning a concept. They can be offered on top of a glimmering piece of fabric, a beautiful tray, a piece of wood, or a mirror. Or they might be in a beautiful box that children can open.

Adding a companion book or photograph with a related visual image adds to the sense of discovery and desire for the children to explore these treasures. The following are some diverse examples.

Playful Possibilities, Seattle, WA

This white tray filled with sparkly crystals (silica gel crystals) bids children to a treasure hunt. They search for colorful pastel letters to spell their names and then scoop and fill the gleaming golden containers with their riches.

Playful Possibilities, Seattle, WA

This teacher offers a variety of colorful objects for the children to investigate. The reflected light glows through the colored shapes as the children arrange them on top of the mirrored surface and in front of the standing mirrors.

Association for the Advancement of Mexican Americans, United Way Bright Beginnings, Houston, TX

Destiny Village Child Care, United Way Bright Beginnings, Houston, TX

The teachers in these two classrooms know that the infants in their care have the ability to see the wonder in the world, so they look for shiny, reflective materials to attract the children to investigate. The first photo shows a collection of little silver boxes with different shiny surfaces, sizes, and removable lids that the teachers gathered and made. These treasures invite the babies to explore the sparkles and rainbows reflecting off of the boxes. The children are also drawn to the serious work of opening the boxes and finding a treasure inside. The other photo shares the element of reflection, but these teachers have added sparkly beads for the children explore. The necklaces make a delightful tinkling sound when the babies move them across the trays. These more unusual objects enhance the babies' attention and joy for learning.

Playful Possibilities, Seattle, WA

A collection of mirrors, metal containers, bracelets, and jewels gives children opportunities to explore how things fit together and inside each other. They can also make designs or move and spin the items. The many mirror reflections from underneath and behind the display and the shiny objects appeal to children's sense of wonder.

courtesy of Deb Curtis, Seattle, WA

This set of drawers with soft, colorful crocheted pieces and spun wool entices the lively minds of the toddlers in this program. They eagerly pull out and explore the soft objects as well as enjoy opening and closing the drawers.

Inventions for Your Program

If the idea of stimulating wonder and intellectual challenge by using light, shadows, mirrors, sound, and motion is new to you, it might be time for some investigations of your own. Gather your coworkers together and try exploring something such as the many ways prisms reflect dancing colors. Or put a mirror on a table and build a Lego block construction on it. Discuss with your colleagues how these small additions enhance your opportunities for new discoveries or enliven your sense of wonder. Begin to notice these things when you are out in the world. Consider one or more of the following elements to enhance your environment indoors and outdoors:

- working with light, color, and shadows
- exploring sound
- investigating motion and gravity
- considering schemas
- providing real tools
- discovering treasures to include in play activities

As you begin to expand the opportunities to provide curiosity and intellectual challenge, be prepared to build on the interests and ideas that the children generate. This might involve gathering some additional resource materials to have in the wings and enhancing your understandings of how to extend key elements of children's investigation into long-term project work.

Children First, Durham, NC

CHAPTER 7

Engage Children in Symbolic Representations, Literacy, and the Visual Arts

Hilltop Children's Center, Seattle, WA

Look Inside

Seeing that some of her preschoolers were interested in board games and mazes, this teacher gathered a set of art supplies and two of the children's favorite games, and then invited the children to make their own board game from the materials. What do you think might have influenced her decision to offer these materials? Once the children were clearly engaged with the materials, the teacher chose to stand back and observe what unfolded, thinking of herself as a researcher of the children's interests, understandings, and capabilities. What questions might she have? What in this picture indicates the teacher's understanding about the relationship between symbolic representation, literacy, and the co-construction of knowledge?

The emphasis in the United States on teaching literacy skills is leading to the dangerous possibility that the necessary stages of literacy development for young children will be bypassed as educators and parents alike are jumping directly to teaching children the forms and conventions of print and phonemic competencies. While children may benefit from this instruction at the right points in their development, they must first be exposed to the joys of literacy.

When children are pushed into reading and writing instruction without being offered a context for its meaning, they typically respond in one of the following ways: lack of interest, memorization with no understanding, stress, or rebellion (Elkind 1987).

In contrast, when they are in an environment filled with diverse, everyday literacy experiences, children come to understand the value and meaning of the printed word, and are then eager to decode and reproduce these symbols in their world.

Young children need to see firsthand the function of print and how it can be useful and pleasurable to read and write. Everyday activities such as writing a note, posting a sign, making a list, drawing a map, and sketching a block structure will demonstrate the value of pen and paper for communication and preserving memories. Another way to help children notice and value print is to read aloud a print or electronic notice, letter, or bus schedule; look up a phone number; check e-mail; or consult a map, dictionary, recipe, or set of directions. For example, think of how powerful the statements that follow are to children who are trying to understand the importance of reading and writing:

- "I think I'll write that down so I remember."
- "Let's look up your phone number so I can call your mom."
- "I can't remember all the letters of that word, so I'm going to look it up in the dictionary."
- "Let me show you where your house is on this map."
- "I want to learn how to write that in Chinese for your grandma."
- "Let's do an online search for the artist Diego Rivera and see his murals to get an idea of how to do ours."

Likewise, taking time to find the weather or sports report in the newspaper or online, sharing a dream or favorite book of visual images, making costumes, and playing music are actions that show children the pleasure and usefulness of the symbolic world.

The educators of Reggio Emilia remind us that the environment is the third teacher. But it can also be said that the teacher is a significant feature of the environment. In addition to creating an environment with multiple opportunities for children to encounter the need for literacy knowledge, teachers have an important part to play in role-modeling and engaging children in meaningful literacy experiences.

With the goal of literacy development, the early childhood field emphasizes creating a print-rich environment. This often leads to excessively labeling everything in the environment in a way that creates environmental clutter and the feel of an institution, rather than home. In our homes we may label our spices in the kitchen or post messages or shopping lists on the fridge, but no one labels their chairs, windows, or microwaves. Classrooms should only use labels to keep things organized and identify individual possessions—just as labels are intended.

Books are of course another form of functional print. Children benefit from having books and other reading material in many areas of the environment, not just in a classroom library or cozy place to curl up and read. Does your classroom have books about architecture, building, math, and engineering in the block area? Does the dress-up area have literature about costume design and occupations? What reading material have you included in the bathroom? Is your classroom technology set up for children to learn how to research things they want to know more about? Children need reading materials that offer pleasure and spark their imaginations, as well as those that provide useful information.

Children simultaneously deserve to have other forms of symbolic representation respected and nurtured so they can continue to develop as creative, flexible thinkers and communicators. As early childhood educators, our task is to strengthen our understandings of symbolic representation and literacy development. Clear thinking about this will lead educators to plan a more conducive environment for the experiences of decoding symbols and for the physical, emotional, and cognitive development that leads to reading, writing, and creative representations. Our efforts to provide for literacy development should include bilingual education as well as visual literacy and image making so children have opportunities to express themselves through and learn to read what the educators of Reggio Emilia refer to as the "Hundred Languages." Indeed, there are so many—at least one hundred—ways to communicate ideas.

As you consider showing children the value of visual arts and literacy, answer these questions:

Nancy Gerber's family child care center, Spokane, WA

1   What in our environment tells children that we see them as readers, writers, and visual artists?

2   How will children know that we value image making and the visual arts?

3   Where can children see adults engaged in meaningful decoding experiences?

4   How many places are there in our room where children can see or write their names and that of their family members and people or objects that are important to them?

5   Where do we offer tools for symbolic representation and image making?

6   Where does our environment have examples of symbols and representations of the same idea or object (for example, a clock or calendar, a book about seasons or the solar system, or a copy of van Gogh's painting *Starry Night*)?

7   Which of the things listed above are available in our outdoor space?

As educators create environments for children that engage them in meaningful encounters with various forms of literacy, children will better understand the function of literacy and will be better prepared to learn the conventions of reading, writing, researching, and representing knowledge.

Invite Living with Elements of Symbolic Representation and Literacy

When you provide children with multiple invitations to construct, express, and reflect on their thoughts and feelings, you advance their understanding of symbolic representation and literacy. Teachers can offer them attractively displayed tools and materials, along with images and props to explore symbolic representations and learn the function of reading and writing. In other words, you can create invitations that offer children many reasons to want to read, write, and engage in symbolic representations through their play and image making. When you offer children materials to present a familiar idea in a new medium (for instance, drawing a block structure or using clay to represent an image that has already been drawn), they will be faced with new challenges for something in which they already have an interest and investment. Their understandings will deepen and expand, and they will become comfortable with the world of symbolic representation and visual literacy.

Most children, even babies, come to our programs already on the road to decoding symbols, such as physical gestures, traffic signs, or product logos or jingles. Building on their keen observation skills, you can create a rich environment for their visual literacy to grow, along with their emerging interest in reading and writing.

Literacy is a huge focus in the early care and education profession, and many programs are struggling with staying developmentally appropriate and meeting increasingly mandated learning outcomes. Those who also embrace the concept of multiple languages and intelligences have been working hard to ensure that the verbal-linguistic arena doesn't overshadow the other important areas for children's identity development and learning. Following are some examples of relevant everyday inventions.

Storage, Display, and Maintenance

As with all the other materials you offer to children, it is important to have a well-planned system for storing and displaying materials for literacy and symbolic representation. When the materials are offered in an attractive manner, the children will be more likely to take an interest in using them and to return them in good condition. Literacy and representational materials are especially important to keep in good condition—when dried-up markers are mixed in with good ones, broken pencils are left unsharpened, paintbrushes are stiff from inadequate washing, and paper is torn and in disarray, children will be less motivated to use the materials with focus and are more likely to treat them with disrespect. Children need a visual reminder of how and where to store work so they can focus and move forward with representational work involving literacy and the visual arts. Books, too, need to be displayed and maintained in a way that communicates discovery and respect. When setting up their rooms and play yards, these programs found a variety of ways to invite children into exploring the printed word.

Nancy Gerber's family child care center, Spokane WA

A simple plastic wading pool outside is filled with pillows and books for the children to enjoy out in the fresh air and sunshine.

Hilltop Children's Center, Seattle, WA

A basket of books next to a couch allows children to stretch out and read on their own or curl up with a friend, teacher, or family member to enjoy a book.

Nia Family Center, Chicago Commons Child Development Program (Head Start), Chicago, IL

Making high-quality board books available for babies helps them begin a relationship with the printed word. Rather than keeping them up high and out of reach, this caregiver places books just far enough away for the children to have to make an effort to retrieve the one that captures their attention. The books are available for the babies to explore on their own or when an adult is available with a lap to sit on. As the baby discovers the parts of a book, the teachers describe each part, offering more familiarity with the concept of book covers, spines, pages, illustrations, and words.

Opportunities for Decoding, Translating, and Reading

Most early childhood programs have a book area, but in many cases, children are discouraged from transporting books around the room. While it is important to help children show respect and care for materials, we also want to help them see all the ways in which the printed word can be useful around the room. Books can be placed in baskets and on shelves in different areas. Likewise, charts, magazines, diagrams, and reference books can be displayed in places next to related materials or play props. For instance, when you set up a new computer, aquarium, video camera, or stereo system, place diagrams nearby that accompany or reference them. Post a list of children's names and phone numbers by a telephone and periodically demonstrate how you find and sequence those numbers on the telephone. In the course of living together, find relevant ways to show children the value of making and reading maps, schedules, diagrams, graphs, charts, and books. Make bilingual and multicultural reading materials an ever-present reminder that there are many languages and ways of living in our communities.

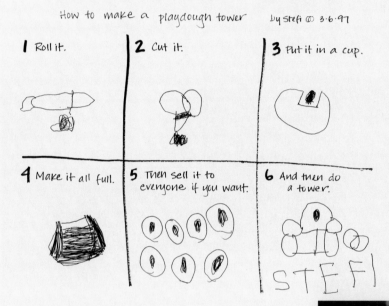

To encourage children's understanding that important ideas and directions can be written down for later reference, this classroom keeps a supply of columned paper available to encourage children to draw the steps they've discovered in learning such things as creating inventions or negotiating how to use materials someone else wants. Here a child has invented a playdough tower and is eager to dictate and illustrate directions so others can make one too.

Hilltop Children's Center, Seattle, WA

For children less interested in using drawing materials, this program encourages them to notice the printed word by including labels with an invitation to take up a task.

Children's Studio, Bellevue, WA

To help children learn to go beyond pencils, pens, and computer notebooks, teachers are finding ways to attractively offer shelves of a wide variety of tools to raise awareness of the language of art. Whether in a classroom, separate studio space, or outdoor area, children can learn more about colors when they see them displayed as a palate. These programs are developing children's skills in learning to use a wide range of materials for representing their ideas.

Paulo Freire Family Center, Chicago Commons Child Development Program (Head Start), Chicago, IL

courtesy of Janis Keyser, Mountain View, CA

Botany Downs Kindergarten, Auckland, New Zealand

Every day, the children watch an adult sign them in and out of the program, so the teachers decided to have a sign-in sheet for the children to use as well. Beside each sign-in sheet are large tags with each of the children's names to use as a reference for their writing. The documentation book of the children's name-writing efforts serves as an encouragement to them, as well as to their parents, to slow down and take the extra time needed to do this important work at the beginning and end of the day.

Mission College Child Development Center, Santa Clara, CA

Botany Downs Kindergarten, Auckland, New Zealand

Early childhood teachers can help children understand that music, too, is a language with written symbols. These programs expose children to music notes, instruments, and recordings. This invites the children to try making their own music and supports their use of written symbols to express what they are hearing and feeling.

Second Presbyterian Weekday School, Louisville, KY

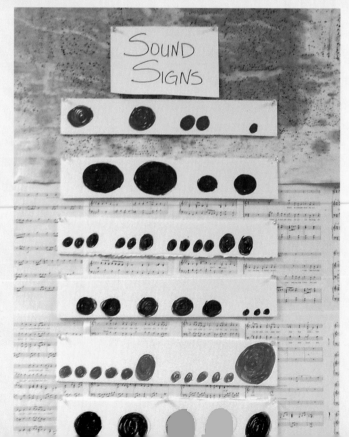

Send and Receive Printed Text

Setting up a system for children to send and receive written messages is a staple of any good literacy program for young children. Message systems provide meaningful ways for children to discover that the spoken word can be written down then read by another person. Message or mailbox systems can be offered in a variety of ways, including phones, clipboards, pens, computers, and individually labeled boxes. Following are examples of mailboxes that programs use for children to send messages within the program or to those on the outside.

In this center, the teachers involved the children in making mailboxes to support their eagerness to write, send, and receive letters from their peers and teachers. Each envelope that is opened provides an opportunity to study the written word as part of their deepening relationships.

Stoneybrook Early Childhood Learning Centre, London Bridge Child Care Services, London, ON, Canada

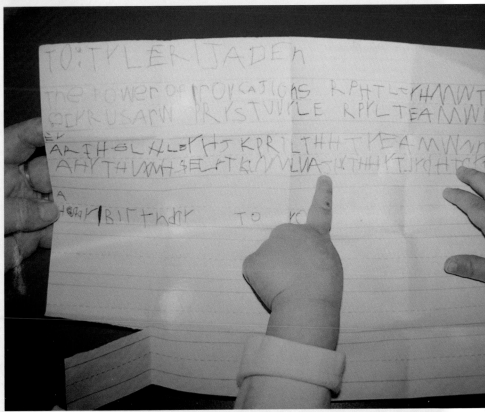

Examples of the Work of Visual Artists, Young and Older

Children benefit from using actual visual arts tools and seeing examples of artists' work, including photos, drawings, paintings, sculptures, books, posters, and note cards. Add visual books and copies of the work of professional artists to your shelves of representational tools and materials. Selectively place the work of well-known artists around your environment and incorporate companion samples of the visual artwork the children create. Consider all the different ways you might do this as offered by the following photos.

Wanting the children to see themselves as visual artists, this program placed attractive framed art prints on the wall alongside a set of empty picture frames purchased at a thrift store and repainted. As the children engage in their own drawing and painting, their images begin to fill the empty frames, helping the children see that their efforts at visual representations are as valued as those of well-known artists.

Pinehurst Child Care Center, Sound Child Care Solutions, Seattle, WA

Rather than leave this staircase alcove as neglected space or use it for dumping things, this program turned it into a small art gallery to display the children's work. Two small benches invite people to sit awhile and view what's in the gallery. Both children and adults can see the visual artists that are emerging in the program.

Rowntree Park Early Childhood Learning Centre, London Bridge Children's Services, London, ON, Canada

Alhambra Head Start, Phoenix, AZ

Wanting to work closely with and represent the children's heritages, this Head Start program includes a continuous display of their cultural artwork, heroes, leaders, and role models. The display generates storytelling and opportunities to honor the children's home languages.

As we use picture books with children, we can help them learn to "read" the illustrations as well as the words, thereby communicating that art is a language. With multiple exposures to a single illustrator, children can learn to express their understanding of the artist's work by creating drawings or paintings in a similar style. The children at this preschool studied the work of Eric Carle and over time tried expressing their own ideas in his style.

Pinnacle Presbyterian Preschool, Scottsdale, AZ

A Studio Space for Focused Representational Work

In her book *Rapunzel's Supermarket*, Ursula Kolbe (2007, 43) reminds us, "Rather than thinking of children's image-making as 'art,' it may be more helpful to see it in a different light. Just as adults use notes and diagrams to assist understanding, so children use images to make sense of things and play with ideas." Likewise, George Forman (1996) describes art as a medium not only for creative expression, but as "a thinking tool." With exposure to the powerful representational work coming out of the atelier (workshop and art studio) of the children's programs in Reggio Emilia, many programs in the United States are now trying to create studio spaces for the focused representational work of in-depth study projects. Having a separate space in addition to the typical art area provides children with an opportunity to receive individualized guidance and experiment with a wider selection of representational media and tools that are often only found in adult art supply stores.

Most programs don't have the luxury of dedicating a separate room or staff person in their building for studio work, but with creativity you can sometimes transform an abandoned storage room or carve out a corner of a larger classroom with some attractive dividers, perhaps adding a door from an adjacent room so that the space can be shared. Studio spaces need good lighting, a sink and source of water, ample shelving for attractively displaying supplies and tools, and storage space for projects that will take place over a period of days or weeks. Visual images and mirrors and attractive displays that spark an interest in colors make studios inspiring spaces for focused work.

Hilltop Children's Center, Seattle, WA

When they moved to a new location, the teachers of this center made it a priority to remodel the space to create a "community studio" near the entryway to demonstrate their commitment to engaging children in ongoing in-depth investigations using various media. This separate space allows ongoing work to be left out yet protected from the classroom spaces that have to be used for multiple purposes. The central location allows everyone to see the children's evolving work.

Pinnacle Presbyterian Preschool, Scottsdale, AZ

With the good fortune of having a dedicated studio space, this preschool selects particular work of the children's to highlight projects they have significantly invested their time and energies in. Here their exploration and representation of flowers is displayed in a lattice structure that also serves as a room divider. As time goes on and other projects are completed, the teachers will feature new artwork.

Invite Learning with Materials for Symbolic Representation and Literacy Activities

Children need to have multiple opportunities to explore the world of symbolic representation, literacy, and the visual arts in the classroom and outdoors. Though they may initially become more absorbed in the sensory and aesthetic aspect of art materials, children often see something in the movement of the lines and color that represents something else they are familiar with. This may become what Kolbe (2005, 15) calls "action drawing and drama," where the child is just engaged in the physical experience of expressing something by moving a pen or a brush across paper, or it may evolve into a representational drawing. Children "make meaning as they make marks" (Kolbe 2005, 8), another way of becoming literate, discovering and communicating what they know. As you watch how children respond to the environment and hear the themes that emerge in their play, you can offer additional materials or suggest the children create them for further involvement in literacy experiences. As you do this, be alert to what children demonstrate that they already know; this will stimulate further ideas for materials and activities to scaffold their learning to the next stage.

When children represent ideas through building, dramatic play, storytelling, drawing, painting, clay work, and three-dimensional sculptures, dance, and music, they show us they understand something about symbolic thinking, a cornerstone of meaningful literacy. Attractive materials for these activities should be in abundance around the room, periodically rotated or added to, and kept in good order. A selection of special materials can be set aside for work in a studio space. Throughout your classroom, writing materials should be available, just as we have them in various places in our homes for easy access to make lists, label things, write letters, and so on. A good balance of handwriting and technology tools should be provided. Examine the photos of these inventors at work and consider how you can add to the learning opportunities of the children in your program.

Writing and Drawing Tools

Many programs have a writing center, but beyond this there are many other ways to invite children to explore the many uses and pleasures of writing. Place a variety of writing tools in various places of the room, arranged attractively so that the children are eager to use them and incorporate symbolic representations into their investigation, construction, and dramatic play. Along with a variety of pencils, pens, markers, and chalk, provide diverse materials for children to write on, including a variety of papers, cards, sticky notes, notebooks, folders, clipboards, chalkboards, and sign-making supplies. Make sure some of these materials are available outdoors on the playground as well.

Children First, Durham, NC

Near a mailbox at this family child care home, a table with writing and drawing supplies and envelopes on the outside deck invites the children to learn about sending personalized snail mail.

One of our goals for literacy development should be to help children "fall in love with words" and have fun with them. Here the children's imagination work with rhyming words is being used to build phonemic awareness and letter-sound association. Posting the work for all to see reinforces its importance and celebrates the fun of it.

courtesy of Janis Keyser, Mountain View, CA

Seeing a squabble begin to emerge among two children wanting to play with their limited supply of Lego blocks, the teacher decided to intervene with clipboards and thin black markers rather than reminders to "be nice and share with your friend." She said to the child grabbing Lego blocks, "You really like his idea, don't you? While you're waiting for him to finish, why don't we draw the structure he's building so we can remember it. Then if you or he wants to build it again, we'll have your drawing to refer to. With a bit more coaching from the teacher, the two boys eagerly took turns drawing the existing Lego block structure and after dismantling it, used the drawing as "the directions" for how to build it again.

Pinehurst Child Care Center, Sound Child Care Solutions, Seattle, WA

Experiment with Color

Adults often talk about wanting children to "know their colors," by which they mean children can name commonly used colors. But there is so much more to "knowing colors." Children benefit from being able to recognize the range of hues and shades of any given color and how light changes color. Why not make an exploration of color part of learning to express different emotions and ideas?

Hilltop Children's Center, Seattle, WA

Organizing art materials by color helps children notice the nuances of their relationship to each other as well as more easily see what colors are available for use. Storing them in glass jars and near a mirror highlights the discovery of colors.

Hilltop Children's Center, Seattle, WA

Rather than buying the paint colors offered in the catalogs, this program purchased only black, white, yellow, red, and blue. Over time they worked with the children to mix and explore a wide range of shades and hues. The children gave each color a name that reflected their understanding of the color and arranged them on the shelves with other materials in the same color palate.

A teacher in this program set up a provocation on a table by covering it with a big piece of white paper and placing containers of drawing utensils—oil pastels, chalk, pencils, and crayons— in grays, white, and black. She was curious how small groups of children would interact with each other and the materials, and if they would engage in what Kolbe (2005) calls "the drama of drawing." This child initially chose a gray oil pastel and made lines that go around and around in circles. Then she chose a darker gray and announced, "I'm making a person." The child added long legs and shaded in the space where the feet might go, saying, "Now it's a mermaid because that's her scale."

Children First, Durham, NC

Develop Observation Skills to Represent What You See

All forms of literacy learning—from letter recognition to computer programming to still life drawing—are enhanced when children develop good observation skills. Children readily love "I spy" games, and with coaching and practice they can develop observation skills for drawing and using other art media.

Kids' Domain Early Learning Centre, Auckland, New Zealand

When drawing materials are available outside as well as inside, the children readily use pen and paper as a tool for investigating and communicating what captures their attention. Here a child has brought a clipboard outside to create a representation of a favorite detail in the garden of their playyard.

Stoneybrook Early Childhood Learning Centre, London Bridge Child Care Services, London, ON, Canada

Children can be encouraged to master their observation skills through still life drawings. This teacher coaches children through the process of "look a little, then draw a little, look a little, then draw." When children are supported in this way to study different sections of an object, the task of representing what they are seeing becomes more focused and detailed.

Casula Pre-School, Liverpool City Council Early Childhood Program, Liverpool, Australia

Teachers can set up an invitation for children to study and draw what they are learning. Picking up on children's fascination with baby chicks, the educators in this program offered a set of interesting materials for the children to closely examine and drawing materials to communicate what they are most interested in.

Children First, Durham, NC

This educator approached the idea of "still life" art in another way, inviting children to investigate a book about trees and then re-create their understanding of the tree at the light table with an invitation of twigs and green beads made of glass. Look closely at the engagement on the children's faces and the details they include in their representation of the leaves on the branches.

Hilltop Children's Center, Seattle, WA

In an effort to help children be aware of how they see themselves and each other, many programs give children mirrors or photographs of themselves to use in creating self-portraits. Posting documentation of the children's conversations as they work offers further insight into how they are thinking about their work. Repeating this self-portrait activity over time and with various materials can reveal children's growing awareness of details as well as their representational skills.

Living in an area with many bridges as part of their surroundings, children in this center were given multiple opportunities to study and represent their understandings of bridges. Their learning culminated in this beautiful work of art that captures many structural details of a nearby bridge.

courtesy of Janis Keyser, Mountain View, CA

Wanting to address the very aggressive play of a group of boys, their teacher engaged them in representational work to help her better understand what they needed from this play. She first gave them photos of themselves and suggested they draw on the photos to recreate themselves as the superheroes of their play. They used their drawings to "tell the story" of their characters, including all their powers, and who and why they need to fight. She brought their drawings to their next meeting and gave them sticks and modeling clay to create "action figures" of their superheroes. They used the action figures to dramatize their stories. Over the course of this representational work, the boys' actual aggressive play significantly diminished.

Epiphany Early Learning Preschool, Sound Child Care Solutions, Seattle, WA

Family Partnerships for Literacy and Symbolic Representations

Some children have home settings rich in literacy experiences, while others don't. Some families are more immersed in oral traditions, the world of dreams, mythology, music, crafts, or visual imagery than the printed word. And many children in the United States have a home language other than English. All of these situations suggest the need for you and your program to have a strong partnership with the children's families if your environment is to be supportive, respectful, and inclusive.

The first step is to learn about each family: what are their values and what is their home life centered around? As you learn about and build relationships with families, you can invite them to contribute to the visual images, language and literacy practices, and representational experiences in your environment. You will also discover what they would like you to be contributing to their child's experiences in your program and in their home environment.

Hilltop Children's Center, Seattle, WA

Living in an urban setting with tall buildings continually under construction, these teachers offered photos of the buildings as the preschool-aged children worked with blocks and other building materials. Because the children's fascination with building ever-taller towers continued, the teachers took the children on a field trip to the observation deck at the top of the tallest building in the city and then had the children create drawings of their experience. The children's families were engaged as well when the teachers requested they e-mail the teachers photos of the outside of their own residence. One evening some of the families came together to study the documentation of the children's ideas about towers and used the various building materials themselves. This engagement of the families allowed the children's exploration to continue within the center and out in the city with their families. They all became more literate with aspects of architectural design and engineering.

As part of the pre-K students' involvement with the church's project to feed hungry people in their community, teachers at this school worked with the children to explore concepts of kindness, generosity, and sharing, which included meeting a visitor from a local food bank. Together with their families, children learned new techniques in clay work, creating symbolic empty bowls for a larger community event.

Pinnacle Presbyterian Preschool, Scottsdale, AZ

Inventions for Your Program

Our profession has long advocated that programs have a print-rich environment to expose children to the value of literacy. As you expand your thinking about the world of symbolic representation, art as a thinking tool, and how this relates to language and literacy development, what are some new insights you have? What changes might you want to make in your environment? Consider these areas:

- adults modeling their creation and use of literacy, symbolic representation, and the visual arts
- opportunities for children to read, write, and decode
- routine use of drawing as a thinking tool
- a studio space with real tools and art media for focused work
- documentation of children's expanding literacy understandings and representational skills
- opportunities to explore the languages of art, drama, music, and dance to communicate ideas and feelings
- ways to engage families in understanding the children's communications with materials

Once you have decided on a focus for improvements, spend some time further developing concepts discussed in this chapter that you are less familiar with. Seek out resources to help you address your goals. As you deepen your insights into the role of the environment and materials in supporting children's emerging literacy with the "Hundred Languages," you will continue to add new elements. Remember to work on your outside as well as inside environment, and your hallways and bathrooms in addition to your classrooms.

Magic Garden Care and Education Centre, Auckland, New Zealand

CHAPTER 8

Enhance Children's Use of the Environment

Look Inside

Take some time to carefully study this photo and the opening story that follows. Then consider the questions we present after the story.

Hilltop Children's Center, Seattle, WA

As the morning began, Ann sat on the floor in a discussion with three children while another group was building with blocks on a wooden platform nearby. The rest of the children were playing in other parts of the room or eating breakfast and having a conversation with another teacher. Ann and the children sat in a flexible area of the room furnished with a number of open-ended materials: unit blocks, logs, a basket of fabric and clips, tape measures, portable screen dividers, two stepladders, two three-square-foot platforms, and two huge cardboard tubes. The children had the idea of creating an obstacle course, and Ann suggested they make a plan.

As the children came up with ideas, Ann restated them for the group's consideration. She asked some initial questions that led the children to the idea of measuring the things they wanted to include in their course. The planning then progressed, with growing excitement and some competing ideas. One child wanted to put a stepladder at each end of a cardboard tube. Someone offered the idea of covering the opening of the tube with fabric. Another child who wanted to clip the fabric as a canopy from the stepladder to the tube refuted this idea. Ann facilitated the discussion by saying at times, "Tell us your idea about how this might work," and "I need to make a different suggestion to make sure you're safe." She kept the group focused by continually pointing to the objects they wanted to use as she restated the ideas they had reached agreement on. As time went on, a few more children approached the group asking if they could be involved too. "Definitely," Ann responded. "Come and help us think about it." As one child struggled to explain his idea of creating an angled tunnel with two tubes, Ann suggested he get one of their reference books to explore how this might look. He brought the book back to the group and began to search through the pages for what he wanted. Ann asked, "Do you want to find it by just going through the pages or look at that list in the front of the book called the table of contents?" Later she suggested he might get a clipboard to sketch a representation of his idea for the group.

As the obstacle course began to take shape, Ann asked the one child still working nearby on block building, "Would you like a screen around you to keep you separate from the obstacle course?" When he said yes, she assisted by putting the screen in place.

Questions to consider:

- What strikes you about the physical environment in this story?
- How would you describe the elements of the social-emotional environment that helped shape this story?

- What routines and practices might be part of how Ann structures time for these children?

- What do you think Ann's values and goals are for living and learning together in this environment?

As you read and reflect on this story and study the photos and ideas in this book, you possibly have some skepticism or doubt in your mind. You might find yourself thinking, "How many children do these teachers have in their room to be able to do these things? Don't the children break or lose things? How do they keep track of everything? And what do they do about cleanup with so much available for the children to use?" These are common questions. We can assure you that the programs shown in the photos of this book have many of the same constraints you do. By and large, they don't have huge budgets, ideal spaces, or extra staff. In order to understand how they have been able to make changes, it's important to examine again how teachers view children and the nature of their teaching work. The teachers in these programs have all spent time thinking and talking about their understanding of their work together and their dreams for the future of that work. They also talk about their vision of the children they work with. Without this careful examination and dialogue among coworkers in a program, the social-emotional environment may suffer and you may be unintentionally undermining children's ability to make productive use of the physical environment you have worked so hard to create.

In programs such as the one in the opening story, the pooling of ideas and the negotiations on how to use the environment do not magically happen on their own. Ann and her coteachers have created an underlying emotional climate that supports the children's use of the environment. A classroom's emotional climate reflects and fosters the teachers' values that in turn shape the children's experience in that classroom. The emotional climate is intricately related to the program's culture of daily routines, use of time, and activity structures, as well as the beliefs, expectations, and choices the adults have for the children. At the heart of a nurturing emotional climate are the strong, caring relationships among the people in it. All of these things together form what our profession commonly calls the social-emotional environment.

Successful educators know transforming the physical environment is only part of the work to be done. Designing beautiful spaces and finding engaging materials is obviously an exciting undertaking, but the social-emotional aspects of creating a wonderful environment for children also require careful attention and nurturing. The social-emotional environment includes how people relate to one another, how time is structured, and how the teaching and learning process unfolds. The climate is shaped by what teachers choose to pay attention to and make visible and their thoughtfulness in setting up routines, choices for children, and teaching activities. There are four areas to examine as you seek to enhance children's use of the environment:

- time and routines
- invitations, special-interest areas, demonstrations, and modeling
- meaningful jobs
- teacher roles

Organize Time and Routines

Once your room is thoughtfully arranged, it is important to plan for long periods of self-directed play. Without time to explore and with teachers who continually redirect their activities according to a schedule, the flow of children's intention and investigation is interrupted, and their earnest desire to demonstrate what they know or care about is disrespected. If children are to initiate their own activities, use the materials in complex ways, and have enough time to work with others, teachers mustn't chop up the day into little boxes on a tight schedule or constantly direct or interrupt children's activities. Children deserve enough time to become familiar with the environment and the ways the materials can be explored and used. They benefit from support and coaching to develop initial communication and collaboration skills. With these things in place, children will be able to make effective use of long, uninterrupted blocks of time to pursue their interests.

Your schedule with children should include stretches of uninterrupted choice times that are at least an hour long and, as the school year progresses, can extend to ninety minutes or more. During these long stretches of play or project time, closely observe the children to distinguish between creative exploration and random, unfocused play. When children are genuinely engaged in a pursuit, they should be respected and not made to stop and clean up before expanding their activity into another part of the room. To prevent the room from getting too messy and children from losing their focus, teachers can continually work to keep order behind the scenes after the children move to a new area. Keeping order doesn't have to mean putting everything away. Sometimes leaving a previous player's creation in an area as an example for another child to draw upon is a way to honor the creation and the creator while inviting another child to participate. This strategy can be used in a single group of children and between morning and afternoon groups using the same classroom.

Ample time should be provided for cleanup at the end of the extended free-choice time. Everyone can participate in cleaning up the entire room, which eliminates the cry of "I don't have to clean up; I didn't play there." When it reflects their lives and interests, children will learn that returning the room to good order can be a source of pride and a productive endeavor that ensures the space is ready the next time they use it. During cleanup, teachers can demonstrate how to care for the materials and how order and organization will alert the group to more ideas during the next play or project time. Consider using cleanup songs that convey these values, such as the Pointer Sisters' recording of "We Are Family" or the Sweet Honey in the Rock song "Oh My Goodness, Look at This Mess!" from their album *Still the Same Me*. Relax and let go of the idea that cleanup should be an orderly, quick, and quiet process—it can be busy and noisy and take a long time. You should allow ample time, have patience, and be actively involved as you work with the children on the important job of maintaining a wonderful environment.

Help Children Focus with Invitations, Special-Interest Areas, Demonstrations, and Modeling

Children's lives today are filled with television, electronic devices, and other games and toys that have been designed for them. They are continually entertained and directed in ways that trivialize their inherent quest for learning rather than earnestly challenged to pursue a love of learning. As a result, many children who come to our early childhood programs don't have experience with self-directed play or with having their pursuits respected and enriched by the adults around them. They grow with guidance to recognize the possibilities for independent use of the environment. And they are eager for assistance in discovering what their peers can contribute to their enjoyment and learning process. The following are approaches you can use to help children learn to focus and work with others.

Design Specific Invitations and Activities

As you explore the values you want reflected in your program and work to design your physical and social-emotional environment to include respect, uninterrupted blocks of time for investigation, and opportunities for problem solving and collaboration, you can also turn your attention to the details of selecting particular materials for exploration or representation. When you believe that children are curious, capable, and eager to make connections and learn, you won't rely on expensive curriculum packages or learning materials to ensure particular outcomes or test scores. Instead, you will draw on your knowledge of child development, your observations of children's play, favorite memories from your own childhood, and a creative eye as you move about the world to discover innovative materials to offer.

There is a delicate balance between offering a range of interesting materials and avoiding clutter and an overemphasis on "stuff." Communicating the value of creating and building relationships instead of acquiring and consuming things involves careful thought and attention to details. When children come upon a cluttered shelf with a pile of materials in textures and colors that have no relationship to each other, they are less likely to be able to see what is available for their use. The way materials are stored and presented sends a message to children about how the environment is valued. If they live in mess, disorder, and clutter, they will likely create more disorder, rather than use the materials thoughtfully. Your selection and combination of materials can provoke curiosity, inventions, and theory building when you take the time to intentionally and attractively arrange things as an invitation for learning. Consider the following guidelines and study the photographs that follow.

- Arrange and store materials in attractive containers and in an inviting, orderly fashion so children can see what is available for their use.

- Highlight a collection of similar materials on an inviting piece of fabric, a mirror, or tray to emphasize the figure/ground relationships and visually frame the activity.

- Suggest new uses for familiar materials by bringing items together in creative ways.

- Display a photo near an arrangement showing how children have used this material in the past. Include a book, diagrams, or photos that suggest or spark possible uses.

Magic Garden Care and Education Centre, Auckland, New Zealand

courtesy of United Way
Bright Beginnings, Houston, TX

Epiphany Early Learning Preschool, Sound Child Care Solutions, Seattle, WA

Second Presbyterian Weekday School, Louisville, KY

Magic Garden Care and Education Centre, Auckland, New Zealand

*Association for the Advancement of Mexican Americans,
United Way Bright Beginnings, Houston, TX*

Children First, Durham, NC

Children's Studio, Bellevue, WA

Kawartha Child Care Services, Peterborough, ON, Canada

Special-Interest Areas

When you notice a recurring focus in children's play, you can extend the possibilities by creating an area for further exploration and study. Displaying photos and examples of previous play and adding new props will keep the play going. As the children arrive each day, they will eagerly seek out ways to continue their pursuits. For example, after watching the children use straws in the water table to blow objects around, you might add a fan and objects to the science area for further exploration of air as a source of movement. This creates the potential for a long-term study of wind or air pressure based on continued observations of the children's pursuits.

Situated in a beach community, this program offers the children a beautiful tray of collected shells along with different backdrops for their sorting, designing, and patterning work. Look closely at the different approach two children chose to work with the materials and you will see their deep respect and intention. They are clearly discovering the inherent beauty in natural materials and the pleasure of working with appealing aesthetics objects.

Bill and Sid Rubin Preschool at Congregation Beth Israel, San Diego, CA

To extend the children's avid interest in woodworking, the teachers offered the group a different yet related activity. They set up a beautiful invitation of wood bases, wood glue, and various materials for collage and wood sculptures.

Children First, Durham, NC

Demonstrations and Coaching

Many cultural groups in the United States, as well as the educators of Reggio Emilia in Italy, have provoked US educators to reexamine the previously held notion that it is damaging to children's creativity to observe teacher demonstrations. When done thoughtfully and with the goal of enhancing children's pursuit of their own ideas, demonstrations can help children understand the possibilities of materials and tools. Former early education college instructor Tom Drummond recommends to his students that they regularly plan times for demonstrations of materials or tools with the children. These demonstrations can be done with small or large groups of children and can last anywhere from five to fifteen minutes, depending on the children's interest. Throughout the year, demonstrations may be extended as the children become eager for more coaching. After the teacher's demonstration, the children are given the opportunity to explore the materials and tools for themselves without further instruction or demonstration unless requested. Examples of demonstrations include:

- a variety of structures to make with an assortment of shaped blocks
- many ways to use a paintbrush
- how to make playdough or goop
- how to make different lines and curves that can be cut with scissors
- ways to examine a flower and draw it
- possibilities for designing with pattern blocks
- how to work with clay and specialty clay tools
- ways to negotiate a conflict

Once a group of children has discovered an effective process or mastered a skill, they can create demonstration charts, direction pages, or instruction booklets for their peers to use.

Offer Opportunities for Meaningful Jobs

If children are to feel a part of the group and be invested in using and caring for the environment, we must give them opportunities to contribute and participate in meaningful ways. Children know the difference between their world and that of adults. In addition to wanting adults to enter their world and play with them, they see adults as powerful and competent and want to be a part of that world. This is especially true when it comes to the materials and tools they see adults using. Children love to be involved with real work. They gain skills and a sense of pride, accomplishment, and ownership from making meaningful contributions to the organization, maintenance, and repair of their environment. Even toddlers want to help carry, fix, build, wash, plan, and organize things. Children develop a strong identity and a sense of both independence and interdependence when they participate in activities that contribute to the classroom and program community.

Rather than trivial jobs made up by the teacher to promote self-esteem, involve children in the real work that needs to be done in your daily life together. Organize and provision the environment for the children to be able to accomplish the work to be done. Children jump at the chance to use real brooms, feather dusters, handheld vacuums, sponges, and spray cleaners as a part of a job. They feel competent and stay on task when they use real hammers, screwdrivers, and duct tape. Strategies that will involve children in taking responsibility for housekeeping and maintenance include the following:

CLEANUP KITS

Let the children do the real cleaning, vacuuming, and washing. Create an area of the room with the tools they will need. Have an accessible storage area for cleaning equipment such as child-sized brooms, dustpans, mini and handheld vacuums, spray bottles, sponges, window cleaner, tubs, buckets, and dish towels. Make sure these tools are visible and well organized for the children's self-direction. Alert the children to the cleaning supplies that are for adult-only use, such as dangerous chemicals, and keep them out of their reach.

MEALTIME PREPARATION, SETUP, AND CLEANUP

Setting the table, serving food, and cleaning up after eating are all valuable tasks. Rather than just an occasional cooking project, provide a system of routines for the children to regularly help with food preparation and cleanup.

CLASSROOM MAINTENANCE AND REPAIR WORK

Have a tool kit or cupboard organized in your classroom so children can help tape ripped books, fix broken toys or equipment, mend fabric tears, change batteries, and so forth.

Choose Teacher Roles to Support Children's Activities

Maintaining the social-emotional environment for children's learning requires teachers to be flexible and responsive. Sometimes you are needed right in the thick of things to model and coach communication skills, the collaborative process, and problem solving. At other times your involvement might send the wrong message: that you don't value or trust what children are doing. The work of a teacher is like that of an improvisational artist—you must continually watch, accept invitations, offer new possibilities, and keep the children's ideas center stage with your attention and curiosity. Many professional resources discuss the roles teachers can play in early childhood settings, including our books *Reflecting Children's Lives* and *Learning Together with Young Children: A Handbook for Planning Your Child-Centered Curriculum.*

In lieu of an in-depth discussion here, consider the following summary of general roles you can play to help children use and work with others in your environment.

PLAYMATE ROLE

Children benefit from having teachers model the use of materials and the social skills needed for cooperative play. As you play with the children, focus on following their lead while also observing and assessing how to support and challenge them to go deeper in their thinking with the activities and with each other.

PROP MANAGER ROLE

As described earlier, an important role for teachers during children's play is to stay alert to the need for reorganizing materials behind the scenes to keep the children's activities and collaborative endeavors going. In addition to reorganizing, you should observe for when to offer an additional prop that might be useful for what the children are doing—either bring it to them or suggest they retrieve or make it. Being a prop manager might also mean cleaning up paintbrushes, bits of playdough, and the like. The idea here is not to be policing the materials, but allowing the children to stay focused and engaged. You might also find a way to include children not yet involved in the play as you move about tending to props.

OBSERVER AND DOCUMENTER ROLE

As the children play, you can watch closely, take notes and photographs, and sometimes video or audio record their activities and interactions. Current technology makes this easy to do. When this documentation is played back to the children, they get a further picture of productive ways to use the environment. They learn more about each other and experience ways to communicate respect for someone else's work. Making visible what is happening creates an attentive, appreciative social-emotional environment, which, in turn, fosters healthy development of individual and group identity. Strategies for this include the following:

- Describe what you see children doing in the moment. Call the children's attention to interesting things other children are doing. Careful observation and study of the children's responses to your comments will help you learn when to offer descriptions and when you should avoid interrupting their focus.

- Use the instant playback on the camera to show and talk about what the children have just done.

- Create displays with descriptive words and photos on the walls, in picture frames, and in notebooks, and place them in the areas where the children have been using the materials. Refer to these photos as sources of ideas and inspiration as the children revisit these activities.

RESEARCHER AND COLLABORATOR ROLES

The observation notes and documentation data collected while in the role of documenter can be studied and discussed with your coworkers and the children's families. This additional examination with others can help you to gain a deeper understanding of what the children are doing, saying, and making. Ideas will likely surface for how you might enrich the environment, rearrange some materials, or invite the children into some further representational work. Teachers who bring curiosity, respect, and responsiveness to their work create a social-emotional environment that communicates a sense of "we," a value children will absorb and begin to offer in return.

COACHING ROLE

Early childhood teachers can often be found reminding children to use their words, take turns, share, and "be nice to your friends." These social skills do not come automatically to children. Just as they must learn to use the toilet, cut with scissors, and read and write, children must learn the social skills we want them to have. They benefit from patient coaching, extended time to practice, and motivational reminders of how these skills will be of use to them. Even babies thrive in an environment where confidence in their social abilities and desire to learn is communicated.

Whatever age group you work with, you can create peer group experiences where children learn to listen to and "read" each other, negotiate ideas and choices, and work together to solve problems. One instance is adapting an activity for small group experiences, as preschool teacher Ann Pelo does. She uses the idea of "spicy work groups," inspired by the Tribes Learning Community (www.tribes.com), to help the children in her full-day program expand their possibilities for collaboration and play with others. Ann periodically invites small groups of children who don't often play together to gather and develop a plan for collaborative exploration of something. She discovered the children love the idea of "spicy" and come to understand it means they might need to try a little harder to work things out with another person. Spicy work groups expand the children's social groupings and help them learn how to work things out when they have different ideas.

You can also promote collaboration by referring children to one another for ideas or help with something they are trying to accomplish. For instance, when children ask you for help, or you notice someone needs comfort or a problem solved, ask which of their peers might like to try helping. Depending on the situation, you might need to suggest some ways to be helpful, or you may trust that the children have enough experience or desire to initiate their own ideas. Eventually you might work with the children to develop a new kind of "jobs chart," one with the names of children who can be turned to for help with tying shoes, pouring water, mixing paint, negotiating conflicts, soothing a hurt, applying ice or a bandage, and so forth.

For many other ideas about creating an environment of inquiry and collaboration, look for the books by kindergarten and first-grade teacher Karen Gallas. For example, in *Talking Their Way into Science*, Gallas (1995) describes how she worked with her group of students to let them know the boys were dominating the class science talks. She developed a strategy of telling the children who were gathered for discussion to look around for anyone who was trying to get a word in. When some boys still found it hard not to dominate the conversation, she assigned them to be "the lookers." Their job was to look around and point to people who were trying to say something so the group would see that someone wanted to contribute. She also suggested the children trying to get in the discussion invent a signal so the others would see them. Gallas offered the children phrases they might use to learn from one another. For instance, she might say to a child, "If you don't understand what someone has said, you could say, 'Do you mean . . . ?' and try to ask a specific question." Finally, she began asking the children to acknowledge if someone's idea triggered a thought for them. She suggested that they say which child's comments led them to this thinking. This helped the children see that they could build on each other's thoughts and develop collective ideas. Rather than making rules, taking charge, and solving problems for them, Gallas's work shows that coaching children into negotiation skills and collaborative discussions and work habits will facilitate their effective use of the environment.

Inventions for Your Program

The social-emotional environment you cultivate, combined with the physical environment, sends a message about your values. Use the following questions to consider your own thoughts and practice and then choose an element you would like to work on in your program:

1   How would you describe your program's social-emotional environment? Have you and your colleagues given collective thought to the values you want your program space and routines to communicate?

2   Are there features in your room that could be expanded to accommodate at least two children? For instance, a bench in front of a computer rather than a single chair; a double easel rather than a single one; a bike with a trailer rather than just one seat; a double baby swing or hammock?

3   What demonstrations of materials or interactions would benefit the children in your program?

4   What new teacher role would you like to weave into your practice?

5   Do you have any new routines for collaborating or taking perspective you want to add to what you offer the children?

6   What changes do you want to make in how you present materials that invite children's investigation and learning?

You are striving to create an environment that respects and honors each child, is free from commercialization, and limits adult direction and control. You may discover this kind of environment is new for children, and they will need some initial guidance and routines to help them use the environment effectively. This is especially true if they are new to initiating, negotiating, collaborating, and problem solving within a group of peers. Studying our book *Learning Together with Young Children* will give you a fuller set of ideas for creating a classroom culture.

Child's Play Family Childcare, San Francisco, CA

CHAPTER 9

Launch the Process of Transforming an Environment

Look Inside

After several weeks of visioning, planning, and collecting, a long weekend was spent transforming this family child care environment. Now it is time to invite the children into the space. Keeping in mind how the environment looked before, what do you imagine the children's response will be as they walk into this beautiful new space?

BEFORE

Child's Play Family Childcare, San Francisco, CA

AFTER

As the children entered the room, I could see looks of wonder on their faces as they discovered the many changes that had been made to the environment. They became quiet and walked around the room looking closely, carefully touching the intriguing new materials on the shelves. Several children turned to me for encouragement to play. I invited them with a smile and a few words to begin to explore the new space and materials.

Now, several weeks later, I've noticed a sense of calm come over the children with these changes in the environment. Their block play has become more engaged and complex. Their creativity has increased with the new natural, open-ended materials, and they stay focused on their play for longer periods of time. They have been collaborating throughout the various areas of the room with little or no conflict.

I have changed along with the children. I am more relaxed, and sometimes I sit back and just watch the children with pleasure. I see their little creative minds working to figure out what else they can do with the materials. Rather than teaching or showing the children how to use materials, I am now coaching while describing what I see them doing. I'm learning when to offer more materials along with information to extend their play and ideas and enhance their experience.

Barbara Manzanares, family child care provider

Starting the Change Process

Meaningful change in your environment isn't just about creating beautiful spaces filled with the enticing materials that you see throughout the pages of this book. Your work, instead, should focus on the children. As the saying goes, "Beauty is only skin deep," and this is true for early childhood environments. You should be clear about the ideas, purpose, and values underpinning any changes you want to make. When you continually think about children's remarkable gifts for living and learning, and design environments to invite their fullest potential, your work will change along with the environment.

Big changes in your environment shouldn't be viewed as "a quick fix." Significant transformation requires observing and listening, careful thinking, and rethinking. You'll need time for visioning and planning, ideally in collaboration to get other perspectives. Big changes always involve negotiation and trade-offs. You'll need to set priorities and continually reflect and revisit your work over the long term, making adjustments as you go.

A protocol for this transformation process can be helpful as you work to observe, reflect, and stay the course while making your vision for children a reality. Consider the following steps:

1. Identify your initial vision and goals for change.

2. Observe and assess how the children are currently using the environment.

3. Study your observations and refine and prioritize your goals for changes. Involve children in the process where possible.

4. Find inspiration to make a plan for change. (Read, visit, or consult with others.)

5. Consider, collect, and order furnishings and materials.

6. Make envisioned changes to the environment.

7. Explore the new environment yourself to test out how things might work for the children.

8. Coach and document during the children's initial encounter with the new environment.

9. Make the principles and story of these changes part of your program history and orientation with new staff and families.

10. Reflect on the change process and your new understandings about the children and the role of the environment.

To explore each of these elements for transforming your environment, look again at the opening story of changes in Barbara's family child care program. Study what unfolded to get a glimpse into this process and identify how the suggested protocol could be useful for your own work.

Identify Your Initial Vision and Goals for Change

Think carefully about where to start. Who are the children you work with? What are their strengths and competencies? What do they enjoy and what do they seem hesitant about? What do you believe the children deserve and would benefit from? Which of your values and goals are you eager to bring to life in transforming your environment? Considering these kinds of questions will help you focus on more meaningful experiences for children rather than just improving your décor.

Begin with a specific focus to keep from feeling overwhelmed. Seeing the impact of small changes will motivate and energize you to do even more. You might choose to focus on changing one area of your environment, such as the entryway, a corner of the play yard, or the classroom block area. Or you might start by concentrating on an element from one of the chapters of this book, such as reducing clutter to create a more orderly, focused environment.

STUDY BARBARA'S PROCESS

Barbara has been operating her family child care for over twenty years, serving children ages eighteen months to five years. At first her program was located in the main area of her home. She later refinished her basement and garage to create a separate space for the children's activities. Over time Barbara's child care environment changed significantly, looking more like a traditional kindergarten program with commercial furnishings, materials, and wall displays. Gone were traces of the homelike atmosphere that she started with. She missed this atmosphere. As a participant in the quality enhancement program Preschool for All, First 5 San Francisco, Barbara received a Classroom Makeover Grant, where she began working with Deb, a consultant with the project. Barbara received a small budget to help with costs but was also expected to contribute her own resources. In their first meeting, Barbara and Deb clarified the initial vision and goals Barbara had for the project. Here is what they came up with:

- Transform the space to feel more cozy and homelike again.
- Ensure the space and materials will work for a mixed age group.
- Expand opportunities for children's cooperative play and learning throughout the environment.
- Get a good rating on the Family Child Care Environment Rating Scale (FCCERS-R) as required by the Preschool for All program.

Observe and Assess How Children Use the Environment

Observe the children, their actions, and their interactions in your environment as you consider how to make their experiences in the environment more meaningful for them. Your observations are a critical part of the change process. Look for where the children are engaged and where they seem to have difficulty. Spend several days observing during various times of the day. Take photographs and notes so you will have concrete data to study. Use the following questions to help you focus your observations and provide important information for your change process:

1. Where in the environment do the children work calmly and with focus for long periods of time? Where do the children seem to have difficulty focusing? How are these areas arranged? What materials are there? What is on the walls?

2. What kinds of materials are in each area? Is there a supply of open-ended materials available? What materials are used often and in creative ways and which ones are neglected or misused? What specifically do children do with the assortment of materials that are available?

3. Where do children use their active bodies and large muscles in the environment? What is the quality of their play in this area? Is it engaged, or is it unfocused and random?

4. Where are the places that invite children to work together?

5. What kinds of interactions do the children have with each other in the different areas?

6. What role do the adults play in each of the areas?

STUDY BARBARA'S PROCESS

Barbara and Deb discovered useful information from observing the classroom activities over several days. In her attempt to score well on the FCCERS-R, Barbara had divided her environment into very small areas, wanting to include all aspects addressed in the assessment tool. However, her and Deb's observations showed that the children rarely used these smaller areas, instead moving materials from these areas to play in other places. The large shelves and furniture used as dividers for the areas made the small environment even more cramped. The children enjoyed playing near each other and often crowded into one area to work together. Barbara saw that the children's actions were inhibited by the limited amount of space for them to spread out. Children were often interrupted in the ideas they were pursuing because someone else's activity got in the way. They didn't stay very long in an area and often needed an adult to help resolve a conflict that occurred from an overcrowded space and inadequate amount of materials.

Play materials were mostly plastic, primary-colored items that lacked texture, natural elements, or possibilities for open-ended exploration. They didn't engage the children for long. The few interesting materials that were

In Barbara's before photos, do you see the small spaces that have been created for children's play? Notice how the walls and shelves look cluttered and disorganized. You can see why Barbara was longing for a homelike feeling again.

Child's Play Family Child Care, San Francisco, CA

available (plastic spools, trains and tracks) were favored, but there weren't enough of them, so conflicts occurred and the play couldn't advance in complexity. Rather than the cozy, homelike atmosphere that Barbara was hoping to offer, the space was modeled after a traditional kindergarten setting, which contributed to the children's lack of focus and engagement in the environment.

Study Observations and Refine and Prioritize Your Goals

When you have collected adequate information through your observations, take time to meet with others, including the children and perhaps their families, to study your photos and observation notes. The following questions can help guide your reflections as you consider plans to change your environment to better support children's lively minds and bodies:

1   How does the arrangement and organization of the environment impact the children's focus and attention and provide for their varied interests and learning styles?

2   How can the environment accommodate children's individual focus as well as working together in small groups?

3   What new elements might create a sense of calm, magic, and wonder and reflect the natural world?

4   What changes will invite children to spread out, pursue their ideas, and use their active bodies?

5   What additional materials will offer children open-ended opportunities to explore and invent using their own ideas and imagination?

6   Are there ways to enlist children in thinking about the environment and how it might be changed?

Find Inspiration to Make a Plan for Change

The programs that contributed their photos and stories to this book have offered many inspiring examples of possible things you can adapt for your own setting. Visiting other programs and browsing the Internet can spark new thinking as well. (For example, go to www.pinterest.com and type "Reggio inspired environments" in the search box.) You can find useful early childhood books about environments, focused on the indoors and outdoors, on the web and at bookstores and conferences. Explore general design and landscape books and websites for new possibilities to inspire you.

Draw a floor plan with cutout shapes depicting any new furniture arrangements you would like to try. Identify several possible arrangements by moving the shapes around on your floor plan to see how each arrangement looks and feels. Clip or print pictures and create a vision board or folder with photos and notes to remind you of possibilities. Take time to think about the children and families in your program, as well as the wider community, and include features that will reflect and welcome them into the space. Consider the identity you are trying to grow in your program. Clarify the budget for your project and other resources you might need, such as professional landscape designers or architects. Develop a plan with a timeline and resource list. If you have limited resources, call on others in your community to help you refurbish, paint, build, or scout for furnishings and materials, and to help assemble and install new purchases.

STUDY BARBARA'S PROCESS

Based on observations and discussions of the children's use of the environment, as well as inspirational new ideas, Barbara and Deb clearly defined some specific changes that could enhance the children's experiences. Together they reviewed photos of other early childhood environments to find examples that reflected elements of what Barbara wanted for her program. The photo below from Deb's former preschool classroom became a guiding inspiration for Barbara as she started her search for furnishings and materials that provide engagement with magic and wonder, nature, open-ended materials, and a cozy gathering space for sitting together. She wanted to include the elements of aesthetics, create focus and order, and add flexible space and open-ended materials described in this book. With all this in mind, Barbara developed her plan for change:

courtesy of Deb Curtis, Seattle , WA

- Eliminate several small areas that children rarely use and re-arrange the environment to create four larger zones for children to spread out in, which include:

  1   a living room with a couch and coffee table to add a homelike feel and create a larger gathering space for children to work with open-ended, manipulative materials;

  2   a block area provisioned with a variety of natural and open-ended materials stored in baskets and wooden bowls;

  3   a drama area with a table as the central focus, provisioned with attractive real items; and

  4   a large table for art, sensory play, and mealtimes together.

- Hang beads to keep two smaller areas—one provisioned as a writing area and the other a quiet corner for books with cozy pillows—separate from the rest of the space.

- Eliminate clutter and distraction to create a calmer feeling by removing most of the plastic, primary-colored toys, materials, and wall displays.

- Add more open-ended and natural materials and real items to expand the possibilities for play, learning, and collaboration among the children of all ages in the program.

Consider, Collect, and Order Furnishings and Materials

A big part of transforming your environment is figuring out the resources you have or will need, and how the work will get done. Most of the examples in this book weren't gathered from traditional early childhood sources. The featured inventors mostly scour thrift stores, garage sales, and garden shops, and ask for help from local business and community members to gather what they need. They also invent ways to reuse and repurpose the treasures they find. If you have funds for your project, the Internet is a fast way to research multiple options and prices for materials and equipment. But you can often look in your own garage and storage areas to discover things you can reuse or repurpose. It takes more time to collect materials than to order them, but the result is often an environment with an evolving integrity and identity that reflects the creativity and uniqueness of the community.

STUDY BARBARA'S PROCESS

With specific ideas for changes in mind, Barbara and Deb went online seeking inexpensive benches with cushions and an attractive rug to define the new homelike living room space. Barbara picked items she liked and also tried to match the light blue color of her existing shelves. They found sparkly beads and mirrors to immediately add magic and wonder to the space. Over the next several weeks, Barbara and Deb both shopped at thrift stores and found baskets and other unusual and natural loose parts, along with real dishes and tools for the drama area.

Make Envisioned Changes to the Environment

Because you don't want the children playing in a construction zone, you need to time your work on the environment carefully. If children haven't been involved in the process, begin to orient them to the new environment that is being planned. Show them the floor plan, vision board, or photo folder of the changes they can anticipate. Take photos of people who are working to make the changes and share them with the children. Invite your coworkers and other folks to help get the work done. Families and other community members are often happy to make a contribution. Sometimes you can identify specific jobs for the children to do with their families. If you are changing just one area, you can close it off with caution tape and make the changes while the children watch, involving them as much as you can in the process.

Consider whether to wait to make changes until you have all of the new materials in hand, or whether your plan can be undertaken in stages. Try to consolidate work parties so that people see immediate changes and don't lose steam for the ongoing work. As you set up the environment and organize the materials, review the principles throughout this book, especially chapters 2, 4, and 8, which discuss ways to offer materials and enhance children's use of the environment.

STUDY BARBARA'S PROCESS

Barbara and Deb took advantage of a three-day weekend to transform the space. First they took everything off the walls and shelves and stored the plastic toys for Barbara's later consideration. Barbara's adult son helped assemble the bench and hang the beads and mirrors. Deb and Barbara moved furniture and carefully arranged materials in baskets for children to discover.

Explore the New Environment

When you take time to consider the changes from the children's perspective, you prepare yourself for support they might need. Spend time moving around, noticing the sensory and aesthetic aspects of the new space. Reflect together with your coworkers and friends. What will the children notice? How might they engage? Explore the materials yourself to see the possibilities for children's investigation and discoveries. How will this new environment support individual children as well as group play? What guidelines do you want to offer to support children in moving toward the possibilities you are hoping for?

STUDY BARBARA'S PROCESS

As the weekend's work drew to an end, Barbara and Deb were thrilled with the results. The changes were dramatic. The space was beautiful, calm, and inviting. Remembering to explore the materials themselves, they considered how to introduce the new environment to the children and what guidance to offer in order to support their involvement. Barbara and Deb couldn't wait to see what the children would do when they came in Monday morning.

Coach and Document the Children's Initial Encounters

During the initial phase of using the new environment, plan to devote time to observing. Approach this as an occasion to discover the possibilities for using the space together with the children. Be alert to what the children notice, and talk with them about their experiences. Observe and take photos of the details of the children's play to research more about how the space is working and discover any needed adjustments. Show the children photos of their activities in the environment. When children see and revisit their endeavors, they expand their repertoire of approaches to play and learning. Revisit the ideas for enhancing children's use of the environment in chapter 8 or dive into our book *Learning Together with Young Children*, which offers multiple approaches and examples of teachers' work to help children go deeper in their learning.

As you work side by side with the children, describe your thinking about the environment and strategies that might be useful. Your words and thoughts can scaffold the children's play and help them stay focused, but remember to be flexible and open to the ideas the children bring. The environment may speak to them in ways you never imagined. Think twice about your own impulse to stop activities you didn't expect. Negotiate with yourself, your coworkers, and the children to expand the opportunities for the space. After all, multiple possibilities and deep engagement were key goals for transforming your environment in the first place.

STUDY BARBARA'S PROCESS

As the children arrived to play in the new areas, Barbara and Deb observed the details of their reactions and the play they initiated. Barbara and Deb described the children's actions to them and joined them in play to discover new possibilities for play and learning in this delightful new space. Interestingly, they noticed the girls spent most of the time in the new block area and the boys in the drama area. Prior to the changes, no one had played in the tiny block area in the corner. And the old dramatic play area was only used for brief periods of time. Now the children were enthralled with the attractive new space and real objects to use in their dramas. The cozy living room area became a gathering space and a place to focus on puzzles, open-ended manipulatives, and building materials.

Barbara and Deb took photos of the children's work to display the next day on the walls in the play areas. The children eagerly studied these images and then quickly refocused to begin again. The new arrangement and materials, along with the calm feel of the space, helped the children stay engaged for over two hours on that first day and even longer the next day. They declined to go outside when it was time, which shocked Barbara, because usually the children couldn't wait for outside time.

Make these Changes Part of Your History and Orientation

It is often hard to motivate change in an early childhood environment and even harder to sustain the momentum when staff and families turn over. Continually enriching and maintaining an environment on behalf of your values and a complex set of ideas about the teaching and learning process requires conscious, ongoing reflection. If you are a director or consultant taking the lead on transforming an environment, involve the staff in the planning and decision making every step of the way. Without engagement in the process, the teachers won't understand the need to regularly invest time and energy into the environment. Orient new teachers who arrive after the transformation so they learn the "whys" of your space and materials. When you document to provide a visible story of how you changed your environment, you help others understand your choices and values. This history of your work can be shared with new families and staff. You can grow a shared vision for living and learning together with children.

Reflect

Changing the environment is just a first step. Ongoing observation and reflection will keep you learning. As you analyze what is unfolding, ask yourself these kinds of questions:

1. How have the children's actions and relationships changed since transforming the environment?

2. Is this what we hoped would happen?

3. Are there things we should reconsider?

4. How have we changed since changing the environment?

5. Do we have any new understandings about materials and the role of the environment in supporting children's engagement and learning?

6. Where do we want to go from here?

AFTER

As you study the photos of Barbara's environment after the changes were made, do you see the much larger areas and zones for play? The clutter, commercial images, and plastic toys have been replaced with neutral walls and inviting natural and open-ended materials. Can you feel the calm and the sense of magic and intrigue in the space?

Child's Play Family Childcare,
San Francisco, CA

Child's Play Family Childcare,
San Francisco, CA

Because Barbara's FCCERS-R assessment was coming soon, she and Deb went through the assessment tool to see how the environment met the requirements and what Barbara might want to change or negotiate. To her delight, once the official assessment was complete, Barbara was told her scores on the FCCERS-R were higher than the previous environmental rating. Barbara and Deb offer the following summary of their reflections on the impact of their work.

Children's Initiatives, Sustained Learning, and Collaboration

Changes in the environment have dramatically impacted the way the children spend their time. They seem more at home and relaxed, as do their families. With more open space, children work together more easily. They use the new materials to build more complex block structures, invent more elaborate dramas, and create intricate designs and visual representations.

Children's Focus and Responsibility

Because the environment is organized and attractive, the children easily see what is available and stay focused on pursuing their ideas. Being

surrounded with beauty and offered more interesting materials helps children feel valued and competent. They show a willingness to develop responsibility to care for the environment.

Math, Science, and Physics Learning

Interesting combinations of open-ended and natural materials engage children's flexible brains as they use the materials to count, sort, classify, and invent. They are learning to plan and organize, draw on past experience, predict cause and effect, and problem solve, thus engaging the executive functions of their brains.

Language and Literacy Learning

Children benefit from a special place for writing and a cozy spot for curling up with a book. They also benefit from having writing materials and reading references present throughout the room. Seeing their own work and ideas reflected on the walls seems to engage them in understanding the value of reading and writing. Rotating and putting their work in binders will continue to provide them with opportunities to see it while avoiding clutter.

Child's Play Family Childcare, San Francisco, CA

Barbara's story reminds us that when done carefully and with intention, transforming an environment can reengage children and families and provide more job satisfaction for providers and teachers. She had the benefit of a small grant and a collaborator to help her identify her vision and plan steps toward reaching her goals. With or without this additional support, the suggested steps for transforming an environment introduced earlier in this chapter are a good resource.

Additional Stories of Transformations

Your plans for change may not initially have support—or even direct involvement—from teachers and families. It is well worth the effort to gain their support. Going slowly and taking the time to involve as much of your community as you can in the change process can lead to an amazing transformation in your environment and new learning and engagement for the teachers as well as the children and families. Inspire your journey by studying the following stories of people who invented their way through changes in a variety of ways.

Reflective Teacher at Work

Sometimes the place to begin in the change process is with your own view of children and the role you play. Read teacher Nadia Jaboneta's story of her work to value, negotiate, and plan for the big-body energy her children arrive with every day.

I have spent a lot of time focusing on my classroom environment and always strive for a place that is welcoming to children, families, and teachers. I use lots of natural materials, warm colors, and wooden toys to create a beautiful place for children. Every year I have a small group of children (usually boys) with endless energy who don't use the space and materials I spend so much time preparing. These children let me know daily that they need more ways to move their bodies, and not just in our yard, as I had always believed. After three years of children with this big energy, and after studying more about sensory systems, I finally realized that what the children deserve are

*Pacific Primary Pre-School,
San Francisco, CA*

spaces both inside and outside to get sensory stimulation. I still struggled with the idea of setting up a big-body sensory area in my classroom. I thought to myself, "Where will I put it? What area would I get rid of? I've worked so hard to set up the space; it would hurt to take it apart to make room for this. Would the Early Childhood Environment Rating Scale (ECERS) approve?"

It took several months of reflecting and planning with my teaching team, and finally we came to share the belief that the children, as well as us, would really benefit from this change. We planned to use Maintenance Day—a day that many families come and help with cleaning and maintenance in the classroom—to put the area together. Not only did we need parents to physically help, but it would also be a great way to collaborate with them and discuss the benefits of having this area in our classroom. Because we decided to use the dramatic play space for our new big-body sensory area, we thought about how to combine dramatic play with the science area. Born was the new idea of the "nature kitchen." We've combined rocks, shells, leaves, and other natural materials with cooking equipment in this area, and the children love it.

In the big-body sensory area, we offer children opportunities to jump, hang, spin, punch, climb, throw, catch, slide, and crawl. We have a variety of textured balls, weighted blankets, weighted stuffed animals, vibrating pillows, and textured pillows. This space is open daily, and the children consistently use it. Our observations have shown that after engaging in these big-energy activities, the children are better able to focus on the other wonderful materials and activities we provide around the room.

Nadia Jaboneta, teacher

Petition to Improve Our Playground

Here's a great story about involving the children in changing their playground. They were major contributors to the process, including advocating for themselves, contributing to the design, and cheering the workers on as they watched them build the new play area.

Every year, Director Leslie turns in requests to a United Way project called Day of Caring to request help with improvements to her child care center. Her center serves children who are living in a long-term homeless shelter while their parents get back on their feet. The program doesn't have many resources. Leslie wanted United Way's help to turn the outside area into a nature playground because the children have little access to the natural world in the neighborhood where the shelter is located. She started Internet research on different structures and items that could be built for the playground. She also turned to directors of other child care programs in the United Way Bright Beginnings program. Then she began to wonder what the children would like to have on the playground and decided to launch a project to get their ideas.

One day during outdoor time, Leslie wrote on a large piece of paper as children answered her questions about what ideas they had for changing the playground. As a part of the discussion, she suggested that the preschoolers and schoolagers write a letter listing their ideas and give it to the people who wanted to help create the playground. To encourage the children to advocate for themselves, Leslie explained that there is a special type of letter called a petition that everyone could sign to request what he or she wanted. The children felt powerful with the idea of signing a petition. Leslie turned in the petition to their design team with all the children's signatures, and the work it listed was mostly included in the final design.

The playground designer, Mr. Todd, came to the center to meet with the children. He showed them how he studied the existing playground so he could create a new plan. The children were concerned that Mr. Todd might not know about all the interesting and fun structures and items they wanted. So they spent time with their teachers over several days cutting out pictures of items from magazines and the Internet and gluing them to paper. Then they voted on all of the ideas to see which ones were the favorites. They posted their work on the wall so Mr. Todd could reference it and include their ideas in his plan.

Mr. Todd drew up the plan for improving the playground and brought it to show the staff and children. He gave the children a copy to keep in anticipation of the many new things that would be built on the playground. Everyone was particularly excited about the bike path and eager to use it to ride the bikes they had voted to purchase.

The children wanted to put a copy of the playground plan in the block center, along with the original petition. One child, Daniel, said, "That's where we do construction, so it should go there." Another child, Connor, said, "And we do destruction in the block center." There were many more conversations guessing what kind of destruction and construction the workers would do. Soon Mr. Todd and his team came to start the work. The children got to watch the ongoing process of change as it happened. They were thrilled and empowered that all of the ideas they had imagined, shared, and advocated for came to life right before their eyes.

BEFORE

DOCUMENTATION OF CHILDREN'S IDEAS

Destiny Village Child Care, United Way Bright Beginnings, Houston, TX

Multipurpose Makeover

This program received a small grant for a single room makeover and chose to transform a community space, which was the room people have to walk through before they have access to all of the classrooms. See if you can find inspiration and practical principles in this image to apply to your own work.

The room chosen for the makeover was a large space used for large-motor activity in lieu of outside play during most of the year. It was also used as a storage area and a dumping ground for broken or unused materials. The center hired Hap Hanchett, a designer with early childhood environment experience, to work with the staff and get the project under way. He was charged with ensuring that the new design maintained the space as a large-motor area, while eliminating clutter. The center also wanted new paint, lighting, storage cupboards, wall art, unified bulletin boards, and a cozy couch area and adult table at one end. The transformation process involved extensive negotiation with the staff. Some staff members had a long history with the program and considerable investment in keeping the things they liked, such as a large mural and places to put material they couldn't store in their classrooms. A process of continually defining values and principles of design helped them begin to accept that a significant change in the space was needed.

Here are the ideas that guided the designer's work:

- Combine design principles with early childhood goals.
- Create a community room and comfortable place for adults and children that is not a hallway.
- De-clutter to provide focus and make space for new possibilities with a sense of aesthetic beauty.
- Store things out of sight or in attractive containers.
- Consider the use of light and color to create cohesion and calm.
- Document the change process and create a binder to help others see the principles that guided the changes.

Hanchett chose a color palate to work with. In addition to painting the walls, he painted some thrift store furniture, covered pillows, and chose lamps in colors that would create a sense of unity. Replacing the bright-colored mats under the climber with neutral colored ones served to reduce the feeling of chaos and overstimulation. The changes completely transformed the feel of the room. The new couch in the gathering area invites arriving families to sit quietly with their children at the beginning or end of the day. It also provides a place for teachers to sit quietly during their break or planning time. Although the designer worked alone over a few weekends, he turned documentation of the process into a binder for others to see, identifying the "why of the changes," the principles he used in the new design, and the solicited feedback about the changes from teachers. The teachers acknowledged that it was difficult to emotionally let go of favorite old things, but they recognized things were shabby and the space was feeling chaotic. Though they weren't involved in the initial transformation process of this room, the teachers became inspired to start changing their own classrooms, hauling out truckloads of clutter and repainting furniture. Seeing the change in the multipurpose room seemed to open up all sorts of creative impulses as the teachers used the principles outlined in the documentation book to guide their work.

BEFORE

AFTER

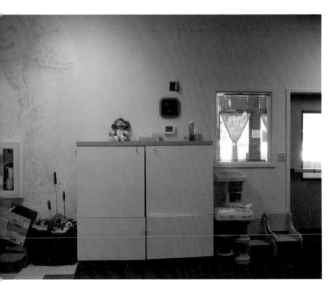

Pinehurst Child Care Center, Sound Child Care Solutions, Seattle, WA

A Journal of Rigorous Change

This next inspiring story is from a center director who worked with one of her teachers to lead the rest of the staff on a rigorous journey of change.

As center supervisor, I asked Darlene, a new teacher I hired, to become a partner and help me lead our team into a "Reggio-inspired" environment challenge—in essence, I wanted to transform her classroom. Darlene and I had an abundance of knowledge surrounding the principles of Reggio Emilia and deeply believe in the philosophy. We led the class's teaching team through a miraculous transformation, educating through professional development, resources, and regular meetings. We sparked their creative spirits by inviting them to make beautiful objects for the children.

Communication was a key element throughout the process. Through ongoing communication, we were able to hear the teachers' reflections, fears, and hesitations, and support their growth. The educators grew from resistant to passionate teachers, excitedly sharing their new ideas, observations, and "aha" moments. It was also rewarding as parents noticed the changes, not only in the environment but in the staff and children's interactions. Families now enter the classroom

BEFORE

Ashton Meadows Child Care, Markham, ON, Canada

more frequently and stay longer. They donate items from home and join us for special evenings to learn about the changes. The classrooms have become inviting places with all the feelings of "home" and full of endless opportunity and, most importantly, calm. Bringing the outdoors in created endless opportunity for sensory exploration and a sense of serenity. The lighting and neutral colors changed the overall feeling in the room. There is a constant buzz of busy children exploring their new environment. The commercialized toys have become scarce. Other teachers are curious and have made changes to their environments too. The children have also changed. They are no longer bored, as staff now collaborate and partner with them to seek their ideas. The teachers have become constructivists rather than instructivists. It is clear that passion helped drive our results, and we see clearly how the environment is the crucial element to a successful program. The staff have transformed their classrooms and adjusted their thinking, and the outcome is phenomenal. This story continues to unfold each and every day. I am grateful to all of the staff who stayed willing and open to a tremendous change. Each of them persevered and became experts of their own environments!

Tammy Nucci, director

AFTER

A Demonstration Room

This story of volunteer work Margie did in a local child care program demonstrates a pedagogical approach to helping teachers embrace transformation of their environment.

Margie and her colleague Larry McMillian were approached by a program aware its environments weren't working well for the children. The program had only $500 in their budget to spend, but they did have an empty room due to low enrollment. With the agreement of the director, Margie and Larry used this empty space to demonstrate principles for creating engaging environments. The program was located on several floors of a high-rise building in a downtown business area. Larry first went around the surrounding area and took photos of things the children and families would see coming to the center so that some of this could be represented in the room makeover. With their limited budget in mind, Margie scouted around the center for extra furniture that could be repurposed and shopped at thrift stores.

After a thorough sweep to clean and de-clutter the neglected classroom, Margie and Larry invested some time and money to repaint the walls. As they began to put their design together, they invited teachers to use their break time to come and see the changes under way and give their input. A notice was put up for families and children to come visit and learn what Margie and Larry were trying to accomplish. When one child exclaimed, "This is starting to look like an apartment!" they knew they were on the right track.

Throughout the week of work, Margie and Larry took before and after photographs. They turned the images into a little booklet outlining the values and design principles they were striving for and left it in the room for ongoing study by the staff. At the end of their work, Margie and Larry did a presentation with these photos and principles and suggested the staff start spending their planning and meeting time in the room to see how it made them feel. They challenged the teachers to begin applying these principles to redesign their own rooms. Before long, two teachers worked with some parents to transform a storage room into a parent reception area with couches, lamps, and photos of the children and their work.

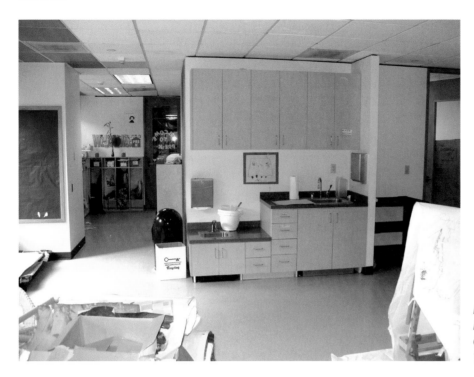

Little Eagles Child Development Center, Sound Child Care Solutions, Seattle, WA

AFTER

Little Eagles Child Development Center,
Sound Child Care Solutions, Seattle, WA

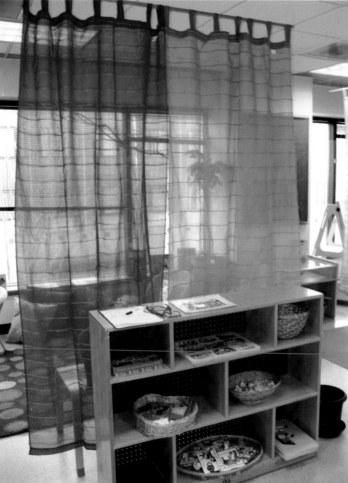

Inventions for Your Program

Examining your own excitement as well as hesitation toward transforming your environment is an important part of the design process. Use these questions and suggestions to reflect on things that may be on your mind after being inspired by our inventors:

1 What were you most excited about in the stories of inventors that you read here?

2 What particular changes were you drawn to and why?

3 In which stories did you recognize environmental challenges that are similar to what you face in your program?

4 What first steps do you want to take? How will you begin?

5 Who in your life can support you in your efforts to transform your environment?

6 Brainstorm a web of specific outcomes you would like to see in your environment as a result of changes you plan to make.

Collaborate with others by getting support along the way from your coworkers, the children, and their families. Keep remembering the larger vision you have for your work with children to keep yourself motivated to move forward. And in the words of poet Eve Merriam, in her poem "A Lazy Thought," remember, "It takes a lot of slow to grow."

Children's Studio, Bellevue, WA

CHAPTER 10

Face Barriers and Negotiate Quality Standards

Look Inside

Anita Rui Olds (2001) writes, "Children are *miracles*. Believing that every child is a miracle can transform the way we design for children's care. When we invite a miracle into our lives, we prepare ourselves and the environment around us. We may set out flowers or special offerings. We may cleanse ourselves, the space, or our thoughts of everything but the love inside us. We make it our job to create, with reverence and gratitude, a space that is worthy of a miracle! Action follows thought. We can choose to change. We can choose to design spaces for miracles, not minimums."

If you approach your work with children in the manner Anita Rui Olds describes as "creating a space worthy of a miracle," how might your thinking and actions change? What strengths do you already have to build on? What barriers will you need to overcome?

Browns Bay Pre-School, Auckland, New Zealand

More often than not, early childhood educators are reluctant to explore bigger dreams for their programs because they feel they don't have adequate resources and have to hurdle too many obstacles. Barriers to reaching your vision can seem daunting and insurmountable. While some programs struggle to stay in compliance with minimum licensing standards, others feel overwhelmed by meeting the accreditation requirements of professional organizations such as the National Association for the Education of Young Children (NAEYC) or National Association for Family Child Care (NAFCC). Any organization seeking federal, state, or city dollars to support their early childhood program (for example, Head Start, state funded pre-K, and Quality Rating Improvement Systems (QRIS)) is subjected to any number of quality rating scales with monitoring visits. Meeting these requirements and creating the required documentation can easily become a full-time focus, leaving little time or energy to explore other dreams for creating quality. But if we are to think of children as miracles, deserving of dreams, rights, and respect far beyond minimum requirements, we must take up the challenge of overcoming barriers and pushing beyond the monitoring visits and limited resources our field is saddled with.

When we first think of barriers, we focus on things such as lack of financial resources, staff turnover, building limitations, endless requirements, and the lack of understanding policy makers have about the support needed to create high-quality programs for our youngest citizens. These are indeed serious challenges, ones requiring tenacity and ongoing activism. But before we can approach these hurdles, we have to face down the barriers inside ourselves—the attitudes, limited thinking, and isolation that hold us back. As you look over the inspiring photographs in this book and consider the examples of strategies for transforming an environment, it's possible that your head is filled with responses such as, "There's no way I can do that. They won't let me," or "That would never fly with my director (or my licensor, or Head Start federal review monitor)," or "There's no way we'd have the money for that." Perhaps you've had real experiences where roadblocks were put in front of something you were trying to do, or maybe you've heard stories of others failing to get approval or money for an innovative approach to improve quality in their program.

But think again. Surely you have a memory of a time you overcame a barrier—something to remind you that this can be done.

Internal Barriers

The most difficult barriers are typically not the external ones, but the ones inside yourself. These can be a fear or a hesitancy to take a risk. You may feel that stepping outside standard definitions of quality would put yourself, children, or your program in jeopardy. Fears are important to examine and face in the light of day. Our first priority is always to keep children and our programs safe. But so often imagined fears take on a life of their own and get entangled with a person's struggle with self-worth, timidity, or a sense of powerlessness.

Other internal barriers can be an unconscious belief that you don't have enough strength or support, that you shouldn't make waves, or that you should stop dreaming and be willing to settle for what you have now. You might find yourself subject to "either/or" thinking, which can create an inability to get past that first "no" and negotiate with differing perspectives. Sometimes a lack of knowledge, information, skill, or experience can be a barrier. All of these roadblocks can be dismantled with determination, perseverance, new understandings, and a healthy sense of humor.

There are five major internal barriers that must be overcome in the early childhood field if we are to successfully tackle the external barriers. These internal barriers often overlap and create a sense of futility and hopelessness in us:

- a fear of taking risks and thinking outside the box
- isolation
- a scarcity mentality
- a feeling of powerlessness
- a limited worldview

Once you recognize any internal barriers that are holding you back from working with a bigger vision, you can begin to join with others in developing action plans for change. This work isn't easy, but it is definitely rewarding and more energizing than living with the status quo.

Take Risks and Think Big

Think of a time when you successfully overcame a barrier inside yourself. Dig through your memory and come up with a specific experience of pushing past some hesitation, a limited self-concept, fear, or prevailing attitude. What was this situation? What made it possible for you to get over the barrier that was in your way? Have you had an experience where facing down your inner roadblocks has led to overcoming a barrier outside yourself, such as a policy, regulation, or lack of immediate resources? Have you ever heard someone else with a story like this? If you were to draw some lessons from this experience, what would they be?

Consider stories of well-known people who have overcome tremendous barriers to reach their dreams. For instance, Wilma Rudolph contracted polio as a young child, which paralyzed her left leg, and doctors told her she would never again walk. With determination and support from her family, she first mastered walking with the use of a brace. Eventually she discarded the brace and went on to become the first American woman to earn three gold medals at one year's Olympic Games. Furthermore, the parade to honor Rudolph in her Tennessee hometown was the first celebration there to include black and white people socializing together. If you were to read her biography, you would learn the elements that allowed her to hurdle the physical limitations before her: strong concentration, determination to never give up, a supportive family, and an enduring faith. Rudolph reminds us of the importance of taking the risk to think big, even as we recognize there are tremendous barriers to overcome.

Form Alliances

There are also inspiring stories of early childhood teachers who have overcome significant barriers as they stretched their respective programs to meet a bigger vision. For instance, Ann Pelo and Sarah Felstiner, two teachers at Hilltop Children's Center in Seattle, Washington, first taught alone in separate rooms at Hilltop and felt tremendously discouraged by the isolation. On separate trips, each of them visited the schools of Reggio Emilia, and they returned to Seattle eager to transform their work. Their program, located on the second floor of a church building, had limited possibilities for transforming the space. They longed to knock down some walls between the classrooms but were told the church would never allow such a thing. So, instead, they knocked down the walls in their minds, schemed to reconfigure the use of their two rooms, and approached their director with all the details mapped out.

Ann and Sarah transformed the smaller of their two rooms into a studio space, put their combined children, furniture, and materials in the larger room, and began to team teach. They have inspired other teachers in their program to make similar changes, and now their work has been featured in numerous videos (*Children at the Center: Reflective Teachers at Work*; *Setting Sail: An Emergent Curriculum Project*; *Thinking Big: Extending Emergent Curriculum Projects*; *Building Bridges between Teachers and Parents*; *To See Takes Time: Growing Curriculum from Children's Theories*; and *Side by Side: Mentoring Teachers for Reflective*

New City Family Center, Chicago Commons Child Development Program (Head Start), Chicago, IL

Practice). People from around the country come to visit their program to draw inspiration for how to transform less-than-desirable spaces into beautiful environments. Fifteen years later, Ann, Sarah, and their colleagues and parent community mounted a capital campaign to move into a newly designed space worthy of their dreams.

We've met scores of early childhood educators across the United States and Canada who have similar stories to tell about overcoming barriers in their own thinking and step-by-step strategically moving forward with their dreams. Each story reminds us that possibilities will always be uncovered when people move out of isolation to work together with a vision and determination.

Kawartha Child Care Services, Peterborough, ON, Canada

Think beyond the Status Quo

Because the early childhood field is so underresourced, we don't typically think beyond the status quo—it is hard to imagine more is possible. Early childhood providers are so used to living with hand-me-down spaces and materials that we begin to think we don't deserve, or have no way to access, something better. The secret is to dream big and then develop clear priorities with strategic planning.

In *The Visionary Director,* second edition, we offer a number of strategies for beginning to nourish a vision for your program, acknowledging the tendency early childhood providers have to keep our expectations low to avoid deep disappointment.

Learn from Other Countries

When you find yourself thinking "They won't let me" or "This is the way everyone does it," we suggest you fortify yourself with research and examples from other countries. Online research can illuminate other approaches that are considered "high quality," and there are a variety of international early childhood study tours and conference to inspire your thinking. Learning to cite other paradigms and definitions of quality can be a powerful tool for self-doubt and strengthen your advocacy work.

Because our profession is full of regulations and rating scales designed to hold providers accountable for children's well-being, and because the United States is a litigious culture, it's easy to adopt the attitude of "I wouldn't dare," or "They would never go for that." While extremely important risk management issues must be addressed, this shouldn't put our thinking in a box or make us think that reaching for a bigger dream is a risk too big to take. One need only to visit other countries to see very different views about the value of risk in children's development. Across the globe, north and south, early childhood educators—and in some cases their policy makers—seem to have sorted out understandings we still struggle with in the United States. Other countries make clear distinctions between the ideas of hazards and risks, and recognize that the well-being and healthy development of children involve offering them both physical and intellectual challenges. They focus on the risks that are worth taking, not just the ones that need eliminating, thereby separating the concept of risk from danger and linking it to recognizable benefits.

Feel Empowered

While it's true that there are barriers outside of ourselves, perhaps the biggest barrier is a person's internal feeling of powerlessness. It's easy to forget that there is a tremendous amount you *do* have power over in your program, starting with your attitude, the organizational climate you create, the physical space you design, and the materials you present to children. You have control over these things. They communicate your values and intentions and, in turn, shape how you feel and behave while in the space.

There's so much more we have control over than we give ourselves credit for. I decided to stop making excuses and start taking action. The first thing I did was to transform our large utility and storage room into a beautiful staff lounge. This was tricky because we never have enough storage, but the room was always such a dumping ground that no one ever kept it organized. I decided to stop being the nag about it and just try something new. I went to several storage supply stores for ideas and also did a search for articles and websites with bright ideas for small spaces. For a little over $1,000, I put in a much more organized and effective storage system, enclosing the washer and dryer and water heater. I set up a work counter with a computer station and got a love seat, two lamps, end tables, and a stuffed chair. There weren't any windows in the room, so I had to settle for painting a mural of a window with a nature scene outside and setting up some grow lights for plants. This was one of the best investments I ever made. It not only gave respect and assistance to the staff, but it gave them a new "can do" attitude. All sorts of other positive changes began to grow out of this first step. When you do something bold on behalf of yourself and your staff, it has a snowball effect for the change process you want.

Janet Reed, director

External Barriers

Facing internal barriers is an important step in actualizing one's dreams. Once you claim your own power to make change, you start on the road to hurdling barriers others may put in your way.

When asked what external barriers they face in their efforts to create the kind of environments promoted in this book, teachers and administrators typically identify one of these concerns:

- shared space with other groups
- licensing and fire marshal regulations
- funding tied to high scores on rating scales
- time to discuss and work on the environment
- lack of resources for improved facilities and materials

You may or may not have a facility where you have to share rooms with another group, such as a church, synagogue, or community center, but you likely face the other four barriers providers listed. While each early childhood setting has its own unique issues, we all face some common aspects in programming for young children.

Negotiate Shared Space

Providers who work in spaces shared with another group find it a tremendous challenge to continually set up and take down the environment they have created. Sometimes early childhood or out-of-school programs use social halls or gymnasiums that must often be cleared out for special events regularly hosted by the organization that owns the building. Many programs just assume that this would be an unfeasible task, so they don't try to create an attractive and inviting environment for children, but operate instead out of toy boxes and locked cupboards. When renting space in a building that is used for Sunday school on the weekends, a secular program may have religious materials throughout the room, creating a dilemma.

Some part-day programs, such as Head Start, nursery school, or pre-K classes, have double sessions with two different groups using the space in one day. When this involves a different teaching staff for each session, a system must be developed for how to organize the room to accommodate the approach and materials each might have. Whatever the particulars, programs that have successfully negotiated a way to share space with another group or teaching team all identify that building friendly relationships, shared understandings, and mutual respect is the key to making it work. Following are examples of some of the things they say.

You have to start by assuming you will have to compromise, but that doesn't mean lowering your standards or giving up your dreams. Approaching each other without resentment or blame is key. I've found that sometimes just beginning to beautify the space in simple ways, for instance with plants, lamps, and attractive rugs, creates an appealing environment for the church group as well as my school-age care group. When I wanted to make bigger changes, such as putting acoustic tiles and fabric banners on the ceiling to absorb the sound and soften the feel of this cavernous social hall, I went to the church with some drawings and catalog pictures and explained how I thought this would be good for both of our programs in this space. A combination of these approaches has worked well for us. Sometimes it has even resulted in sharing the cost of improving the space.

Mari Kennedy, after-school program coordinator

Every Friday we need the preschool to take down and store all their materials so that we can use the space for our church functions. The preschool tried on numerous occasions to persuade us to allow them to leave some things up, but our deacons were never willing to agree to that. The preschool purchased a number of rolling cabinets and installed hooks and Velcro strips in various places on the walls to facilitate their setup and breakdown process. Still, each Friday and Monday it took them about an hour and a half to go through this routine. Our attitude was that this was just their problem to deal with. At some point, we realized that if we wanted them to stay—and we do benefit from the rental income—then we needed to meet them half-way. We devised a plan where we paid our custodian to come in to do that ninety-minute breakdown each Friday, and the preschool paid for the ninety-minute setup person on Monday mornings.

Cassandra Wilkins, church pastor

For years I grumbled about the things I couldn't do because of the double sessions in our Head Start, where a second set of children and another teaching team use my room each morning. At the beginning of every school year, we'd meet to set up the room together according to the curriculum we use, and it stayed that way all year long. But then I'd get new ideas when I'd go to conferences or see photographs of other classrooms, and it would start to irritate me that I couldn't make any changes because the morning teachers wanted to keep things the same. I kept thinking that maybe someday we'd get some new, creative morning teachers, but that just didn't happen. Finally, my coordinator came up with the idea that all morning and afternoon teachers in the same room should go together to attend the same workshop sessions at the conference. She also made it a policy that every three months we would evaluate how the space was working in our room, taking turns as to who had the final say over what we would change. We did this for a couple of years and then gradually began to be more open to each other's ideas and desired changes. I think the real turning point came when I got to get rid of the busy, bright-colored carpet in the room and add a couch and some lamps to make the place more homey. This just mellowed out the behaviors in the morning as well as afternoon group, and before long one of the morning teachers came in with a big plant she wanted to find a place for.

Reba Kaushansky, Head Start teacher

Helensville Montessori, Helensville, New Zealand

Partner with Licensors and Assessors

There are many compelling reasons to be a strong advocate for highly regulated early childhood programs, not the least of which is educating providers and holding them accountable for the health, safety, and education of young children. In nearly every state in the United States, a monitoring agency (or agencies) oversees group care of children and usually includes some combination of fire, health, safety, and staffing regulations. In some states the requirements are bare minimum, while in others they are more fully developed, incorporating aspects of accreditation criteria into their requirements. The overall intent of regulating, licensing, and monitoring programs is to keep providers and teachers aware and accountable for managing risk and ensuring the well-being of children.

As state agencies responsible for regulating programs for young children have expanded and reorganized, most have begun to require their monitoring specialists to have an early childhood education background. This is an important development all of us must continue to advocate for, particularly at the state licensing and QRIS levels, because monitors with specific early childhood programming experience usually understand not only the intent of the regulations, but also what well-meaning providers are trying to accomplish when they seem to step outside the letter of the law. Our field must learn to value the thoughtful observations and "research" of teachers alongside that of outside research-based experts, recognizing there are a variety of ways to meet the components of high-quality environments. Hopefully there will be fewer stories of rigid interpretations that misdirect the intent of regulations—for instance, thinking that a child-centered classroom means there is no adult furniture, or keeping things at children's eye level disallows a model of a solar system to be hung from the ceiling.

Most regulations are written as general guidelines for providers to follow to ensure that children will not be subjected to any undue risk and that activities will be age appropriate. Because many of these guidelines are subject to interpretation, some regulators, with the goal of being consistent and fair, have taken it upon themselves to create a specific definition of how the requirements should be translated into practice. Some want to eliminate any trace of risk potential and thus require strict adherence to their understanding of the regulations. Others focus on the intent of the regulations and are open to different ways the regulations are met. In either case, it is a regulator's job to hold us accountable for the lives of children in our care, and we should be grateful that they take their work seriously. As one fire department inspector said, "If you have had to carry a child in flames out of a burning building, you will never be lax about fire safety regulations."

Magic Garden Care and Education Centre, Auckland, New Zealand

Providers, teachers, directors, regulators, and monitors are all trying to do what they think is best for children. Conflicts arise when they have differing priorities and interpretations about what this means and discount teacher knowledge. Rather than assuming antagonistic positions, forming a partnership between regulators and programs on behalf of children's well-being should be the goal. A partnership, by necessity, always involves mutual respect, good communication skills, negotiation, and a willingness to compromise or develop alternatives together. As QRIS and universal pre-K systems attach funds to scores on rating scales, an appeal process should always be in place for the voice of educators to be heard and taken seriously. We want equity in our standards for high quality, but not standardization that leads to look-alike programs. As programs try to implement the ideas in this book, typical issues around which this partnership must come into play include:

- hanging fabric or any potentially flammable materials in the room
- ceramic or breakable glass objects
- freestanding tall furnishings or cabinets
- repurposed loose parts
- ladders, lofts, swings, or multitiered structures
- freestanding or tabletop lamps
- plants, animals, rocks, logs, sticks, or water sources
- ropes, nets, hammocks, tires, hoses, or adult tools
- holes in the ground
- hiding or jumping places
- culturally relevant features in the environment
- furniture and lamps in hallways

Browns Bay Pre-School, Auckland, New Zealand

- documentation displays hanging throughout rooms and hallways
- real tools and technology
- environmentally friendly, less toxic sanitizing chemicals

Important issues arise around the use of these materials, and in each case, the negotiation process must take into account such things as the following:

- overall compliance with health, safety, and risk management issues
- philosophy, core values, and goals of the program
- size, age, and competence of the group of children
- adult-child ratios
- staff training and proximity and skill of adult supervision
- solid communications and partnerships with families
- culturally appropriate practices
- space configuration and established protections
- safety audit, sanitation, and maintenance systems
- provisions made for geographic susceptibility to hazardous acts of nature such as earthquakes, tornadoes, and floods
- overall rating scale scores needed for funding

An Internet search for "risk taking in early childhood" displays that most of its advocates are from outside the United States. Across the globe, north and south, early childhood educators—and in some cases, governments such as those in the United Kingdom—seem to have sorted out understandings we still struggle with. They make clear distinctions between the ideas of hazards and risks and recognize that the well-being and healthy development of children involves offering them both physical and intellectual challenges. They focus on the risks that are worth taking, not just the ones that need eliminating, thereby separating the concept of risk from danger and linking it to recognizable benefits. For instance, in Aotearoa New Zealand, the government states that planning should always consider the implied questions children's development suggests; they are asking us, for instance, "Will you let me fly?" (Podmore et al. 2001, 9)

Hilltop Children's Center, Seattle, WA

In the United Kingdom, instructor and expert on outdoor environments Helen Tovey (2014) takes the discussion of providing for risk taking in early childhood a step further by talking about the dangers of safety. She writes, "An environment that is safe as possible, where all possible sources of risk of harm are removed, is actually an unsafe environment because it offers little value in terms of play and learning and denies children the necessary experience to develop and practice the skills to be safe. . . . Instead of promoting a 'safe' environment, we should focus on creating an environment that is 'safe enough' for children to act on, transform, seek out challenges, and take risks."

In England, the National Children's Bureau (NCB) and the government's Health and Safety Executive (HSE) have collaborated on a very useful guidebook, *Managing Risk in Play Provision: Implementation Guide*. The guidebook takes into account general safety standards, legal frameworks, and the needs of children. It advocates for all early childhood education programs to do a risk-benefit assessment, stating, "Risk-benefit assessment means that the provider considers two goals alongside each other: the goal of protecting children from avoidable serious harm, and the goal of providing them with stimulating, adventurous play opportunities" (Ball et al. 2013).

In the United States, professional safety auditors who work with the National Playground Safety Institute and follow the guidelines of the Consumer Product Safety Commission rate the seriousness of hazards from a priority number-one hazard, which can cause death or permanent disability, to a priority number-three hazard, which may cause minor injury such as scrapes or splinters. Drawing on this model, when their licensing office took over responsibility for outdoor play space inspections, a group of licensors in Washington State led the effort to educate other licensors and develop resources for this new work. They put together a guidebook, a training for licensors, and a notebook for orientations that includes the accident pyramid (see below).

It is critical that we look at programs situationally and get the bigger picture of what they are trying to do. We need to help them acquire the knowledge, skills, and abilities they need. Let's look at the intent of the regulation. What's good for children's development? We need to get away from a strictly prescriptive, one-size-fits-all approach and gather a body of knowledge. How could this look different than what I imagined and still meet children's needs? I once worked with a licensor that made a program take out their rosebushes because they had thorns. Now I'd kind of like kids to discover that thorns will poke you and you need to be careful around them. We have to notice where the true risks are and focus on preventing life-changing accidents while allowing childhood to flourish in all its many dimensions.

Marjorie Johnson, a child care licensor in Washington State

Johnson and the other licensors in her department used this Accident Pyramid for their trainings:

ACCIDENT PYRAMID

Class 1 Injuries
- death
- brain damage
- permanent paralysis
- loss of vision
- loss of speech
- loss of limb
- organ destruction

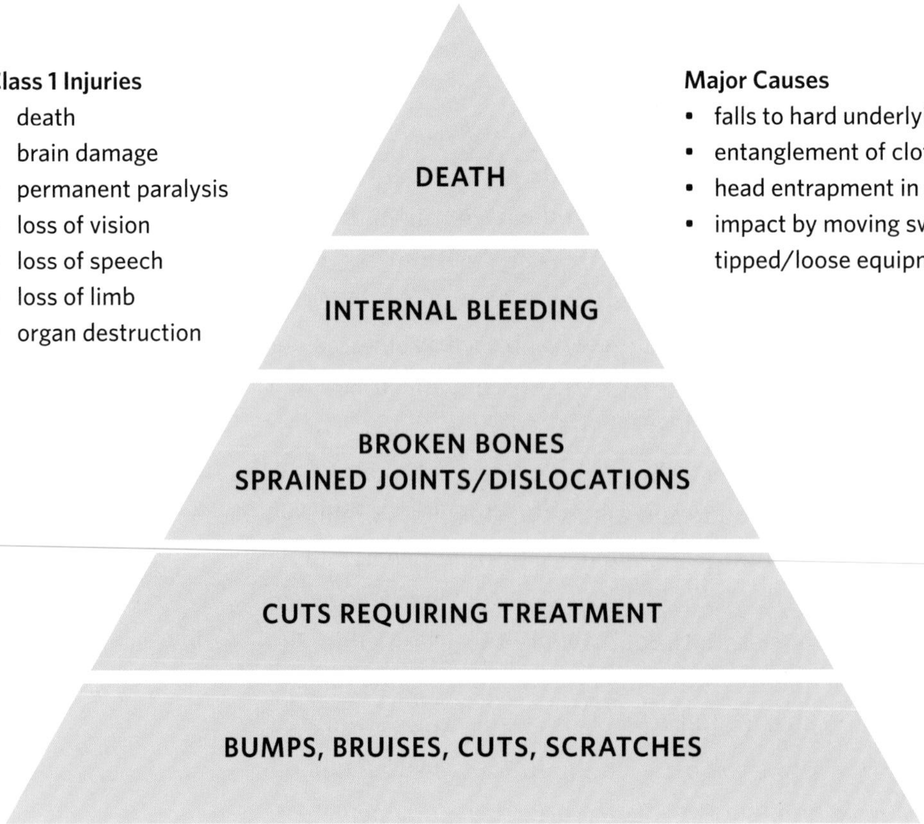

Major Causes
- falls to hard underlying surfaces
- entanglement of clothing, strings, or ropes
- head entrapment in equipment openings
- impact by moving swings or by tipped/loose equipment

DEATH

INTERNAL BLEEDING

BROKEN BONES
SPRAINED JOINTS/DISLOCATIONS

CUTS REQUIRING TREATMENT

BUMPS, BRUISES, CUTS, SCRATCHES

- Most injuries are at the bottom of the pyramid.

- Fewer injuries are at the top of the pyramid (Class 1 injuries).

- We cannot prevent all bumps, bruises, minor cuts, and scratches. They are part of the experience of childhood.

- We *must* prevent Class 1 injuries by identifying the major causes and eliminating the hazards that tend to cause them.

In speaking with other licensors and program directors around the country, we have heard some wonderful examples of the attitudes, relationships, and thoughtful negotiations that create meaningful partnerships between providers, regulators, and monitors. We share some here for your inspiration.

My licensor recognizes that I have gone through a long, tedious process to make these changes. She sees that I work with a vision and not a catalog as I create the environment I want for the children. For instance, seeing that I had a chicken in the backyard for the children to interact with and feed didn't alarm her. She saw that we are always on guard when the children are out there and we aren't lax about washing hands when the children come in. I now feel good about my work. I can look people in the eye and say with pride, "I'm an excellent family provider." My licensor thinks so, too, because she brings new licensors to visit our program.

Vic McMurray, family child care provider

Negotiating is what it's all about. Providers need to know that. They can negotiate with us. They really can. Providers come up with options all the time. I always tell them, if you have a good idea, I'm going to put it in my little album to show everybody at the new provider orientation meetings. Two examples come to mind. One provider found a way to create the required barrier between the diaper changing stations. She put up a piece of sheet metal and then used hook magnets to hang clipboards with the diaper changing charts on them. That was real neat. Another provider wanted to put infants on the second floor and was faced with what to do about the requirement for an evacuation crib for babies. She did some research on the Internet and found an "evacuation apron" made in Quebec and approved throughout Canada. The apron has pockets for putting the babies in and easily carrying them in an emergency. That was such a good solution, and she came up with it. Of course we would accept that, and I'm going to recommend it to others.

Marge Sorlie, state public health specialist

My experience shows that if you can get the people with clout *into* your center, it goes a long way toward solving the dilemmas that come up. Even before our official licensing visit, we contacted our licensor to give her some information about the Reggio approach and how we were approaching curriculum. We said, "Why don't you just come in and visit apart from your monitoring role?" She spent a lot of time reading our documentation panels and began to understand that our approach to planning involves responding and documenting what happens, rather than using the required weeklong planning approach. We use webs to hypothesize about the meaning of what is happening and add items from it to our daily plan. This plan actually is our log, because we often change things as the day evolves. We include in our plan a box that says, "changes to make to the environment." Her response when seeing all this was, "If there are new ways you want to do it and I can see that rich things are happening for the children, then that's enough for me."

That taught me that if we want to do something we believe is good for kids, then we should challenge a regulation and see what happens. These people are human beings. As long as you have a rationale that you can show them, you can change these old scripts. Government agencies can be very intimidating, but no one is going to take away

Browns Bay Pre-School, Auckland, New Zealand

your license if they see a good program. If enough of us question some of these things, they are likely to go back and reexamine the regulations. They need to evolve, just like we do.

Susan Stacey, program director

If a provider calls me for a consultation or a request for a waiver, when I am in agreement with their intent and am convinced that there is no logical reason to prevent an approval, I will seek the support of people above me to address their concern. Where there was no precedent, for instance, in the case of a program that wanted a ferret for a pet, we consulted with an expert in the field and negotiated from there. From the vet we learned that ferrets are able to be vaccinated, so we could approve this with that stipulation. I've negotiated fixing loft railings that are too far apart with sheets of Plexiglas. We were able to flexibly interpret the intent of bolting cabinets to the wall by allowing a hook and eye security system to allow more flexibility for rearranging the furniture. As people are trying to make things more aesthetically pleasing, they may inadvertently raise a fire safety hazard. It's interesting to notice my first reaction and then with further thought, to be willing to work with them to meet their goals.

Kathy O'Neill, child care licensing specialist

There are things I take far more seriously now than I did as a director, for instance, having visual, not just auditory, access to the infant napping area. When I sign my name to that piece of paper as a licensor, it means I'm responsible for saying that this is a good and safe program for children. There have now been five sudden infant death syndrome (SIDS) deaths in child care programs in our state. This hadn't happened when I was a director. Given my caseload and the time I have available to observe in a program, I find I have lowered my expectations, especially compared with doing a day-long NAEYC accreditation validation visit. I mainly have to focus on health and safety issues. When I see something alarming, like the way ropes have been hung like nooses on a playground, I have to tell myself to keep breathing, just to bring my tension down. This breathing helps me remember I need to observe carefully to see how skilled and effective the teachers are at supervising the children, and then to negotiate with, rather than jump on, them. I'd really like to see rails on risers and protective padding around any thin edges. But I also want to educate providers to know they can negotiate with me. Lamps make me nervous, but I'll accept them if they are held down with sturdy Velcro.

Jean Kasota, child care licensor

Kids' Domain Early Learning Centre, Auckland, New Zealand

Every director in the room told me I was crazy to want a little stream or pond on my play yard. What I've discovered is that because nobody has done these things, it's assumed this won't be allowed. But no one has attempted to ask or offer their own way to address the intent of the regulations. I ask my licensor, "How can I do these things? Please talk to your supervisor."

Dee Jammal, child care director

For many years, the fire marshals in our state oversaw these inspections with no early care and education background. All they knew was health and safety. It reminded me of the proverb that says something like, "If all you have is a hammer, then everything looks like a nail." I think most problems with licensors arise when we don't know how to ask about what we are seeing. When something concerns me, I've trained myself to say, "Tell me what goes on here," and to observe very carefully. Maybe it doesn't meet the licensing regulation, but maybe it's not as scary as I thought. I'm looking for providers to tell me, "Here's what we do. Here's why. And here's how we keep kids safe." That's the first step in getting a waiver approved when you need one.

Charlotte Jahn, child care licensor

Negotiate Rating Scales (ERS) and Rating Systems (QRIS)

As the importance of early childhood education has gained more credibility and political viability in the United States, more public dollars are available for programs serving young children, and with that funding comes mandated use of external assessments. With the nationwide adoption of quality rating and improvement systems, administrators and educators have to negotiate a relationship with the tools and process of assessment. Again, the voices of those directly engaged in this negotiation offer us food for thought.

Being assessed can be like going to the dentist for a checkup—we get a snapshot of our health and how well we take care of ourselves. It's important, but almost no one looks forward to it. Some dread it. The first time can be terrifying if you don't know what to expect.

The stress of assessment and the pressure of doing "well" is very real. At any time in our city, there are teaching teams engaged in a marathon of cleaning, rearranging furniture, removing books, and counting blocks over the weekend because their assessment is coming. We do not need to love the tools. But we do need to learn to live with the tools, know their uses and their limitations, gain perspective about their importance in the equation of what drives quality. As an administrator who sees staging and borrowing of materials prior to assessment, I can advocate for funding to adequately equip our classrooms. As a teacher, I can explore how reusing materials in new ways can enrich what is in the classroom when budgets are tight. Building our self-esteem and self-confidence as educators can counter the effects of anxiety and eliminate fear of change. We need to find ways to recognize excellence and competence when an assessment score does not tell the whole story.

What gets measured in a single day will never replace what teachers see every day. More importantly, not everything that is important can be measured by a tool. The environment's relationship to inquiry, creativity, empathy, curiosity, sense of belonging, and the presence of joy all require teachers to be observers, learners, and decision makers. We can learn to be guided by the tool *and* remember to be guided first by how the children are learning.

Lisa Lee, director of training and technical assistance

As a person hired to administer rating scales with child care centres, I try to meet with them first to familiarize them with the scale and assessment process. I talk about how ECERS/ITERS can be useful and what the scores mean. I acknowledge I am aware that they will be nervous and I will take this into account and may ask more probing questions to help me more fully understand what is happening. I reassure them that we do not live and die by the scores, that the most important part is the reflections around the scores and the importance of the ideas and reasons for some of the indicators. I talk about how they can think about the "whys" of the quality indicators and possible actions, pointing out that it is not all about purchases or workshops, but could be about providing time to talk among themselves and decide on values they have for the children and their practice. (I often discover this is a major omission and staff really need these conversations.) I insist with the director that educators do not have to miss their breaks to talk with me.

After I have administered the scale, I give them a detailed report, along with the scores, including a detailed account of what was present in the classroom and what was not present. This helps educators see how quickly a small tweak in the environment can change a score and effect a practice. My emphasis is on their practice more so than on "stuff." I do point out how certain materials can meet many needs and am often ready with handouts of possible "loose parts" that could be gathered and used. I strongly recommend that they do *not* try to fix everything at once. Prioritize and include the parents, community, and other educators in the discussions.

In my province, I've strongly advocated that administering these scales should not be a "one off" event with little or no support for staff and administrators to interpret or work on next steps. I believe staff should take an active role in writing their own action plan from the scale results and in setting their own timelines for achieving their objectives. When educators have autonomy over their actions they are most likely to "stick" and be understood. Finally, while I do think the scores can be used as a beginning conversation to look at quality within a centre, it is evident that some quality indicators in the scales may fall short of what innovative centres are actually doing, for instance, a Reggio-inspired program or one using a reflective, emergent curriculum. With these kinds of programs, I encourage reflection on the scales as a means to achieve the values identified within the centre.

Elizabeth Hicks, private consultant

In our state, participating in the quality rating scale is mandatory if you are a program receiving subsidy payments. State funding levels are tied to star achievement, so site evaluations can feel like high stakes testing. Programs have an option for an automatic two-star rating if they are in compliance with licensing, and with this, they can request technical consultations and a technical rating, which can move them up to a three-star rating without an environment rating scale (ERS) evaluation. However, if a program is seeking a four- or five-star rating, it must have at least one observation with an ERS tool.

Most programs have multiple hazards according to the tool and do not score well in the safety categories. Two common ones are insufficient cushioning, indoors and outdoors; and glass and certain other items accessible to children. I have never seen a program that didn't have some hazards and therefore cannot score higher than a two in the ECERS for safety. So, I say, embrace that—remove the hazards that truly are hazardous, such as chemicals, but then "have your program." If children have strong interactions with staff and peers; adults use thoughtful, responsive language with children; a variety of materials are thoughtfully placed; and staff engage with children in their play, hazards aren't going to keep the program from doing well overall. The ERS tools are criticized for being somewhat mechanistic in that materials and interactions are counted but little guidance is offered from the tool about how materials can be thought about or valued. If I value sanitation above all, or uniformity, or possibly cost, then the bulk of the materials will likely be plastic. If I have identified other values that I want to uphold, then I have a different starting place for choosing materials in my space. Offering interesting materials (blocks, dramatic play materials, collections of natural items) in thoughtful, beautiful ways can have a large impact on living into one's values. Teachers are in the driver's seat when a program has a strong vision that is lived into and they have support from the administrators who are not pressuring them for numbers but rather are focusing on examining what children and adults actually experience in the program. My experience has been that the "numbers come" when the humans are the focus.

Kelly Matthews, Department of Children and Families rating observer

When *Designs for Living and Learning* was first published, several teachers I know raced out to purchase table lamps, wicker baskets, live plants, and sheer fabric to hang in their classrooms. They wanted to "cozy things up." They wanted their classroom environment to look like the amazing images in the book, but I'm not sure how much they reflected deeply about the intention behind these additions to the space. The same is true with the ERS. Teachers want to earn high ratings but often do not take the time to reflect on why the items are considered indicators of quality or self-assess how their classroom environment meets the quality indicators. In order to make truly meaningful quality improvements, there must be some level of reflection and teacher learning embedded in the process. There needs to be a curiosity and interest in creating an optimal environment.

There are many different ways to achieve quality, but there needs to be a process for considering possibilities for improvement. The ERS assessment tools were designed to assess *process quality*—what children directly experience in programs that impacts their learning and development. This includes the various interactions that take place between teachers and children and among the children themselves, as well as the interactions children have with the materials in the environment. It also includes features such as space, schedule, and daily activities that support these interactions. Sadly, there are many environments that limit very fundamental learning experiences—things that should be considered basic childhood rights. For example, there are some early childhood programs that do not allow children to make any decisions about where they play, how they use materials, and with whom. The desire seems to be on maintaining strict order and control. How might we help these teachers become more intentional in helping children interact and engage with materials and one another?

The aim should be to put teachers in the driver's seat on the path toward engagement in continuous quality improvement. Too often the perception is that these assessment tools are being imposed on them rather than looking at the tools through the lens of how they relate to the important work the teacher is already doing with children. It seems to me the issue we all should be attempting to address is the teacher's voice (or lack thereof) in today's classrooms. How do we empower teachers to trust in their own ability to inspire children's learning?

My experience is that teachers who have identified their own set of core values and have the capacity to be intentional in their work do quite well in securing high ratings on assessment tools, accreditation validation visits, and program reviews. They have the greatest chance of using a QRIS as an opportunity to engage more deeply in quality improvements. When a QRIS assessor enters a program for an observation and is greeted with, "We are so excited you are here," chances are the director and the teaching team have a good sense of their mission and want to learn and grow. Not too surprisingly, this often stems from the director's attitude about their participation in QRIS. As we at the McCormick Center for Early Childhood Leadership like to say, "When it comes to quality, leadership matters." My question is how can program directors support teachers in embracing a process of continuous quality improvement? What opportunities can they provide teachers to investigate and explore children's learning and the environment? I believe it is vital that program directors use their leadership role to empower teachers to find their voice and create meaningful learning environments for children.

Ann Hentschel, director of quality assessment

My first year as a lead teacher using the ECERS tool was quite stressful. Although I understood the intention, I was confused about the amount of time, effort, and money that was spent to get a "good score." Teachers were spending large quantities of money on toys and materials from catalogs and making big changes in their classrooms. Our director supported this by giving us the budget, time, and encouragement to make all these changes. I will never forget my disappointment as I read the results of my first ECERS assessment, which gave me a low score for including several books that were "scary" with some having "cultural stereotypes." One was a book about dinosaurs (which the children loved) and the other was a book that a child in the classroom donated when her grandfather, a mariachi player, came to play music for us and tell us about his work in Mexico.

It has been a long journey since this incident, and what I learned from this, and many similar incidents year after year, is that I need to find a way to use the ECERS tool successfully and find its strengths and commonalities. I have become an advocate for how to work *with* the tool, not against it. One of the main things I do and also emphasize to other teachers is that if we already have a quality environment, we should not be changing our entire classrooms to prepare for the assessment. If we are not doing things that are on the indicators, let's think about why and if there is something we should change. If there is something I am doing that ECERS says I should do differently, I really take the time to think about it and talk to my team and director. Is it really something we support and believe in? Do we really want to change it? As I look at the tools more reflectively with my observations, I sometimes make changes that go against my score. For instance, ECERS says blocks need to be on the shelves organized by shape. I saw the children were no longer using the blocks, saying, "It's too hard to put them away and it takes too long." This really broke my heart, and I chose to change this to support the children who really love using the blocks! I feel that once ECERS comes around again, I am ready to explain and support my decision and describe all the other ways children are classifying, sorting, and learning about shapes.

Nadia Jaboneta, lead teacher and consultant

Each of these professional voices working in different settings and geographical regions from across North America brings forth some key points to keep in mind when you are negotiating QRIS assessments:

1   Focus on the process of learning from the tool, not just the score you are after. How can the careful review of your environment open up new understandings and changes you might want to make?

2   Consider the "why" and values behind each requirement and compare with your program's core values and philosophy. Have you neglected something, or do you just have a different way of providing for this?

3   Understand the assessment score is only one window on the experience children are having in your program, but use it to reflect on your work from that perspective. How are the children using the required number of materials, and do you want to offer them in alternative ways?

4   Provide time for teachers to take leadership and ownership of the process without neglecting what brings them joy in their work. Have you created structures and support systems to make the process manageable and meaningful rather than a distraction from their primary work of engaging with children and families?

5   Recognize that while the ratings may add extra stress, programs can use the process as an opportunity to do some seasonal cleaning and "get ready for company." Do you have ways to support, appreciate, and celebrate the big effort involved?

6   Reflect on your environment throughout the year, not just when assessors are coming. Do you have regular meeting time with colleagues devoted to examining some aspect of the environment?

7   Examine whether following "the letter of the law" (for example, posting three pieces of art for each child on the wall or ordering blocks by shapes on a shelf) eliminates or creates problems in your environment. Have you added too much clutter or discouraged children from wanting to use any of the materials?

If we want rating scales and QRIS assessments to prompt meaningful dialogue for quality improvement, these tools should be used for reflection, not just an assessment for compliance. In her QRIS work, Ann Hentschel at the McCormick Center for Early Childhood Leadership at National Louis University has developed tools to help providers reflect on the rating scales and develop action plans. Several of these are reprinted with permission in appendix B.

Most states have coaches or technical assistance specialists as part of their QRIS. These specialists, along with program administrators, can create opportunities for educators to learn from their work with the tools. For instance, Kelly Matthews suggests technical consultants start by asking teachers to identify their favorite and least favorite parts of the environment and then explore how these preferences might be impacting potential scores on ERS items. Then have educators consider their rooms and outdoor play space from the child's point of view by gathering documentation of who plays where and whether a space needs to be redesigned to better engage all children.

Try stirring up curiosities about the environment with possible teacher research questions related to some ERS items. What materials are helping children form relationships in the block area? Are there any conversations the children are having that suggest you need to strengthen the representation of cultural diversity in your environment?

Those striving to make rating scales and QRIS meaningful offer us an important insight: the negotiation process is needed and will always be with us. It is inherent in the very nature of our work, and indeed, in life. Once we learn to embrace, rather than bemoan or rail against, this truth, we can mobilize our creativity and courage to do what we think is best.

Capital Investments to Improve Facilities

However useful rating scales and QRIS are, quality improvements can only go so far in an ill-designed building with no resources for renovations. This understanding is at the heart of the tireless work of Carl Sussman and his colleagues who have founded the National Children's Facilities Network (NCFN) to bring together community development financial institutes interested in providing financing for early childhood education facilities in low-income communities. They've also been active in lobbying for federal and state ECE quality enhancement funds to include capital investments in physical facilities. The research and resources they have amassed can be useful for any early education group seeking to raise funds for improved facilities. Visit www.ncfn.org to learn more about NCFN and www.ofn.org for a description and listing of community development financial institutes.

Provide Time for Dialogue and Work on the Environment

The work and stress within one child care program is usually so overwhelming that directors and teachers have a hard time getting out of their own buildings and connecting with others in the profession. The job can be very isolating, with little time or energy left over to explore what others are doing to improve their quality, overcome barriers, or keep their dreams moving forward. When people are tired, they don't remember that getting out and exercising their bodies and brains will energize them, not further

Southwest Early Learning Center, Sound Child Care Solutions, Seattle, WA

exhaust them. Likewise, when people are short on time, they forget that making time to explore other ideas will expand their sense of possibilities.

Getting together with other providers is a terrific way to discover these shared issues, hear strategies that have been successful, and develop a collective voice to advocate for change. Through professional organizations, study tours and publications, web searches and social media, you can discover groups that have formed around a common context or set of circumstances, such as campus-based or church-housed programs, military programs, programs located in Jewish community centers, or out-of-school programs. Connecting with others will bring you out of isolation and give you a support system for concerns particular to your situation.

Within programs, one of the major frustrations teachers express is that more and more is expected of them to be compliant with standards and accountability tools, but rarely are they given paid time to do this extra documentation work or to reflect on these tools in a meaningful way. As authors, we've heard numerous stories about administrators hiring substitutes so they can pull their best teachers away from their work with children in order to prepare for an accreditation or QRIS visit. From our perspective, this undermines the approach to quality that these tools are designed around. Quality doesn't come from completing paperwork but rather from carefully thinking about intentional work with children. One of the biggest challenges programs must undertake is budgeting for off-the-floor time, beyond breaks, for their educators to engage in meaningful dialogue together about their work. This requires setting up staffing patterns so that not only are educators free to step away from their rooms, but the staff who relieve them provide consistent relationships with the children.

With regard to the environment, teachers need time to observe and discuss how the space and materials are working for the children and their curriculum. They need extra paid time when given additional responsibilities to work with assessment tools and rating scales and encouragement to see it as "research" work, not just getting in compliance. Beyond the work of a daily custodian, teachers require time to ensure the room and materials are well cared for and in good repair. Both the indoors and outdoors need regular attention, not only with an eye on maintenance needs, but from the perspective of the environment as the third teacher. If teachers are to get creative with repurposed and open-ended, nontraditional materials, they should have planned time and a budget for scouting out interesting furniture and materials, and time to clean, paint, and get the furniture ready for children. When teachers are given time to organize, declutter, and create storage systems, the environment works better, and so do they. Consider the following approaches to steadily move toward providing the kind of time teachers deserve in order to work as professionals.

- Begin to design staffing patterns with permanent floaters or substitute teachers to cover regularly scheduled afternoon release time for teachers to discuss what their observations suggest about changes needed to the environment.

- Dedicate a portion of each staff meeting to discussing improvements the team might want to make in the environment.

- Make it someone's job to regularly plan and provision the outdoor environment, whether as a rotated responsibility or part-time staff position.

- Form a consortium with other programs to share a regular maintenance person to help with needed repairs, small carpentry jobs, and landscaping in the environment.

- Budget for quarterly or biannual closure days for in-depth cleaning and improvements to the environment.

- Set up in-house work teams who specialize in different aspects of the environment, such as environmentally friendly practices, landscaping, technology, organizing and storage, and lighting and color design.

Transform Your Thinking about Resources

It is hard to imagine an early childhood team who feels they have enough resources. Whether working at a for-profit or nonprofit, large or small, nearly every program feels they can't get closer to their dreams without additional resources. Programs always need more money, time, and staff. They also need leaders and educators with more vision. And as programs grow and refine their visions, they will uncover resources they never imagined.

Sometimes there are resources right under our nose that we haven't tapped: ideas to inspire us, models to visit, expertise from other fields, stories and relationships to nourish our souls. While it's true we need more money, money alone isn't what's holding us back. We need to transform our thinking about resources and expand the field of vision we work with.

> Most programs wait until they have money before they work on clarifying their vision. I've learned how important it is to write down our vision and continually refine our goals and action plans. I don't want to settle for small results. We are going for more than what seems possible at any given moment.
>
> *Karen Haigh, Head Start director*

Creating a rich environment in your program takes a significant amount of time if you don't have a lot of money and resources. It takes

Nia Family Center, Chicago Commons Child Development Program (Head Start), Chicago, IL

time to collect low-cost, interesting equipment and materials, and time and patience to stumble across a great bargain, treasure, or find! It also takes a change in your mind-set about what materials and equipment would enrich your program. Move away from an institutional school mentality and think about the kind of place you want to spend your days with children. This means shopping in places other than early childhood catalogs or children's stores. Thrift shops, garage sales, creative repurposing and surplus stores, and estate sales can be great sources of materials and equipment. Make sure you choose things that are clean and in good repair. Just because something is secondhand doesn't mean it needs to be junky.

Some of the best sources of wonderful materials, furnishings, and other items can come from the families in your program or members of your community. You may make specific requests for donations from these people or explain the general idea of what you are looking for. Many families are willing to donate good quality furniture or carpets that they may be replacing in their homes. In fact, they may have a garage or basement full of useful items that they would love to donate. Community organizations have volunteers who are often willing to donate money or labor to a project you would like to complete. Asking people to be involved in your program, with specific requests, gives them a way to be a part of a community of people who support children and childhood.

Rather than only viewing limited resources as a barrier, consider this as an opportunity to go on a treasure hunt. Base your choices on things that will extend what you see children already doing or discussing, or things that will give them a new perspective on something familiar. Remember the value of promoting a focus on relationships rather than consumption and amassing "stuff."

Inventions for Your Program

We hope your journey through the pages of this book has sparked some new thinking and inspiration for how to design environments for young children. But inspiration doesn't create change in and of itself. You have to mobilize your sense of possibilities, determination, and working partners to develop priorities and specific action plans. Consider these questions to bring your dreams alive:

- What mind-set and mantra do you want to move forward with?
- Who in your community can you partner with for creative problem solving and innovative, out-of-the-box thinking?
- What do you want to hold yourself accountable for beyond basic requirements and rating scales?
- What would it take to see yourself on equal footing with outside regulators and assessors?
- Who can you engage to assist you in strategic planning with short- and long-term goals for improving your environment?

If we think of children as miracles in our lives, they will inspire us to hurdle barriers and transform things that aren't worthy of a miracle. Miracles tend to beget miracles, so once you take this approach to designing your program for living and learning with children, be prepared for some new joy and satisfaction in your work. And, goodness knows, your attitude and transformative work is likely to have a ripple effect, changing the tide in how early care and education are viewed and practiced. Seeing children as today's citizens, not just tomorrow's, shifts our thinking about the environments they deserve in the here and now.

Ashton Meadows Child Care, Markham, ON, Canada

CHAPTER 11

Seek Children's Ideas about Environments

Look Inside

If a child showed you this drawing in answer to the question "What makes our program so special?", what new insights might you get about how she views the space you have created for her? As you look at the details in the drawing, what do you notice is important to her? What might you want to explore further with this child, and how might you go about it?

Ashton Meadows Child Care, Markham, ON, Canada

Throughout this book we've offered a set of ideas and principles to guide early childhood educators in planning program environments for the kind of childhood experiences our youngest citizens deserve. Under the heading of "Invite Living," we've included "macro" ideas about the larger environmental features, and under "Invite Learning," there are "micro" ideas focused on materials that can engage children's minds and bodies. Each chapter has offered a variety of examples from what we call "Inventors at Work," people across the profession who are trying to use these principles in their work settings.

We would be remiss, however, if we ended this book without seeking ideas from the children themselves. As citizens, they not only deserve to have a voice, but a right to participate in decisions that affect them.

In setting standards for quality, the early childhood field is focused on assessing and rating environments and interactions, but rarely do we actually explore the children's ideas on our "best practices." Chapter 1 of this book offers an assessment strategy for you to use to consider a child's perspective when examining your environment, and there are additional versions of this tool in appendix A. But we believe it is important to go a step further. While any definition of best practices must keep children's curiosity, competence, developmental interests, and sociocultural context in mind, you should also consider children's rights and actually find ways to invite children's ideas into the planning and assessment process for your environment.

Finding a pathway into children's thinking is a delicate process for educators, deserving careful planning and reflection. We recommend you start with close observation of how children are really using your space and materials, where their self-initiation takes them, what they do with various materials, and what they talk about. As you observe, pay close attention to the details of body language and behavior, because children often communicate more through these nonverbal methods than through words. When you decide to use conversation to collect their ideas, formulate questions that clearly invite the children's ideas without any tone of interrogation, testing, or seeking agreement with your idea. Use phrases such as, "I'm curious" and "I wonder."

Ann Pelo, a masterful teacher in inviting young children's ideas, offers these thoughts on seeking children's ideas about your environment:

I'd work with one or two children at a time and start a conversation about what makes our classroom/playground/hallway/bathroom special? Other questions I'd imagine asking include:

1 What makes our space beautiful?
2 What makes it an interesting place for children?
3 What's an important place in our program?

4   What part of our space makes you feel good/happy/curious/ excited/proud?

5   What do you think your mom/dad really likes here?

6   What would you want a new child to see or do first the first time she visited?

7   What makes our environment a good place for children?

I'd have a good, full conversation in relation to these sorts of questions. While listening, I'd make notes about the child's thoughts and pay attention for ideas that hold good possibility for representational work, then jump on that: "I'm wondering if you will draw a picture that shows that idea." "Please draw a picture of that part of our classroom or play yard."

As authors not currently engaged in daily work with children, we forwarded Ann's thoughts about seeking children's ideas to the early childhood educators who generously offered us photos and examples of how they have been designing their program environments. Some have a regular practice of exploring children's thinking, while others haven't yet focused their work in this way. Even those with experience in this practice acknowledged that they hadn't often, if ever, directly sought children's ideas about their space. As they sent us their children's drawings and conversations, we replied with questions seeking their reflections:

1   What did you learn that seems most important to the children?

2   Did anything the children said or drew surprise you or confirm what you already know about these children from your observations?

3   Did you get any new insights on how your environment does or doesn't engage the children the way you'd hope?

4   Are there any common themes that prompt you to reconsider the design of your space?

5   What have you learned about seeking children's ideas and how to take that process deeper?

Because children's verbal language and representational skills don't always match the intricacy of their ideas, adults must listen and look carefully and study the details of their drawings and actions. Then engage colleagues and perhaps the children's families in interpreting the deeper meaning of what the children are expressing. You can practice with the following examples educators have offered as they invent their way into this work of seeking and understanding children's ideas, honoring the voices and rights of our youngest citizens.

Stories of Inviting Children

Educators following the approach Ann suggests above invited children to think about their environment in conversations and in drawing. The documentation and reflections that follow show that some children had detailed ideas to offer, while others had to be coaxed into saying more, with the adults trying out new questions to solicit their thinking. Some gave children cameras as another way to capture what they find important in the space.

As you read their words and closely study their drawings, you will see the children expressing some of the same concepts we focus on in this book. These include enjoying spaces that are cozy and homelike, experiencing a sense of belonging, staying connected to their families and culture, being able to focus because of the order, exploring with their senses, relating to the natural world, and delighting in physical and intellectual challenges.

Darlene Nantarath and Makayla, age five
Ashton Meadows Child Care, Markham, ON, Canada

Darlene writes: I asked Makayla to draw her favorite part of our classroom, and she immediately took up the task. I was especially curious about her perspective because she is only with us part-time and has a number of transitions in her days. We talked about her drawing.

> MAKAYLA: I like this classroom. There are lamps. My other classroom doesn't have lamps, and this one does. Feels like I have friends over there and here; I feel like I have a classroom and friends.
>
> DARLENE: I love how you sketched your favorite part of our classroom and I was wondering how the lamps make you feel so special in our classroom.
>
> MAKAYLA: They are mats and light. I like them just the way they are, because they are difficult. The mats are difficult. Yoga moves are hard to do. When I do yoga, it feels better than lights because it gives me more energy.
>
> DARLENE: When you walked into our classroom this morning, how did it make you feel?
>
> MAKAYLA: It makes me feel like I want to cuddle with my mom.

Darlene reflects: In her very initial comment, "my other classroom doesn't have lamps, and this one does," I feel that perhaps Makayla's naturally becoming observant and in tune with her emotions because of having to transition between four places within a week. She said the classroom makes her feel like she wants to cuddle with her mom, and this is exactly why I am so focused on creating and designing environments that spark these emotions. When she initially drew the yoga mats, I was curious as to why she added the mats into her sketch, because she spoke of the lamps and not the mats. Perhaps she connected soft lighting to yoga? Did the lighting bring a calmer aura, as yoga did?

I did add three more lamps in addition to the two that we had. This eliminates the need for the overstimulating fluorescent lights and softens the room up to a homelike feeling so that the transition from home to school is less drastic. Adults such as teachers, college professors, early interventionists, and parents have given positive feedback, saying that they didn't want to leave the room!

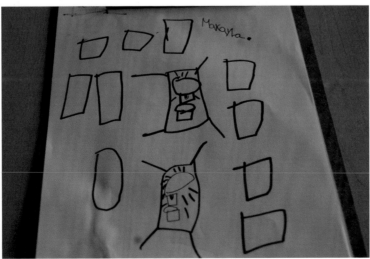

Cassie Tondreau and Audrey, age four

Hilltop Children's Center, Seattle, WA

Cassie writes: At our center, the environment we create for children is vastly important to our work. Recently I opened a discussion with several four-year-olds about what they feel is important to making their room a great space for living and learning together. Through my conversations with them, I discovered several interpretations of the space, and most importantly what children need to experience it in their own way. The underlying messages of their discussions about favorite objects, times of day, people, and places in the room underscored a message of specific desires and needs for their time in the classroom.

I started by asking children in the River Room, "I'm wondering what makes our River Room feel special to you. What do you love about the River Room?" As our discussion progressed, I offered the children paper and pens to help their thinking through illustration.

> AUDREY: I love the studio. I love the paintbrushes because they remind me of wands. I felt good when I saw them.
>
> CASSIE: What do you need to make a classroom great?
>
> AUDREY: You need a clock, and you need glitter, because it's glittery and sparkly. You also need naptime so you can rest, because kids get tired sometimes.
>
> *Cassie reflects:* Audrey drew as she spoke about the room, and I noticed her focus moving to an image of herself at naptime, snuggling on her nap mat.
>
> AUDREY: I'm under the blanket, but I'm not asleep! I'm pretending to be asleep, but I'm just cozy.
>
> CASSIE: What do you need to feel really cozy at naptime?
>
> AUDREY: Well, you need the lights off, and you need books. And you need nap toys! You can play with them on your mat, or you can just sleep.

Cassie reflects: Audrey's ideas confirm the importance of comfort in the space and joy in provocations. She expresses a need for autonomy in her space. The need for her to make her own choices, be it choice of provocations, or simply whether or not to sleep at naptime, is evidently very important to her. She also needs a great deal of aesthetic stimuli in the room, describing objects she feels are important to display, as well as colors she prefers in the room.

Megan Arnim and Ben, age four

Epiphany Early Learning Preschool, Sound Child Care Solutions, Seattle, WA

Megan writes: I was pretty honest with Ben, and explained that I have a friend who is really interested in what makes classrooms good places to be, and that, in fact, my friend is writing a book to help teachers if they aren't sure what would be good to put into their rooms. I told him that my friend is particularly interested in what children thought about this subject. He got pretty excited about that and started telling me about trampolines and cannons, and I realized I had to qualify things a little more. I told him that those things do indeed sound exciting, but that I was thinking about our room, and thinking that it was a pretty good place to be, and was wondering what it was about our room that made it "really cool." As an additional prompt, I added, "If someone asked you what your favorite part of our room is, what would you say?" He thought about this for a few minutes before answering. With a little more prompting, he added some words about why the couch is a good thing to have in our room. After I had written down what he said, I told him that I really thought my friend would love to see a drawing of the couch, and would he be willing to make one so that I could send it along with his words: "The couch is important. The couch holds you when you read stories."

Ben has been exploring representational art a lot lately and was happy to help me out with this. I think that he must have continued thinking about my original question while he did his drawing of the couch, because as soon as he was done, he started in on a new feature of the classroom, our Lego blocks saving shelf. Ben made a picture of our bright blue Lego block shelf and told me, "You need a place to keep Legos. A Lego shelf. So people won't step on them. So they don't break."

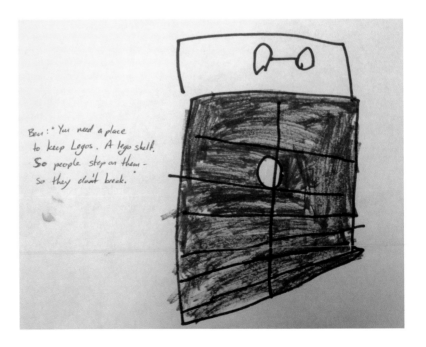

Angela Woodburn and Daniel and Ella, both age five

West Huron Early Childhood Learning Centre, London Bridge Child Care Services, Zurich, ON, Canada

Angela writes: We took up Ann's suggestions and asked Ella and Daniel about what makes this center special.

Daniel talked about how on the other side of the creek, there is a rain forest, and that they need to wear boots when they go into the creek. Several children mentioned the number of mosquitoes in the woods and that you had to have a coat or long pants or the mosquitoes would get you. Daniel said, "Sometimes the creek has a little bit of water, sometimes lots. When the sun is out it soaks into the ground. When there is no sun then there is water. It's really muddy when there is water in there."

Ella suggested that the woods are one of her favorite places to be. She shares that her favorite place to play in the woods is hanging from a tree branch. She draws a picture and describes how there "is a log down here, I swing my leg up, then swing the other leg up and hang like a koala, and move slow like a sloth." Ella's teachers say that they often see her doing exactly what she describes in her drawing.

Daniel and Ella's drawings reinforced the value of the outdoor classroom. This center has been open for two years, and we have been documenting the children's journey in the woods—from exploration, to building climbers and shelters, as well as the infants' exploration of the outer perimeters.

While Ella's drawing is clearly representational and easier for us to interpret, I often find when looking at even younger children's drawings that we see an experimentation of color and motion, seemingly random marks, made without much thought to them. Some might look at the paper afterward and only see scribbling, but as we watched and listened we learned that the marks they made were representative of their ideas expressed in a very concrete way. We have come to understand that young children often draw in verbs, their marks depicting actions instead of nouns. For instance, a child drawing a fast car often draws the "fast" path of the car but not the car itself. When we spend time watching children draw and looking at their work from this perspective, we see a connection between the children's ideas and the marks they put on the paper. These marks represent not only the beginning of literacy development but are also an outlet for the expression of creativity and imagination. They are not random; they are the process of their thinking made visible.

Terry Haye and Eli, age four

Clark College Early Learning Center, Vancouver, WA

Terry writes: We went outside and the children picked a comfortable spot to sit in "the forest," their name for the outdoor play space. I prompted them to spend some time looking at our new building and noticing what it looked like. Then they were invited to get up and feel the outside of the building and walk around it to notice it "up close." After that I gave the children clipboards with paper and pen and asked them to draw what they see and what they wonder about, asking, "What do you see when you look up the river at our new building? What do you like about it? What do you want to know more about?"

Eli immediately looked at the stonework on the side of the building. He said, "I never saw rocks on the building before; I only saw trees from the window!" He was referring to the view he sees daily from the window of his classroom that overlooks the creek bed and "forest."

This made me wonder about perspective and how to intentionally offer opportunities for children to take the time to change their perspective and really notice the environment around them. When I asked Eli to tell me about his drawing and what he noticed and observed, he made a distinction between the small river rocks and the large boulders. He showed me where he drew the smaller trees that "are smaller than the very tall building." He also pointed out the large beam that runs across the top of the building. Eli said, "I think it's a good idea to have rocks on the building, and wood. I want to make my building picture with rocks!"

Sadie Parrinello and her age-four class

Ventana School, Los Altos, CA

Sadie writes: In the Sun Room, we are encouraging children to give careful thought to what they like to do at school and where they like to play. Within the first month of school, we started thinking about and reflecting on our classroom, playground, and nature area/trike yard and materials, such as tape, pencils, blocks, and the like. Children were given photos showing these areas and materials. I asked children as a group and individually to look at the photos and to choose one that depicts where they enjoy spending their time at school and what they like to do or what specific material they enjoy using, and to talk about how they use the material or why the space was important for them. Our intention was to support children in reflecting on the spaces they share with each other within our classroom community as a way to define a sense of belonging. We were interested to see if individual children would choose photos representing the places and activities we have observed them being most invested in.

I see that their drawings reflect variations of the actual images they chose. Some children included themselves within the drawings, while others drew only the material or space. Upon reflecting on this activity, I find it compelling that some children drew themselves in the environment, while others didn't. I wonder how their depictions of themselves, or not, speaks to how they identify with a sense of belonging within the environment shown in their drawings.

The majority of the spaces children strongly identify with are outdoors. The nature area and the monkey bars are important parts of their experience. However, for some children, classroom materials, such as colorful masking tape, are what they strongly identify with. Children generally selected images representing the places and materials they gravitate toward interacting with the most. When they did in fact select images reflective of the places and experiences they enjoy, I feel that this spoke to the quality of their self-understanding and ability to be self-reflective.

We put documentation of this work adjacent to the sink where children gather at least two times a day. Children often look at their drawings and the photos, reflecting on the spaces and materials depicted. In my view, documentation in this instance serves as a powerful tool, providing a framework for children to feel known and valued.

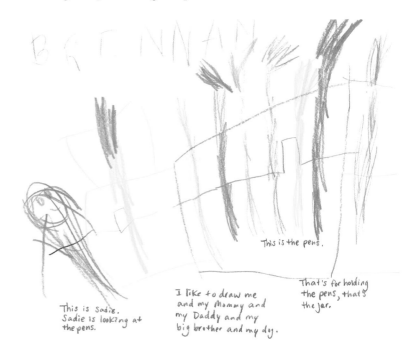

This is the pens.

This is Sadie. Sadie is looking at the pens.

I like to draw me and my Mommy and my Daddy and my big brother and my dog.

That's for holding the pens, that's the jar.

Nadia Jaboneta and Frankie, age five, and a few other children
Pacific Primary Pre-School, San Francisco, CA

Nadia writes: I sat down with Frankie early in the morning as a few other children played.

> TEACHER NADIA: Frankie, you've been at this school for a long time now. I bet you have a lot of ideas about what makes the Coyote Classroom special.
>
> FRANKIE: Yeah, I've been coming here since I was a baby because I have a big brother. I know a lot about this school.
>
> TEACHER NADIA: What do you think is different and special about the Coyote Classroom?
>
> FRANKIE: The sensory area. I really, really, really, really, really, really like it. I like to jump on the big box and climb up the punching bag to get the chain. I like that I don't have to visit anymore because now I'm a Coyote [name of the classroom]. Other kids can visit though—they check it out. They should check out . . . anything.

Ellis hears the conversation and joins in: I think the people make the classroom special, but the toads do too. They can climb the glass. The art area is also special because you get to make interesting things like with the smelly markers. The yellow one is my favorite; it smells like lemon cake. Oh, I can't forget the "Wall of Kindness," because it spreads kindness.

Bram then walks over to us and says: I like our punching bag and mat. Nobody else has that. We can play basketball and jump at the same time.

Ryder walks into the classroom.

> BRAM: Ryder, we're talking about what's special in our classroom. What do you think?

Ryder pauses for a little bit and then responds: The sensory area, because I can do flips in the air. The other rooms don't have a sensory area. Everybody wants to visit our classroom to go to our sensory area. I do boxing too.

As children were dropped off, Bram became the interviewer. Riley walked in and Bram ran to him.

> BRAM: Riley, what do you think is special about our classroom?
>
> RILEY: The Legos. I like connecting them and making stuff. I like that it's a giant container, because I could just put chairs there and I don't have to dig them out of a basket.

I then brought out paper and markers and asked the children if they would draw their ideas. Nora was not in our group when we were having this discussion, but apparently she was listening. Later that morning she handed me her drawing that she had made in our art studio and said, "I like the sensory area too. It's so creative. This is my brother, and he's covering his eyes. The calmness place is important too, because it helps people calm down." (The calmness place is a wooden cube for one person with a big bean bag pillow, things to squeeze, notebook and crayons, music boxes, lavender bag, and other calming items.)

As part of my regular practice, I reflect with the children about our project work and other interests. I have regular conversations with them about their discoveries and what else they are curious and wonder about. Reflecting with the children about our classroom space was something new to me. Taking a closer look at the children's words and drawings, I was able to make the connection and understand how important our sensory area is to them. It felt gratifying that a space that I, along with my teaching team, worked so hard to create last year is a space the children really love and use daily.

I now consider our classroom a sensory friendly space. and have materials throughout the classroom to meet children's sensory needs, not only tactile (which seems to be the most common sense), but the seven senses: touch, sight, hearing, smell, taste (oral), proprioception, and vestibular activity. We have this "sensory area" open daily with opportunities for the children to engage in big-body activities such as jumping, spinning, and sliding. To help with vestibular and sensory integration issues, we add such things as textured balls and pillows, weighted blankets, and stuffed animals. The benefits of this type of input are something we teach the children about too; they are quite knowledgeable on the topic.

I also want to note how Ellis's response really warmed my heart. At first I was surprised to hear her say that the people are what's special, but then felt like the work us teachers are doing to help the children remember their kindness and see the strengths in their peers was really paying off. This has been a huge part of our curriculum this year, so it was wonderful to hear this from her.

Susan Stacey and Genevieve, age four
Junior Primary Programme at Halifax Grammar School, Halifax, NS, Canada

Susan writes: Genevieve is a very quiet child who does not speak unless asked a question, and usually engages in solitary play. Through her actions with materials and play, we can see that she is highly intelligent and notices everything in her environment.

One day, she quietly went off by herself, and drew slowly and carefully, as if with intention. When she slowed down as if finished, I asked about her drawing. She told me it was a map of the classroom. Hearing her explanation, I realized that she included not only the physical aspects of the classroom, but also the daily routines. Genevieve drew morning meeting, with mats in a circle and a teacher's chair. She had noticed minute things, such as the teacher's drawer in the desk. The teacher's desk at first

included only the computer, but the second round of drawing now shows a desk drawer full of stuff. All areas of the classroom are there, including the exit door, clearly labeled with Genevieve's printing.

When I examine Genevieve's drawings, I realize that she has included all the spaces that are important to her and the routines that she enjoys. For instance, she is one of the children in my small group where we do activities that are inspired by not only the children's interests, but also their level of development. Although we consider interests and development throughout the day, small-group time might, I realize, be reassuring and comfortable for a quiet child like Genevieve, since she is one of only five children in this group and therefore is able to have one-to-one conversations with me as well as listen to the others in a more relaxed setting. I wonder, how could I provide more relaxed situations for Genevieve through the busier and noisier parts of the day?

In conversation with Genevieve whilst revisiting these drawings, she commented that the studio space—in particular the easel—is her favorite place to be "because it has paint. My best choice is painting. I wish I could paint at the easel lots of times every day!" she said. This comment was rather puzzling to me, since the easel is very accessible most times during the day. Therefore, I have to wonder if Genevieve realizes that she can go there at any time or is waiting to be invited. Something to watch for and consider further.

Lindsay Sparkes and Andrea Dewhurst, and Grace and Hayden, both age four

Stoneybrook Early Childhood Learning Centre, London Bridge Child Care Services, London, ON, Canada

LINDSAY: What makes our classroom beautiful?

HAYDEN: The writing center, because it's like all sorted so nothing's not in order. We make pictures for our moms and dads.

GRACE: To draw stuff for Mommy and Daddy. If we didn't have markers, we couldn't draw.

LINDSAY: What do you need in the art center?

GRACE: Markers and pencil crayons and pencils.

LINDSAY: Why so many different things?

GRACE: So we can draw what we want.

Lindsay reflects: When materials are neatly sorted and presented in a visually appealing way, they invite children in. Having a variety of materials available allows children to fully explore their thoughts, ideas, and creativity. It is important to have more than one chair in the writing center so that children can work together and inspire one another.

Laura Edwards and Kathy Dutton and ten children, age four

Second Presbyterian Weekday School, Louisville, KY

Laura and Kathy write: We used the analogy of going to a museum to get children to look closely at our classroom environment and identify what is important to them.

MRS. EDWARDS: Have you ever been to a museum?

Chimes of "yeses" were heard throughout the group.

WILL: We use museum hands.

MRS. DUTTON: Museum hands are used because it helps us observe with our eyes. That means we are looking at things that we may have never seen before.

MRS. EDWARDS: Our room is kind of like a museum. It is filled with many beautiful things that you may have never even noticed. Not only is it filled with your artwork, but there are many other interesting parts of our room.

MRS. DUTTON: Let's take a few minutes to walk around our room in silence and look with our eyes for things we may have never noticed.

The children walked around the room silently observing with their eyes. Then we gathered together again and shared the things we observed.

GRAY: I liked the pictures of the letters made by us. My favorite was the letter *G* because I made it!

NAN: I noticed the names of our school family. They make me happy.

AMELIA: I noticed the painting in the block area that I painted because they are hearts.

ELLA: I saw the bird, and it made me feel happy inside.

WILL: I noticed all the different colors on the marbles.

GRANT: I liked the picture of all the crayons.

MRS. DUTTON: Did you notice how it was made?

Grant ran back to look.

GRANT: It's a puzzle!

CHARLES: I like the picture on the wall. I noticed the words on top and the people holding hands. They are all smiling.

SUMMER: I liked the hanging stars because they are colorful. They are yellow.

CHARLIE: I saw the family pictures in the block area on the shelf. I saw my family and I liked that.

LUKE: The flowers in the window had such pretty colors.

Laura and Kathy reflect: Several of the children decided that they would like to recreate the things they noticed in the classroom. We were especially touched to see Ella, who used markers to draw the bird hanging from a branch; and while she was writing her name, she said, "The *E* sits on the branch, the *L* sits on the branch, the other *L* sits on the branch, and the *A* creeps down the side."

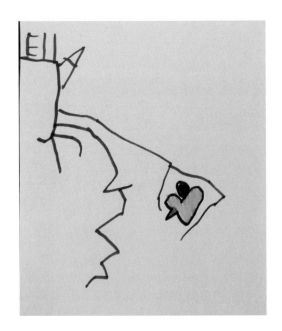

We were thrilled that several of the children were drawn to items in our room that reflect our school "family." We have worked from day one to develop a sense of family in our room. For example, we considered taking down the names the children made with small beans in the beginning of the year, yet we, as teachers, love how they look, and we know how hard each child worked to spell out their name with the small beans. So instead of taking them down, we have added quotes by their names, which we change periodically to reflect their thoughts on our different studies. The names were the first thing Nan noticed. They have meaning to her, and we are now glad we have made them a permanent part of our room. We were surprised by several items the children noticed. At first we thought Will liked the marbles simply because he always plays with them. But then he talked about all the different colors inside the marbles. Luke liked the flowers in the corner of the windowsill because of all the colors, and Summer was drawn to the stars over the snack table because they are yellow. Color seems to be an important theme for drawing children to certain objects. While we strive to keep our environments neutral, we fill them with items of color as well, which become sources of interest for our students. Finally, we were not surprised that several of the children were drawn to their own artwork that was displayed in various places around the room. Four-year-olds are typically proud of the things they create! However, the sense of pride also comes from the fact that the teachers, too, thought it was display worthy! Shouldn't we always display their efforts regardless of how the final product looks? On some level, we feel our students have a sense that items in our room have a purpose, their own artistic contributions are valued, and we really are a "family." The environment most definitely is a third teacher!

Bridget Towle and the children of her program, ages four and five

Kids' Domain Early Learning Centre, Auckland, New Zealand

Bridget writes: Relationships are the foundation of the learning community at our center. We place great value on building authentic, meaningful relationships with others and the environment. Our intention is to nurture a sense of belonging and to cultivate ecological identity within ourselves and the children. Over the past couple of years, we have been focusing on developing sustainable living practices within the center, and children have been involved in the planting, care, and harvesting of vegetables and flowers. We have also spent time exploring and connecting with our local natural environment, the Auckland Domain.

The conversations I have shared with the children have surprised and intrigued me, particularly the abstract level of conception in which some children perceive our environment. When I asked, "What makes our center special?" Scarlet replied, "Love." Intrigued, I asked, "Where can you see love?" "In the air," she replied. I asked if she could tell me more, and she said, "The air outside clears stuff and blows it away, but inside its got energy." When I asked Adreus what makes our center special, he answered, "Playing together, playing with our friends." I then asked what makes our center beautiful, and he said, "Nature. The sun makes our *kindy* [kindergarten for four- and five-year-olds] beautiful."

We have recently designed and developed a new garden area with planter boxes and fruit trees, and when I asked Scarlet and Adreus what they think is an important place in our center, they both said, "The new garden." Scarlet said it's because "it's got baby grass. The grass is not able to survive. It won't live, so you need to water it and not stand on it for a while." I asked Adreus what he thinks is beautiful about this area, and he said, "The love of nature and the trees and the grass and all of the plants." When I asked what makes it interesting for children, he said, "the butterflies." When I asked Scarlet how we could make the garden more beautiful, she said, "A plant that's already grown with wood. Dig its roots out and plant it in a hole. Put it in the middle of the garden. It needs to be big, not little, so the children will see it." "What's going to be important for the children about this tree?" I asked. "It's going to be a fruit tree so they can enjoy eating it," she answered. These thoughts suggest to me that Scarlet and Adreus are drawn to this new space by a mix of curiosity and wonder, and a sense of compassion and responsibility to nurture and connect with it.

I invited Scarlet and Adreus to draw the garden. Scarlet drew the whole scene, whereas Adreus chose to focus his attention on his favorite planter box.

As Adreus sat drawing, I asked him how the garden made him feel. "Happy . . . and sometimes sad." "Why?" I asked. "Sometimes everyone's in there," he replied. This left me thinking about children's need for natural spaces that offer peace and sanctuary. I was left wondering how we can offer time and space in natural environments that nurture relationships with others whilst also offering moments of silence and solitude.

On another occasion, Isabelle said that the construction area is an important place in our center. Of particular significance to her are the photos the children use to identify ownership of their work that is either completed or being revisited later. When I asked her why these images are of particular importance, she said, "Because everyone's on it." Isabelle then paused and thought before adding, "If there are no blocks, you can't build something, and then you can't play with anyone. You'll have to be all alone with nothing." Isabelle was talking about times when all of the resources in the space had been used by others before she had arrived. Isabelle's reflection illustrates to me the significance and impact of rituals that can become established around particular spaces. While Isabelle seems to value the inclusiveness of having everyone's image reflected in this space, the rituals around the use of these images seem to leave her feeling excluded at times.

David Sobel writes, "If we want children to flourish, to become truly empowered, then let us allow them to love the Earth before we ask them to save it" (1998). I believe the sentiment of this statement is reflected in the children's responses to my inquiry about their personal perceptions of our learning environment. The conversations shared with the children over the past couple of weeks have opened my eyes to the importance of including their perspectives

in designing living and learning spaces. The children have taught me how deeply they consider their environment and its impact on themselves and others. I am left feeling surprised at myself for the assumptions I have made about *what I think I know* about the children's perspectives on their environment. I have been left asking myself how we can be more inclusive of each other's ideas and thinking so we can coconstruct a truly authentic and organically evolving learning environment. I am left feeling humbled with a lot to think about!

Donna King and Everett, age four, and Justice, age five
Children First, Durham, NC

Donna writes: My approach was to sit with a few children and start our conversation like this: "We have two friends named Margie and Deb who write books to help teachers make schools good for kids. They want your opinion about what makes a good school."

Our conversations went like this: Everett and Justice agree that if they were going to choose a school, they would really want it to have a bathroom. They think about what the bathroom would need . . .

> JUSTICE: Soap!
>
> EVERETT: Toilet paper.
>
> JUSTICE: Towels!
>
> DONNA: What makes the Children First bathroom nice?
>
> JUSTICE: It's nice that you have doctor stuff; I think that's cool. (*Justice is talking about the first aid basket. I remember times when he's taken a lot of comfort in coming into the classroom and asking for help with an injury, and settling in the bathroom with a teacher and the healing basket.*)
>
> EVERETT: And I like that you have that kind of spray.
>
> JUSTICE: The spray to help you.
>
> EVERETT: The spray that takes the smell out of the air.
>
> JUSTICE: It smells good.
>
> DONNA: What do you usually look at when you're in the bathroom?
>
> JUSTICE: I look at the mirror a bunch.
>
> EVERETT: I look at the fish when I'm washing my hands.

Donna reflects: I invited the children to draw and take photographs of the bathroom. In his drawing, Everett shows the water coming out of the faucet over a person's hands, and the fish in its bowl. When Everett photographs the bathroom, he captures the fish, then asks me to take out the spray. I so appreciate Everett's identification of the "no smell spray" as important! This spray is an unscented product that actually removes smell from the air (not a spray that covers smells with another strong smell). I know that for me, smell has a powerful effect on my ability to relax and settle into a place. If an environment smells "institutional"—either strong bathroom smells or pungent food smells or overly perfumed smells—I feel tense and self-protective. And in our small classroom, the bathroom is very accessible—so of course, any smell in the bathroom is accessible too.

We have taken care to make sure the bathroom looks and feels attractive and homey, but a bad smell trumps all when it comes to how our sensory system responds to the environment.

Alison Maher and Ellen Hall and a group of children, age four
Boulder Journey School, Boulder, CO

Alison and Ellen write: As a school community inspired by the schools for young children in Reggio Emilia, Italy, and the people who participate in the World Forum Working Group on Children's Rights, we have chosen to engage in ongoing research alongside children. One example of this research occurred when teachers observed four-year-old children stacking stumps and tires in an effort to see over the fence that surrounds our school playground. Teachers noted that the fence, intended to keep children safe from traffic, was in opposition to their right to participate in the world around them. To better understand the children's thinking, teachers invited children to discuss and draw their frustrations, along with proposed solutions.

The teachers' analyses of children's conversations and representations revealed their idea of building a tree house that would give them visual access to the things that lived beyond the fence: cars, bikers, animals, houses, people, and so on. Teachers invited children to display their drawings and subsequent three-dimensional models in the school hallway. The visibility of their work generated school-wide enthusiasm for the project, as well as suggestions from other children, teachers, and families. The children seriously considered the suggestions, which included making the tree house both fun and safe for even the youngest children, integrating musical elements, and selecting construction materials that would mirror its location outdoors. The final design was a tree house, low to the ground, filled with wind chimes, and made of wood and branches. Construction by children, as project managers, families, and educators took place over several weekends. A quote from one parent captures the value of children's active participation in the design of their world: "The fact that you take children through the journey of concept to closure and give them responsibility through each leg of the road is so impressive. I relate it to my daily work environment. My team typically has a better appreciation for an end product when they have been part of the process that gets us there. Thank you for providing our children with exposure to that process at such an early age."

Inventions for Your Program

It takes practice to find concrete ways to acknowledge children's rights and, indeed, to uncover their thinking, preferences, yearnings, and meaning of their instinctive actions so we can honor them. Involving children in planning and assessing your environment is a concrete step you can take, even as you collaborate with other adults (and children) to interpret what they are communicating. Consider these questions to provoke your thinking about seeking children's ideas:

1   What observations have we made that give us an indication of how children are experiencing our environment?

2   How can we further engage the children in giving us their ideas about whether the environment is working for them?

3   What specific questions or activities might we offer to better understand new ideas children could offer us about our designs?

4   How can we better analyze what we are doing in light of rights we believe children should have as our youngest citizens?

Some years ago we met Paula McPheeters, an early childhood teacher who continually thinks about the rights of the children in her program. She created an environment to honor the children's right to have dual language learning, which enabled their Spanish learning to keep pace with their mastery of English. This also supported their right to stay better connected to their families, communities, and cultures.

Because many of the children's families feared deportation, she created a supportive social-emotional environment for families in her classroom, making visible their hopes and dreams for their lives. She responded to the challenge Loris Malaguzzi, founder of the schools of Reggio Emilia, proposed: that educators think carefully about a "Charter of Rights." Paula worked with her program's studio coordinator to develop a long-term project called "Considering the Rights of Children, Families, and Teachers" (Carter 2013). Paula's approach reminds us that our work to empower children must extend beyond our early childhood settings into our wider communities and the world at large. Supporting this notion, our colleagues in Aotearoa New Zealand challenge us with these questions: When you think of a child as a citizen, what comes to mind? How does that image influence your teaching?

To learn more about the wider activism around children's rights, explore the work of the World Forum Working Group on Children's Rights, which has been focused on amplifying children's voices, both verbal and nonverbal (www.worldforumfoundation.org /working-groups/childrensrights).

Afterword

Reaching the end of this book, we offer a final thought for how you might use *Designs for Living and Learning* with the children themselves as a way of honoring their right to offer their thinking about environments they would like to have. This idea was prompted by our visit to Paula McPheeters's classroom some years ago. Paula prepared the children with the news that some authors would be coming and put out a copy of what is now the first edition of this book, along with some sticky notes and pens. She suggested that in the days leading up to our visit, the children find something in *Designs for Living and Learning* that they wanted to talk with us about, writing their names on a sticky note and putting it on the related page. Indeed, we barely got in the door when several children rushed to us with the book. We were disadvantaged as English-only speakers, but their enthusiastic welcome and engagement with the book needed no translation. They clearly had many thoughts they wanted to offer us.

We encourage you to explore how you might use this book as a way to give further voice to the children you work with. It is both their and your right to have their assessment of desirable learning environments hold as much influence as any measured evaluation tool.

Notes

Ball, David, Tim Gill, and Bernard Spiegal. 2013. *Managing Risk in Play Provision: Implementation Guide.* London, UK: National Children's Bureau. http://www.playengland.org.uk/media/172644 /managing-risk-in-play-provision.pdf.

Barret, Peter, Yufan Zhang, Joanne Moffat, and Khairy Kobbacy. 2013. A holistic, multi-level analysis identifying the impact of classroom design on pupils' learning. *Building and Environment* 59:678–689.

Carter, Margie. 2013. Teachers as Leaders and Activists. *Child Care Exchange* 209 (January/February): 37.

Elkind, David. 1987. *Miseducation: Preschoolers at Risk.* New York: Knopf.

Forman, George. 1996. Negotiating with Art Media to Deepen Learning. *Child Care Information Exchange.* (March): 56–58.

Gallas, Karen. 1995. *Talking Their Way into Science: Hearing Children's Questions and Theories, Responding with Curricula.* New York: Teachers College Press.

Gandini, Lella. 2002. *Teaching and Learning: Collaborative Explorations of the Reggio Emilia Approach.* Edited by Victoria Fu, Andrew J. Stremmel, and Lynn T. Hill. Upper Saddle River, NJ: Merrill Prentice Hall.

Greenspan, Stanley. 1999. *Building Healthy Minds: The Six Experiences that Create Intelligence and Emotional Growth in Babies and Young Children.* Cambridge, MA: Perseus Books.

Kolbe, Ursula. 2007. *Rapunzel's Supermarket: All about Young Children and Their Art.* Byron Bay, Australia: Peppinot Press.

Kolbe, Ursula. 2005. *It's Not a Bird Yet: The Drama of Drawing.* Byron Bay, Australia: Peppinot Press.

Kritchevsky, Sybil and Elizabeth Prescott. 1977. *Planning Environments for Young Children: Physical Space.* Washington DC: National Association for the Education of Young Children.

Lehn, Barbara. 1999. *What Is a Scientist?* Brookfield, CT: Millbrook Press.

Louv, Richard. 2008. *Last Child in the Woods: Saving our Children from Nature-Deficit Disorder.* Chapel Hill, NC: Algonquin Books of Chapel Hill.

Lucas, Christopher G., Sophie Bridgers, Thomas L. Griffiths, and Alison Gopnik. 2014. When children are better (or at least more open-minded) learners than adults: Developmental differences in learning the forms of causal relationships. *Cognition* 131:284–299. http://www.alisongopnik.com/papers_alison/Lucas %20et%20al..pdf.

Olds, Anita Rui. 2001. *Child Care Design Guide.* New York: McGraw-Hill.

Podmore, Valerie N., Helen May, and Margaret Carr. 2001. *The "child's questions": Programme evaluation with Te Whāriki using "Teaching Stories."* Wellington, NZ: Institute for Early Childhood Studies, Victoria University of Wellington.

Shonkoff, Jack P., and Deborah A. Phillips, eds. 2000. *From Neurons to Neighborhoods: The Science of Early Childhood Development.* Washington DC: National Academy Press.

Sobel, David. 1998. Beyond Ecophobia. *Yes! Magazine.* (November). http://www.yesmagazine.org/issues /education-for-life/803.

Tovey, Helen. 2014. All about risk. *Nursery World* (January): 21–24.

van Wijk, Nikolien. 2008. *Getting Started with Schemas.* Waitakere, NZ: New Zealand Playcentre Publications.

Tools for Assessing Your Environment

- Assessing from the Child's Perspective

- Assessing for Family-Friendly Environments

- Assessing Your Environment for Infants and Toddlers

- Assessing Your Work Environment for Staff

- Herramientas para la Evaluación del Medio Ambiente Evaluación Preescolar

- La Evaluación de los Entornos Acogedores para Familiares

- Evaluando el Medio Ambiente de Infantes y Párvulos

- La Evaluación de su Entorno de Trabajo para el Personal

Assessing from the Child's Perspective

Draw a floor plan of your current facility. Put yourself in the shoes of the young children who spend their days in your space. Consider the statements below from a child's perspective and use them to assess your space. Write the numeral of each statement in all of the places on your floor plan where you are confident the statement is true.

1 = I can see who I am and what I like to do at school and at home.

2 = I see places that are comfortable for my tired mommy or daddy, grandma, or auntie to sit and talk with me or my teacher.

3 = The natural world can be found here (such as objects from nature, animals, or living specimens).

4 = There is something sparkly, shadowy, or wondrous and magical here.

5 = My teacher leaves a special object out here every day so I can use it many times and try to figure out more about its properties and how it works.

6 = There are materials here that I can use to make representations from what I understand or imagine.

7 = I can feel powerful and be physically active here.

8 = I can learn to see things from different perspectives here, literally and through assuming roles in dramatic play.

9 = There is a cozy place here where I can get away from the group and be by myself.

10 = I see my name written, or I get to regularly write my name here.

11 = I get to know my teachers here—what they like, how they spend their time away from school, and which people and things are special to them.

Now examine your coded floor plan. Did you have trouble finding any of these components in your room? If so, you will probably find new ways to think about transforming your environment in this book.

Draw a floor plan of your current facility. Write the letter of each statement in all of the places on your floor plan where you are confident the statement is true.

L = Families and children can see their interests, languages, and **lives** reflected here.

E = Families can see here what their children have been **engaged** in at the program.

R = Children and families can strengthen their **relationships** with each other in these spaces.

S = Children and families can learn more here about the **staff** and their lives.

N = Children and families can learn here about what is happening in their **neighborhood** and larger community.

C = Children and adults can sit **comfortably** together in these spaces.

A = Family members can stop and talk with the program **administrator(s)** here.

Now examine your coded floor plan. Reflect on the results and identify changes you want to make.

Draw a floor plan of the infant and toddler room(s) and write the following letter codes in all the places where these elements are present.

I = Children's **identities**, family lives, and cultures are reflected and nourished here.

H = Parents can feel **at home**, relaxed, and respected here.

R = Places where **relationships** can be nourished with special time, sharing, and enjoyment between adults and children are here.

SD = Children can have **sensory discoveries** and experiences (encountering different textures, light pools, colors, shadows, smells, and sounds) here.

LM = Children are encouraged to have **large-muscle** activity (climbing, crawling, pushing, pulling, sliding, bouncing, hiding, throwing, going up/down, up/over, in/out, and so on) here.

SM = Spaces where **small-muscle** skills (grasping, banging, poking, stacking, shaking, squeezing, patting, pouring, fitting together, taking apart, and so on) can be developed are here.

C = Places that are soft and **cozy** and where a child can get away from the group to rest or watch are here.

P = Children can feel **powerful**, independent, important, and competent here.

A = **Adults** can relax, enjoy, and share their lives with the children here.

S = **Systems** for communication and record keeping among the adults about the infant or toddler's time in the program and at home are found here.

Reflect on the results and decide on any goals you want to set to create changes.

Draw a quick floor plan of your building. Write the numeral of each state-ment in all of the places on your floor plan where you are confident the statement is true.

1 = Here is a dedicated place to welcome new staff members into the program.

2 = There is evidence here of who the staff members are and what they do in the rest of their lives (their passions and values).

3 = Families and visitors can learn the history of the program and its people here.

4 = Staff can easily store their personal belongings in this place.

5 = Staff have easy access to technology—for example, a phone, a com-puter with e-mail, camera(s), multitouch mobile device(s)—and technical training and support available here.

6 = Adults are nurtured by beauty and a relationship with the natural world (fresh air, natural light, plants, shells, and so on) here.

7 = Staff work space with accessible, well-organized resources here.

8 = Here is a comfortable place to meet with families.

9 = Staff can learn here what is happening with coworkers' and chil-dren's activities taking place in other rooms.

10 = There is evidence here that staff members are engaged in profes-sional development.

11 = Here is a place for staff, away from children, to relax, put their feet up, and have some quiet time to think over how the day is going.

12 = Places for staff to have uninterrupted discussions with each other are here.

13 = Here there is evidence of accomplishments by the staff.

14 = Here you can see ongoing efforts to improve wages, benefits, and working conditions.

Reflect on the results and identify changes you want to make.

Póngase en los zapatos de los de los niños de tres a seis años de edad, que pasan sus días en su espacio. Utilice las siguientes afirmaciones (todas desde el punto de vista de un niño), para evaluar su espacio acerca de un ambiente amigable para niños. Escriba el número de cada declaración en todos los lugares en el diseño de su salón dónde usted tiene la certeza que la afirmación es cierta. Reflexione sobre los resultados y decida que metas desea establecer para hacer cambios.

Ponga un **1** en donde me puedo ver a mi mismo/a, mi lengua materna y mi cultura, y lo que me gusta hacer aquí y en casa.

Ponga un **2** donde haiga lugares cómodos donde mi mamá o papá cansado, la abuela, o la tía puedan sentarse y hablar conmigo o con mi maestro/a.

Ponga un **3** en donde se puede encontrar el mundo natural (por ejemplo, objetos de la naturaleza, los animales, los seres vivos, luz natural, aire fresco).

Ponga un **4** en donde hay algo brillante, sombrío, o maravillosa y mágico.

Ponga un **5** donde mi maestro deja un objeto especial todos los días para que yo pueda seguir tratando de averiguar más acerca de sus propiedades y cómo funciona.

Ponga un **6** donde hay materiales que puedo utilizar para hacer representaciones de lo que entiendo o puedo imaginar.

Ponga un **7** en donde me puedo sentir poderosa/o y estar físicamente activo aquí.

Ponga un **8** donde Puedo aprender a ver las cosas desde diferentes puntos de vista, literalmente, y por medio de asumir roles en el juego dramático.

Ponga un **9** donde puedo encontrar un lugar acogedor para escapar del grupo y estar sola.

Ponga un **10** donde veo mi nombre escrito, o me pongo a escribir regularmente mi nombre.

Ponga un **11** en donde conozco a mis maestros - lo que les gusta, cómo pasan su tiempo fuera de la escuela, y que las personas y las cosas son especiales para ellos.

Ahora examine su plano codificado. ¿Tuvo problemas para encontrar cualquiera de estos componentes en su habitación? Si es así, probablemente encontrará nuevas maneras de pensar acerca de la transformación de su ambiente en este libro.

Dibuje un plano físico de su programa actual. Evalúe los componentes favorables a las familias de acuerdo a los siguientes elementos y códigos de letras. Reflexione sobre los resultados y decida las metas que desea establecer para los cambios.

Pon una **V** en todos los lugares donde las familias y los niños pueden ver a sus intereses, su lenguaje y su **vida** reflejada.

Ponga una **O** en todos los lugares donde las familias pueden ver en lo que sus hijos se han mantenido **ocupados** en el programa.

Marque con una **R** en todos los lugares donde los niños y las familias pueden ver las **relaciones** que se están fortaleciendo en el programa.

Ponga una **P** en todos los lugares donde los niños y las familias pueden aprender más sobre el **personal** y sus vidas.

Marque con una **VC** en todos los lugares donde los niños y las familias pueden aprender acerca de lo que está sucediendo en su **vecindario** y su **comunidad**.

Ponga una **C** en todos los lugares donde los niños y los adultos pueden sentarse **cómodamente** juntos.

Pon una **A** en todos los lugares donde los miembros de la familia pueden hablar con los **administradores** del programa.

Ahora examine su plano codificado. Reflexione sobre los resultados e identifique los cambios que quiere hacer.

Dibuje un plano físico de su salón y escriba estos códigos de letras en todos los lugares donde éstos elementos están presentes. Luego reflexione sobre los resultados y decida las metas que desea establecer para los cambios.

Ponga una **I** en todos los lugares donde la **identidad** de los niños, la vida familiar, y la cultura se reflejan y se nutren.

Marque con una **C** en todos los lugares donde los padres pueden sentirse como en **casa**, relajado, y respetados en el salón.

Marque con una **R** todos los lugares donde las **relaciones** entre niños y adultos se pueden intercambiar, disfrutar, y ser alimentadas con un tiempo especial.

Marque con **DS** en todos los lugares donde hay **descubrimientos y** experiencias **sensoriales** para los niños (como diferentes texturas, piscinas o mesas de luz, color, sombras, olores, sonidos).

Marque con **MG** todos los lugares donde se fomenta la actividad de músculos de **motor grueso** (escalar, arrastrarse, empujar, tirar, correr, rebotar, ocultar, lanzar, pasar hacia arriba / abajo / sobre, adentro/afuera, y así sucesivamente).

Marque con **MF** todos los lugares donde las habilidades de los **músculos** de motor **fino** se pueden desarrollar (agarrar, golpear, picar, apilar, temblores, apretando, acariciando, vertido, encajando, desmontar, y así sucesivamente).

Ponga una **TA** en los lugares que son **tranquilos** y **acogedores** y donde un niño puede alejarse del grupo para descansar y observar.

Ponga una **P** en los lugares donde los niños puedan sentirse **poderosos**, independientes, importantes y competentes.

Ponga una **A** en todos los lugares donde los **adultos** pueden relajarse, disfrutar y compartir su vida con los niños.

Ponga una **S** donde haiga **sistemas** de comunicación y mantenimiento de registros y documentación entre los adultos sobre el tiempo del bebé en el programa y en el hogar.

Reflexione sobre los resultados y decida sobre los objetivos que desea establecer para crear cambios.

Dibuje un plano de su salón y escriba estos códigos de letras en todos los lugares donde éstos elementos están presentes. Luego reflexione sobre los resultados y decida las metas que desea establecer para los cambios.

Ponga un **1** donde se demuestra como un nuevo miembro del personal recibe una bienvenida en el programa.

Ponga un **2** donde haiga información acerca de quienes son los miembros del personal y lo que hacen en sus vidas afuera del salón (sus pasiones y valores).

Ponga un **3**, donde se puede conocer la historia del programa y de su gente.

Ponga un **4** donde el personal puede guardar fácilmente sus pertenencias personales.

Ponga a **5**, donde el personal tiene acceso fácil a la tecnología: por ejemplo, un teléfono, un ordenador con el correo electrónico, cámara, IPAD, y que tenga la capacitación técnica y el apoyo disponible.

Ponga un **6** donde los adultos se pueden nutrir de belleza y relacionarse con el mundo natural (aire fresco, la luz natural, las plantas, conchas y así sucesivamente).

Ponga un **7** donde hay un espacio para trabajar con recursos accesibles y bien organizados.

Ponga un **8** donde hay un lugar cómodo para reunirse con las familias.

Ponga un **9**, donde el personal puede aprender lo que está sucediendo con los compañeros de trabajo "y actividades de los niños que están en otros salones.

Ponga un **10** donde haiga evidencias de que el personal está comprometido en el desarrollo profesional.

Ponga un **11** donde haiga un lugar para que el personal, lejos de los niños, se pueda relajar, elevar sus pies, y tener un poco de tranquilidad para pensar en cómo le está yendo el día.

Ponga un **12** donde haiga lugares donde el personal puedan tener conversaciones ininterrumpidas entre ellos.

Ponga un **13** donde hay pruebas de los logros del personal.

Ponga un **14** donde se pueden ver los esfuerzos para mejorar los salarios, beneficios y condiciones de los empleados.

Reflexione sobre los resultados y decida sobre los objetivos que desea establecer para crear cambios.

"That's where we're looking out the window at the top."

"That's the lunchroom where we ate."

RCIN
AA

"That's when we're on the elevator."

"That is where we came in."

11-8-13

Tools to Reflect on Quality Rating Scale Components

 Taking a Closer Look at an Infant or Toddler's Daily Schedule

 Getting to Know the Assessment Tool

 Evaluando tus rutinas en Tomando un vistazo más cercano al horario de Infantes o Párvulos (Niños de edad aproximada (12-30 meses)

 Conociendo la Herramienta de Evaluación

Children First, Durham, NC

Taking a Closer Look at an Infant or Toddler's Daily Schedule

Directions: Select a child in your program between 6 months and 30 months who typically spends an extended time in your care. Fill in the time and activity log below based on the daily schedule of the child you selected. In the first column put the time segment (e.g., 9:00–9:15 am). Then describe what the child is doing during that specific time frame. Routine care activities include such things as feeding, diapering, and naptime. Other activities include all the other play and learning experiences during the day such as playing with blocks, being read a book, and working on a simple puzzle.

Child's name _____

Time	Routine care activities	Other activities

FROM: McCormick Center for Early Childhood Leadership, National Louis University (McCormickCenter.nl.edu). Reprinted with permission.

After you have completed the child's daily schedule, answer the following questions:

How much time does this infant or toddler spend in routine care?

What is the total time during the day that this child spends in bouncy chair, exersaucer, swing, or high chair?

How much time did the child spend in group activities such as story time, music time, or teacher-directed group art projects? What were the child's options if he/she did not want to participate in a group activity?

How often during the day does the child have access to soft, cozy places?

When did the child have an opportunity to engage in active play?

How much time did the child get to actively explore the world outdoors? (Stroller rides are not considered active play).

How much time did the child get to enjoy unstructured free play indoors?

What insights did you glean from analyzing the content of this infant or toddler's daily schedule?

FROM: McCormick Center for Early Childhood Leadership, National Louis University (McCormickCenter.nl.edu). Reprinted with permission.

Purpose: This activity provides an opportunity for teachers to reflect and discuss their understanding of the quality indicators in a particular assessment tool like the ECERS-R, ITERS-R, or CLASS Pre-K. The activity offers a format to self-assess and consider changes for improving classroom quality.

Directions: Teachers work in small peer learning teams. Peer learning teams are best defined as ongoing groups of four or five teachers who meet regularly with the focus on increasing understanding about children's learning. For this activity, the learning team determines which item in the assessment tool they want to work on. Once that is determined, each person on the team independently completes the attached handout titled "Getting to Know the Assessment Tool." It is fine to use the assessment tool books to guide their thoughts in completing the handout. It is important that the handout is used as an individual tool for reflection and is completed prior to meeting as a group. This allows the learning team to hear varying perspectives and interpretations from one another.

Once each member of the team completes the handout, a learning team meeting is scheduled for discussion. In round-robin fashion, each person shares one or two components from their completed handout that were of particular interest to them. Once each person has had a turn, the group responds to the guided questions below:

> What are common beliefs we agree upon relating to this item of the assessment tool?
>
> Are there any areas where we have differing points of view?
>
> What resources might help guide our group to a better understanding of this item?
>
> Are there steps we'd like to take to improve this item in our classrooms?

The group generates a list of what they do well and possible next steps to implement or improve this item in their classrooms.

FROM: McCormick Center for Early Childhood Leadership, National Louis University (McCormickCenter.nl.edu). Reprinted with permission.

Getting to Know the Assessment Tool

Teacher:	Date:

Assessment tool:

Item or dimension:

Why does this item matter for positive child outcomes?

Key questions prompted by the item	The environment includes	A child will experience
·	·	·
·	·	·
	·	

When you think about this item in your own environment, what questions come up?

What steps are necessary to implement or improve this item in your environment?

Getting to Know the Assessment Tool

Assessment tool: CLASS Pre-K

Item or dimension: Instructional Learning Formats

Why does this item matter for positive child outcomes?

While we want children to have fun play experiences, we also want them to be actively learning.

Key questions prompted by the item	The environment includes	A child will experience
• Am I involved, asking meaningful questions and expanding children's interests? • Do the children have a wide range of hands-on materials that peak their curiosity? • When I scan the room, are children actively engaged in activities? • Can the children explain what they are learning?	• Teachers moving around and working with the children • Lots of materials and experiences for kids to explore, like the new recycled art materials I put out on the art shelf this week	• Never being bored or sitting around waiting! • Active, hands-on learning

When you think about this item in your own environment, what questions come up?

I think I do a pretty good job with the dimension Instructional Learning Formats during free choice time. But I'm not so sure how well I do during group time. It feels like I spend a lot of time correcting children's behavior and trying to get them to listen. They often seem tuned out. I wonder what a high score in this CLASS dimension looks like during group time.

I would also like to learn more about the effective facilitation indicator within this dimension. What do they mean by "effective questioning?"

What steps are necessary to implement or improve this item in your environment?

Perhaps I could observe one of Sam's group times? During our learning team sessions he has described some pretty interesting things he's done with the children when they gather as a whole group.

I wonder if our learning team could review some of the CLASS video clips that focus on effective facilitation. The videos might offer some concrete examples. If I'm not sure about this concept, others might be struggling too

FROM: McCormick Center for Early Childhood Leadership, National Louis University (McCormickCenter.nl.edu). Reprinted with permission.

Instrucciones: Seleccione a un niño en su programa de entre 6 meses y 30 meses de edad que normalmente pasa un tiempo prolongado en su cuidado. Rellene el formato a continuación con la hora y registro de actividades sobre la programación diaria del niño/a que ha seleccionado. En la primera columna de ponga el segmento de tiempo (por ejemplo, de 9:00 - 9:15 am). A continuación describa lo que el niño está haciendo específicamente durante ese periodo de tiempo. Actividades de atención de rutina incluyen cosas tales como la alimentación, cambio de pañales y la siesta. Otras actividades incluyen todos los otros juegos y experiencias de aprendizaje durante el día, tales como jugar con bloques, cuando se les lee un libro, y trabajar en un rompecabezas sencillo.

Nombre del Niño/a: _____

Time	Routine care activities	Other activities

Después de haber completado la programación diaria del niño, responda las siguientes preguntas:

¿Cuánto tiempo se gasta el bebé o párvulo en la atención habitual de rutina?

¿Cuál es el tiempo total durante el día, que este niño pasa en la silla mecedora, columpio, brincador, o en la silla de comer?

¿Cuánto tiempo pasa el niño en actividades de grupo, como la hora del cuento, el tiempo de la música, o proyectos de arte de grupo dirigidas por el maestro? ¿Cuáles eran las opciones del niño si él / ella no quería participar en una actividad de grupo?

¿Con qué frecuencia durante el día tiene el niño acceso a los lugares suaves y acogedores?

¿Cuándo tiene el niño la oportunidad de participar en el juego activo?

¿Cuánto tiempo exploro el niño activamente el mundo exterior al aire libre? (Paseos en cochecito no se consideran juegos activos).

¿Cuánto tiempo llego el niño a disfrutar el juego libre no estructurado en el interior?

¿Qué ideas has espigado después de analizar el contenido de este horario diario de infantes o párvulos?

FROM: McCormick Center for Early Childhood Leadership, National Louis University (McCormickCenter.nl.edu). Reprinted with permission.

Propósito : Esta actividad ofrece una oportunidad para que los profesores reflexionen y discutan su comprensión de los indicadores de calidad en la evaluación de una herramienta en particular, como ECERS -R, ITERS -R o CLASS Pre -K. La actividad ofrece un formato para autoevaluar y considerar cambios para mejorar la calidad del salón de clases.

Instrucciones: Los maestros trabajan en pequeños equipos de aprendizaje entre pares. Equipos de aprendizaje entre pares se definen mejor como grupos en curso de cuatro o cinco profesores que se reúnen regularmente con el objetivo de mejorar la comprensión sobre el aprendizaje de los niños. Para esta actividad, el equipo de aprendizaje determina con qué elemento de la herramienta de evaluación quieren trabajar. Ya que hayan determinado, cada persona en el equipo debe completar independiente el formulario adjunto titulado " Introducción a la herramienta de evaluación." Esta bien utilizar los libros de la herramienta de evaluación para guiar sus pensamientos al rellenar el formulario. Es importante que la hoja se utilice como una herramienta individual para la reflexión y que sea completada antes de la reunión como grupo. Esto le permitirá al equipo de aprendizaje escuchar diferentes puntos de vista e interpretaciones de otras personas.

Una vez que cada miembro del equipo haya completado el formulario, una Se programa una reunión del equipo de aprendizaje para una discusión. En "round- robin", (juego de consenso) cada persona comparta uno o dos componentes de su folleto completo que hayan sido de especial interés para ellos. Una vez que cada persona ha tenido su turno, el grupo responde a las preguntas guiadas a continuación:

> ¿Cuáles son las creencias comunes en las que estamos de acuerdo en relación con este tema de la herramienta de evaluación?

> ¿Existen áreas en las que tenemos diferentes puntos de vista?

> ¿Qué recursos puede ayudar a guiar a nuestro grupo a una mejor comprensión de este artículo?

> ¿Hay pasos que nos gustaría tomar para mejorar este tema en nuestros salones?

El grupo genera una lista de lo que hacen buen trabajo y posibles pasos a seguir para implementar o mejorar este tema en sus salones.

Conociendo la Herramienta de Evaluación

Maestra/o:	Fecha:

Herramienta de evaluación:

Elemento o dimensión:

¿Por qué es importante este tema para los resultados positivos del niño?

Preguntas clave impulsados por el tema	El ambiente incluye	El niño/a va a experimentar
•	•	•
•	•	•
	•	

Cuando usted piensa acerca de este artículo en el entorno de su medio ambiente, que preguntas surgen?

¿Cuáles son los pasos son necesarios para implementar o mejorar este tema en su medio ambiente?

FROM: McCormick Center for Early Childhood Leadership, National Louis University (McCormickCenter.nl.edu). Reprinted with permission.

Conociendo la Herramienta de Evaluación

Maestra/o: Martha	Fecha: Septiembre 23

Herramienta de evaluación: CLASS Pre-K

Elemento o dimensión: Formatos de Instrucción de Aprendizaje

¿Por qué es importante este tema para los resultados positivos del niño?

Si bien queremos que los niños tengan experiencias de juego de diversión, también queremos que estén aprendiendo activamente.

Preguntas clave impulsados por el tema	El ambiente incluye	El niño/a va a experimentar
• ¿Estoy involucrado, haciendo preguntas significativas y expansión de los intereses de los niños? • ¿Tienen los niños una amplia gama de materiales de manos que cumba su curiosidad? • ¿Al escanear el salon, están los niños participando activamente en las actividades? • ¿Pueden los niños explicar lo que están aprendiendo?	• Los profesores se movilizan y trabajan con los niños • Un montón de materiales y experiencias para que los niños exploraren , como los nuevos materiales de arte reciclados que puse en el estante de arte esta semana	• Nunca se aburre o se sienta a esperar! • activo en el aprendizaje práctico

Cuando usted piensa acerca de este artículo en el entorno de su medio ambiente, que preguntas surgen? Creo que hago un buen trabajo con las dimensiones de Instrucción formatos de aprendizaje durante el tiempo de elección libre. Pero no estoy tan seguro de lo bien que hago durante el tiempo de grupo. Se siente como si me paso un montón de tiempo para corregir el comportamiento de los niños y tratando de conseguir que me escuchen. A menudo parecen estar sintonizados a cabo. Me pregunto qué sería tener una alta puntuación en esta dimensión CLASS durante el tiempo de grupo.

También me gustaría aprender más sobre el indicador de facilitación efectiva dentro de esta dimensión. ¿Qué quieren decir con " el cuestionamiento efectivo?"

¿Cuáles son los pasos son necesarios para implementar o mejorar este tema en su medio ambiente?

Tal vez pude observar una de las reuniones grupales de Sam? Durante nuestras sesiones de aprendizaje del equipo él ha descrito algunas cosas muy interesantes que ha hecho con los niños cuando se reúnen como grupo.

Me pregunto si nuestro equipo de aprendizaje podría revisar algunos de los clips de vídeo de clase que se centran en la facilitación efectiva. Los videos pueden ofrecer algunos ejemplos concretos. Si no estoy seguro acerca de este concepto, otros también podrían estar luchando.